THE NATURE OF DEVELOPMENT

THE NATURE
OF DEVELOPMENT

*A Report from the Rural Tropics on the Quest
for Sustainable Economic Growth*

Roger D. Stone

Alfred A. Knopf   New York

1992

THIS IS A BORZOI BOOK
PUBLISHED BY ALFRED A. KNOPF, INC.

Library of Congress Cataloging-in-Publication Data

Stone, Roger D.
The nature of development : a report from the rural
tropics on the quest for sustainable economic growth /
Roger D. Stone. — 1st ed.
p. cm.
Includes bibliographical references.
ISBN 0-394-58358-2
1. Economic development projects—Developing
countries. 2. Environmental policy—
Developing countries. 3. Economic development—
Environmental aspects. I. Title.
HC59.72.E44S76 1992
338.9′00913—dc20 91–53122
CIP

Manufactured in the United States of America
First Edition

A Council on Foreign Relations Book

The Nature of Development was completed by the
author while he was the 1990–91 Whitney H. Shepardson
Fellow at the Council on Foreign Relations in New York.
Designated "A Council on Foreign Relations Book," this
book is, in the judgment of the Committee on Studies of
the Council, a responsible treatment of a significant
international topic worthy of presentation to the public.

This volume is dedicated to these people,
and to their values:

Dalmiro Cortez
Ian Craven
Maria de Lourdes Davies de Freitas
Marjory Stoneman Douglas
Surapon Duangkhae
Yance de Fretes
Robert J. A. Goodland
Kenneth Green
Albert Hirschman
Dale Lewis
Jim "Diego" Lynch
Heather Macleod
Jeffrey A. McNeely
Godfrey Mubita
Flywell Munyenyembe
Patson Mwimanzi
Jorge Orejuela
John Parrott
Allen Putney
Nikhom Putta
Yves Renard
Alberto Salas
Deborah Szekely
Sarah Timpson
Carlos Villarreal
Mike Wright

Contents

Introduction

૨✿

Seven hundred and fifty million of the world's poorest, most destructive, and most creative people inhabit the Third World's rural tropics. In their daily battles for survival, often using grimly ingenious techniques, these villagers cut ever deeper into tropical forests to create farms and pastures, strip abundant mangrove areas along the coasts, and ravish the coral reefs that lie offshore. Despite the ongoing rush to cities in poor and rich countries alike, the stress they are placing on their environment is bound to become heavier as their numbers increase. According to some sources, the total number of rural poor in the Third World may reach 1.25 billion—more people than now live in the entire industrial world—by about 2015.

The villagers' actions bring to those responsible for them neither food security nor hope. At the same time, they do heavy damage to the world's most important genetic storehouses. Of all species of plants and animals, of which there may be as many as 100 million, 90 percent or more exist only in tropical regions of the Third World. The pressures that people are placing on these tropical habitats are causing losses in biological diversity, which responsible scientists estimate to be taking place at one hundred or perhaps even one thousand times any previous rate. In this crisis, the most severe spasm of extinctions since dinosaurs disappeared 65 million years ago, 25 percent of all species now in existence may vanish by the year 2015.[1] Since scientists have identified and begun to describe fewer than 1.5 million species, moreover, we have only the vaguest idea of what is being sacrificed.

1. See Peter H. Raven, "Our Diminishing Tropical Forests," in Edward. O. Wilson and Francis M. Peter, eds., *Biodiversity* (Washington, D.C.: National Academy Press, 1988), pp. 119–22.

This loss, the biologist Edward O. Wilson has stated, is the sin for which current generations can least be forgiven. The health and productivity of agriculture is dependent on germ plasm that comes from the wild, and much of our industry depends on nature's shrinking genetic pool. Some people like to argue that biotechnology's impressive progress is rendering the conservation of wild germ plasm ever less important to the world of medicine, and add that if it *were* of cardinal importance the profit-oriented drug companies would be swarming over the world's jungles. But penicillin, aspirin, and many other commonplace drugs now made artificially originated in nature—and every year brings new discoveries of medicines based on natural products. Not all of them can be synthesized in the lab. This evidence comes, moreover, from only the tiny fraction of species that scientists have yet studied. It is thus difficult to disagree with Wilson about the sheer folly of discarding, unopened, what nature has given us.

To alleviate human poverty in the rural Third World would, then, serve several major purposes. It would bring relief to a large share of the world's most desperate people. The integrity of the planet's most fragile ecosystems, and the wide biological diversity (often referred to as "biodiversity") within them, would be far better protected. The accelerating rate at which the Third World's rural people are migrating to already teeming cities would also slow down, along with the pace of migration from developing to industrial nations.

In recent years many people living in the Third World's backlands have begun working hard to avoid the ecological abysses toward which, as they know better than anybody, they have been headed. Conservationists and donors of aid have arrived with unfamiliar technologies and agricultural innovations to help—or sometimes hinder—these efforts. What will result, proponents hope, is something called sustainability. The term, fashionable throughout the 1980s, was given additional prominence in *Our Common Future,* a report published in 1987 by the World Commission on Environment and Development, chaired by Gro Harlem Brundtland, Prime Minister of Norway. In this benchmark document, sustainability is defined as a commitment to sustaining both economic health and the resources of the natural world on which that health and growth ultimately depend, as using the earth's resources in a manner which "meets the needs of the present without compromising our ability to meet those of the future." Beyond this clear statement of intergenerational equity, other definitions abound. What they have in common is the goal of slowing or stopping the world's current movement toward degradation, extinction, and human misery.

Many theorists believe that achieving sustainability will demand an unprecedented burst of growth—the elixir for economic improvement that, since the end of World War II, has dominated conventional thinking about development. Overall, according to Jim MacNeill, the environmentalist who served as secretary-general of the Brundtland commission, a five- to tenfold increase in economic activity is "required over the next 50 years in order to meet the needs and aspirations of a burgeoning world population, as well as to begin to reduce mass poverty."[2] Others believe that it is not possible to achieve such rapid human advancement without precipitating a breakdown in the earth's ability to support all forms of life. Dismissing the vision of sustainable growth as a "bad oxymoron," the environmental economist Herman Daly of the World Bank recommends an era of "sustainable development" during which the world would mount "a serious attack on poverty." Central to any such effort would be measures, such as population control and income redistribution, that might be applied without causing ecologically unsound increases in overall economic activity.[3]

MacNeill and Daly both have a point. While I lean toward the latter view, the world is a complex place where the frenzy of development that might bring long-term prosperity to one region would lead quickly to ecological collapse in another. Generally, my evidence suggests a strong correlation between progress toward the goal of sustainability in the rural tropics and the degree to which local people are involved in designing the pathways. But even with the villagers' energetic participation, and with the establishment of an environmentally sound local rate of economic growth, distant people and institutions will need to cooperate if small successes are to have broader meaning. National

2. As stated in his "Strategies for Sustainable Development," *Scientific American,* September 1989, p. 156.
3. See Daly's "Sustainable Growth: An Impossibility Theorem," in *Development* (Journal of the Society for International Development), Vol. 3, No. 4 (1990), pp. 45–46.

governments of developing countries will have to abandon their stubbornly held notions about the importance of central power, military dominance, and the role of the state. The few rich countries holding the balance of the world's economic power have done much to bring about the agrarian crisis that, one way or another, exists within nations at every stage of development. These nations will have to make major adjustments in what Mrs. Brundtland has called "geo-economics"—worldwide patterns of trade, investment, and capital flow—for these mean far more to the well-being of most Third World economies than current levels of development assistance. Significant progress in the rural tropics will, in short, require that national leaders and Third World peasants share common goals.

At the heart of this book lie stories about remarkable people I have met on the extreme margins of the developing world, and about the techniques they are working out, often with some help from outside, to avoid their own disappearance as well as that of their environment. These tales make up almost all of Chapters 5, 6, and 7, and portions of several other chapters. While I would hardly contend that they constitute comprehensive country or regional analysis, there may be broad lessons to be learned from what I found happening in the remote villages, on three continents and several islands, that I visited. I saw important and replicable synergies—instances where the introduction of environmentally benign practices has resulted in better incomes for people in desperate need *and* less pressure on the natural environment. I believe, in other words, that a combination of intelligence, technology, and sound management can enable the poor farmers in today's Third World to avoid contaminating their own environments in different ways as they consume and pollute more. Short-term economic sacrifices are sometimes required if environmental gains are to be achieved in these places, and at times environmental goals will need to be modified as well. But overall, I found the ideological and practical walls separating those punch-drunk old enemies to be breaking down. The coincidence of both success and failure on both sides has been too frequent to justify any other conclusion.

An opening chapter offers contrasting "good" and "bad" examples of sustainability in rural development in the Third World. In Chapters 2 through 4, I show how environmental and development assistance organizations, far from successful when working alone to save nature or help poor people, achieve better results when they join forces. After the reports from the villages in the central section of the book, in Chapter 8 I draw together some more general thoughts about the techniques of "development" (a word even more frequently redefined than sustainability) I observed that seem especially promising. In three final chapters, I outline the broad shifts in outlook and behavior that both the South (a term often used to indicate the community of less developed countries) and the North (the rich industrial nations) will have to consider so that the principles behind the small grass-roots efforts have a fair chance of blending into the broader flow of human thought and activity. A major test is the June 1992 United Nations Conference on Environment and Development (UNCED), in Rio de Janeiro, successor to the pioneering 1972 Stockholm Conference on the Human Environment. Whether the 1992 "Earth Summit" and work done in its aftermath achieve fruitful and lasting results will say much about how disposed the world is to bend in these directions.

While emphasizing the direct links between the byways of the Third World and the First World's capitals, I have chosen to skirt a number of other pertinent issues. I do not closely examine environmental degradation in the rich parts of poor countries, usually brought about by industrialization or excessive agribusiness development. Of critical importance to the planet's future environmental quality, but exempted from my discussion here, are thoughts about energy planning for the huge coal-burning nations—India and mainland China—or for the gluttonous United States. On these pages you will find little about the fast-growing problem of urban poverty in developing countries. Each of these subjects merits a book in itself.

My purpose is hardly to encourage concerned people in advanced nations to disregard *their* local issues, as some have done, and focus exclusively on global questions requiring less immediate personal commitment. Conserving energy and resources, assiduous attention to recycling and the proper disposal of wastes, are the First World's equivalents of saving the rhino or the rainforest. Rather, my hope is to persuade my readers, whether they be in Washington or Berlin, Warsaw or Mexico City, Jakarta or Beijing, of the importance of what happens both close to home *and* far away. I especially intend to demonstrate that achieving better lives for the Third World's peasants is in everybody's interest—and that their defeat, should it occur, will be a profound setback for the planet and every soul upon it. While the prescriptions here recommended may not be palatable to all, they are designed for everybody's benefit.

PART I

TOWARD
CONVERGENCE

❧

CHAPTER I

The Meaning of
the Difference

After a night of heavy rain, a soft misty dawn rose over the Awá Indian settlement of Mataje, in the northwest corner of Ecuador on the Colombian border. Here, in a small clearing surrounded by lush green lowland forest, only a few miles inland from the coastal town of Esmeraldas, parrots and parakeets screeched in the lofty trees, and red, yellow, and black toucans gurgled and swooped gracefully from branch to branch. I had spent the night in the wood-and-thatch house of Belisario Canticus, an elder in the group. Around me in the large open front room of the communal dwelling, Awá of several generations stirred. Half a dozen men and boys rose quietly from the floor, where they had slept in a tidy row. In a smaller room at the rear of the house, one of but three or four buildings in the small compound, women heated water, to cook rice, in pots resting on an open wood fire. Pigs and chickens ranged in mud under the house, whose living quarters rested on stilts above the ground.

Dr. Roland Dameron, a French-Ecuadoran fieldworker for a Quito-based agency called the Unidad Técnica Ecuatoriana del Plan Awá (UTEPA), was up as well. From a large red backpack he extracted medical supplies that he had carried with him to Mataje, a strenuous

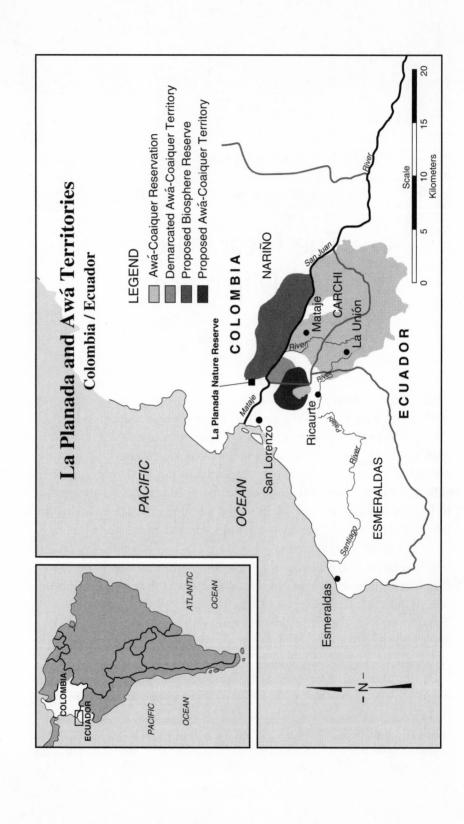

La Planada and Awá Territories
Colombia / Ecuador

LEGEND

- Awá-Coaiquer Reservation
- Demarcated Awá-Coaiquer Territory
- Proposed Biosphere Reserve
- Proposed Awá-Coaiquer Territory

PACIFIC

OCEAN

COLOMBIA

NARIÑO

CARCHI

ECUADOR

ESMERALDAS

San Lorenzo

La Planada Nature Reserve

Mataje

La Unión

Ricaurte

Esmeraldas

San Juan

Mataje River

River

Palabí

Santiago River

River

Scale

0   5   10   15   20

Kilometers

COLOMBIA

ECUADOR

ATLANTIC

OCEAN

PACIFIC

OCEAN

N

eight-hour walk along a hilly, muddy, root-strewn footpath from the nearest roadhead. To Belisario and other members of the family Dameron distributed vitamins and pills, and spoke about how to use them. Then the bearded Dameron climbed down a primitive ladder that led from the house to the ground, and took a brief stroll within the hamlet. He paused at a small, healthy nursery where Awá farmers, with help from a volunteer provided by the Australian government, had been experimenting with two hundred plant and tree species new to them; they were accustomed to planting little but maize. Then Dameron visited Mataje's new two-room primary school, where Belisario's son Aurelio taught twenty-four children and thirteen adults, some of whom were commuting by foot from as far as two and a half hours away to attend the half-day sessions.

After his brief tour Dameron entered the *casa comunal* (community house), where formal meetings are held. Here Dameron brought official greetings from UTEPA, which since its founding in 1987, with backing both from abroad and from the Ecuadoran government, has been a link between Ecuador's three thousand Awá and the world beyond their forest homeland. He also intended to gather information about the Mataje community's needs and complaints to incorporate into a management plan for the entire region on which he and his Awá partners had been working. Elected leaders from Mataje and other Awá villages had already agreed upon the general outlines of what they wanted. Now, Dameron said as the meeting got under way, the task was to arrange this information to suit the requirements of the many faraway organizations that had expressed interest in helping the Awá.

What he needed, he continued, was a list of Mataje's specific needs. "A road good enough for horses," said Julián Canticus, Belisario's nephew and president of the Awá Federation's Mataje chapter at the time of my visit. "A zinc roof for our *casa comunal*," said another man. "We have to walk a long way to get the kind of thatch we use, and carry it here on our backs. We put it up and then it quickly rots and must be replaced." Books, maps, other school materials. Medical supplies. ("It's always the same things," Dameron told me later. "Education, health, access to markets.") After he had completed his list and raised a few other matters, Dameron introduced me as a writer working on a book about conservation and economic development in distant rural corners, and suggested that I ask questions. How, I began, were the Awá organized before there was a Federation and a UTEPA? "Before 1981 no one paid any attention to us. We had no organization at all," Julián replied unhesitatingly in the Spanish we were all using, which many Awá would now rather speak than their own unwritten language. "Every family lived separately, in its own place. We had no way to work or make decisions as a group." Now, he and others continued, increasing help is coming from outside. Long ignored by the Quito government, the Awá recently were given *cedulas* (citizenship cards) and titles to their land within a 101,000-hectare[1] reserve that shields it from the assault of timbermen coveting its valuable tropical-forest hardwoods. The Federation meets every three months, its officers gathering from the small settlements like Mataje dotted through the reserve, to review and reach decisions about matters of common interest.

By midmorning the meeting ended. Under a brightening sky Dameron and I set forth on a second full day's journey through the forest in the company of several heavily laden Awá, including Julián and Aurelio. For most of the way we walked, using sticks for balance as we made our way down steep slippery inclines to small *quebradas,* or streams, fording them, then clambering back up to respites of more nearly level terrain. At Julián's house, high above a broad river, we stopped for a luncheon of bananas and dry, vinegary-tasting corn mush. Julián's wife appeared, extracted a baby from the straw basket she had been carrying on her back, and began to feed it. Barefoot, she and the baby joined us as we proceeded, Dameron beginning to complain of blisters and a sore knee. At one point, no longer able to tolerate our ponderous pace, two young Awá pushed off from the crest of a long hill and, slaloming fast down the muddy slope on black rubber boots, soon disappeared from sight. As daylight faded, Dameron now hobbling, we made our way into La Unión, the settlement that was our destination. I stripped and gratefully swam in a deep pool of the crisp, clear Río Palabi, one of the many rivers within the Awá forest, which flows past this village.

---

1. A hectare equals 2.47 acres. Since the hectare is the most commonly used unit of measurement for large areas, it will be used throughout this volume, in preference to acres.

"I'm going to *dance* tonight," a sixteen-year-old Awá boy had told me earlier in the day. The principal house at La Unión was decorated with blossoms from the forest for the final hours of a five-day *chutún*. This is a ceremony in which an ailing man works with a *curandero,* or healer, to relieve his own tensions—and those of his neighbors—with the help of music, dancing, fermented corn liquor, called *chicha,* and a final predawn river bath to liberate evil spirits. Now, as Dameron and I settled into the small enclosed back room of the house that we had been given as our quarters, the party was getting started by the flickering orange light of kerosene lanterns and a wood fire. Four older men began to play insistent music on a marimba, guitar, wooden flute, and drum. Teenage couples (my friend prominent among the boys) ventured out onto the wooden floor and danced in formal stiff-legged little steps. Mothers and young children sat in clusters around the edge of what had become the dance floor. Julián, Belisario, and other men turned to the *chicha*.

As the *chutún* approached its climax, the *chicha* ran out. The Awá began to buy *aguardiente* from a black river trader who had arrived earlier in the evening, been driven off by Julián ("We don't want him ruining our party"), but later succeeded in installing himself, along with his wife, a young daughter, and a red plastic five-gallon container, on one side of the dance floor. Before dawn several men, Belisario principal among them, were tottering at each other in feeble efforts to settle old scores. Wailing and moaning replaced the music. The teenagers disappeared. So did the ailing man to complete his cure. Daybreak revealed a tawdry scene, most of the men passed out, Julián still standing but slugging from a small bottle and passing it among the women, who remained stoically ranged among the debris with sleeping or crying babies. Belisario staggered over to the balcony, unbuttoned his fly, and dribbled urine down his trouser legs. Julián vomited, then took another swig. *"Es bueno,"* the black man told me cheerfully, nodding toward his jerry can. *"Puro ecuatoriano."*

Not long after, Dameron managed to rally a few of La Unión's leaders, including one wearing a baseball cap who had not attended the *chutún,* and conducted an open-air meeting similar to the one he had held in Mataje. Julián gamely participated. Then we boarded a dugout canoe to continue our journey downstream back toward the coast. Three young boys, the only willing boatmen, poled and pushed us over

*Dr. Roland Dameron and local guide travel
by dugout canoe on a river in the Awá
Indian reserve, northwest Ecuador.*

the rocky shallows of the Río Palabi, one of the most beautiful rivers anywhere. Tall trees soared above its banks, their upper branches linking at midstream. Kingfishers of several species, screeching, bored up and down the river, and herons settled into little marshy patches. Before long, after traversing the neck of a large oxbow on foot, we boarded a second boat and were soon beyond the realm of the Awá and their sadly fragile yet promising condition.

Now we were within the Pacific coastal municipality (township) of San Lorenzo, an isolated outpost that was founded late in the sixteenth

Evidence of continuing logging operations near San Lorenzo

century by survivors from a wrecked slave ship. Still predominantly populated by blacks, San Lorenzo is the principal community in the "zone of influence" bordering the Awá reserve. The municipality, whose sixty thousand citizens suffer from malaria and federal neglect, can still be reached only by boat along the coast or by "train"—a battered, always overcrowded diesel-powered bus on steel wheels that often derails as it makes its precipitous, swaying daily journey through the Awá forest between the inland city of Ibarra, high in the volcanic Andes, and the town of San Lorenzo. Now, as we continued our descent of the widening river toward this destination, we passed growing numbers of older black men and topless women standing chest deep in water as they panned for scarce flakes of alluvial gold dust washed down from high in the Andes. An ancient mufflerless municipal truck, a large hole in the center of its battered windshield, met us at a settlement called Ricaurte, where a local dirt road ended. We bounced, past subsistence farms, into downtown San Lorenzo.

Prospects for this municipality seemed less gloomy during the 1950s, when government logging concessions created new jobs and when the railroad line from Ibarra—a considerable engineering feat—was completed. But the port, which the railroad was designed to serve as a connection between the sea and the highlands, was never built, and the mangrove-lined channels to the ocean have since silted up. As the 1980s began, only small ships of ten thousand tons or less could reach San Lorenzo from open water. The explosive growth of shrimp-pond aquaculture projects had caused grievous losses to the mangroves. Since these nutrient-rich areas are important in the life cycles of wild shrimp and other seafood species, San Lorenzo's small-scale fishermen had also suffered. Most devastating was the assault of the loggers, who by the late 1980s had reduced the accessible supply of uncut timber to less than 10 percent of what it had originally been, initiating a drying trend in the local microclimate and disruptions in supplies of fresh water. The complete end of the local logging industry, on which fully 85 percent of the population had come to depend, could be foreseen by the year 2000.

Ecological degradation disguised as "development" was, in short, putting San Lorenzo on a collision course toward economic and social disaster. Were events to take what has regrettably become the "natural" path in most of the rural Third World,[2] the San Lorenzan reaction would be to press deeper into Awá territory to clear land and establish subsistence farms, driving the vulnerable Awá ever closer to extinction, while giving them only temporary relief from the environmental collapse that wanton forest clearing would soon bring about. But as UTEPA and other outsiders were doing what they could to strengthen the Awá, San Lorenzo too, a decade ago, began its search for a more promising future.

"We had no choice but to act," the forceful community leader Dalmiro Cortez told me. "If we do not create alternative ways to get income there is no future for us." Son of a farmer, a farmer himself, Cortez watched the forest disappear and the streams dry up. He saw

2. This term, considered outmoded by some as global relationships have undergone profound change since the late 1980s, is used in this volume to mean poor countries, with annual per capita incomes of $370 or less, whose citizens remain dependent on agriculture and natural resources.

Dalmiro Cortez, head of FETANE in San Lorenzo,
points to progress in construction of a new building
for the growing association.

the grim future. He saw also that the principal need was for people to relearn farming skills that were soon forgotten when quick money was to be earned in the logging camps. After a long and wearying legal battle, with assistance from the AFL-CIO's American Institute for Free Labor Development (AIFLD), he founded the Federación de Trabajadores Agrícolas Autónomos del Noroccidente de Esmeraldas (FETANE) to plan an ecologically sound development program for the municipality.

In its brief lifetime FETANE has become a formidable local institution. In 1990, only eight years after it began to take shape, it had four thousand members in thirty-nine subdivisions within the municipality. The handsome Cortez gave us a few glimpses of what goes on within the organization. At an evening meeting, a locally trained young woman explained her department's techniques of extending and managing agricultural credit—the first ever available in this corner of Ec-

*"Train" preparing to depart San Lorenzo, northwest Ecuador,
for Ibarra in the highlands*

uador. Another official described how FETANE agronomists were ranging the territory teaching farmers individually about the proper use of chemicals and methods of agricultural diversification new to the region, many of them based on experimental work at a FETANE-run tree nursery that spreads over several hectares. Riding to the outskirts of San Lorenzo, again aboard the township's wheezing truck, we debarked and walked these fields. With a $150,000 grant from the United States Agency for International Development (USAID), FETANE had installed a mill (San Lorenzo's first industry not based on logging) to process *yuca,* a plant commonly cultivated here, into a white meal used as chicken feed. We toured the tidy premises. Animal husbandry, environmental education, health services for members plagued by malaria and other debilitating ailments of the tropics—nothing seemed beyond eager FETANE's grasp.

At a newly opened restaurant in San Lorenzo we ate excellent coriander-flavored seviche and broiled fish. At an adjacent table were several tourists: backpacked European youth. After dinner we repaired to Cortez's house for a farewell Cuba libre. As we were returning to the hotel the town's undependable diesel-powered electrical system failed and we walked the remaining distance under a bright full moon.

The next day, seated aboard the "train" to Ibarra, I had more than eight hours to think back over my time in the forest and in San Lorenzo. Relations between FETANE's members and their Awá neighbors are not entirely smooth, I had discovered. If the Awá do not protect the forest within their reserve, the San Lorenzo agro-ecosystem is bound to suffer further degradation. But Cortez complains that the Awá, with better land than San Lorenzo's blacks, still do not use it properly, and are not yet ready to receive the kind of assistance that FETANE's overworked agronomists can provide. For their part, despite the demarcation of the reserve and the granting of land titles, the Awá remain apprehensive that Cortez and his fellow blacks are really after the Indian land. Still, the socio-environmental interventions that have taken place in both communities offer far greater hope for the people of the region, and for its biological treasures, than the disaster that seemed imminent not long ago. Precarious though these experiments still are, northwest Ecuador today is far more likely to survive ecologically and progress economically than it was just a few years ago.

Economics and environment march together in northwest Ecuador. Not so, I was to rediscover on a recent visit, to the Brazilian town of Parauapebas, a raw Amazonian settlement located some 320 kilometers south and a little west of Belém on the Pará River. In the 1970s Parauapebas had no name and practically no population. Its site was part of a thick unbroken tropical forest where local Indians lived in small settlements. Only a few outsiders entered to hunt or to harvest Brazil nuts from the tall trees that bear them, once plentiful around here. Then came a mighty burst of activity. A road pushed into the forest toward a nearby range called the Serra dos Carajás, where the world's largest deposit (18 billion tons) of high-grade iron ore had been discovered and where a mine and railroad terminal would be constructed. At a fork near the mine, another road was built to provide access to what became the famous gold mine at Serra Pelada, from

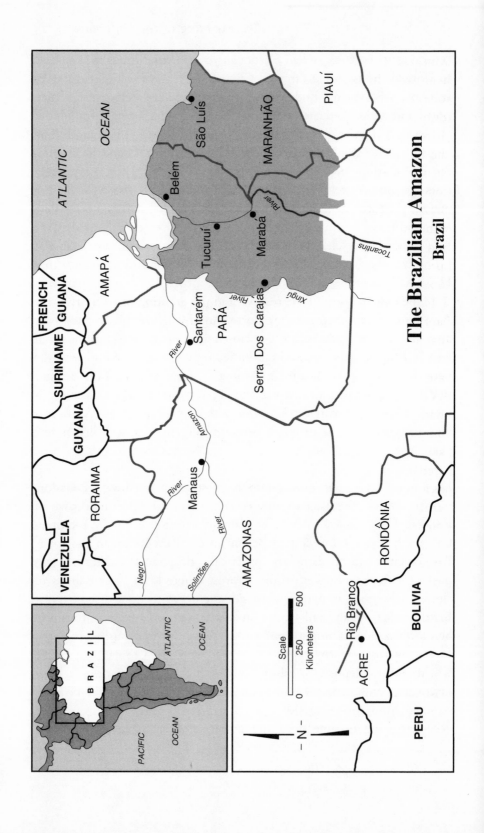

The Brazilian Amazon
Brazil

which vast quantities of the metal, comparable in tonnage to the peaks achieved during the California gold rush, were extracted before the lode began to peter out in the mid-1980s. In photographs circulated globally a decade ago you could see sweating human ants at work there, hauling heavy sacks of gold-flecked mud up wobbly ladders from the bottom of a slimy pit. That was when I first saw Parauapebas, then little more than a camp to house construction workers for the company, Companhia Vale do Rio Doce (CVRD), designated by the Brazilian government to develop the iron mine. Several years later I returned to find a town of ten thousand people, afflicted with poverty and disease and bereft of hope, who had been attracted there by the spreading news of a regional bonanza. Early in 1990 I took a third look.

I went westward by car from the small city of Marabá on the Tocantins River, a major Amazon tributary. Founded in 1916 and for many years a sleepy Brazil-nut port, this place has undergone haphazard and ugly growth as a result of the nearby mining boom. When I last had driven the short distance from there to Parauapebas, in 1985, CVRD had newly asphalted the road. After the mine was built, the road reverted to local management and became badly potholed; one of its more important wooden bridges was barely passable on a single lane. No less run-down than the highway was the flat landscape that stretched to the horizon on both sides: ravaged ground that only a decade ago had been untouched tropical forest was now reduced to scruffy weed and pasture grass, with only an occasional blackened spire of a tree jutting forth as a reminder of the past. The small herds of cattle grazing among the stumps, though healthy in appearance, served as evidence that, because of poor soil quality, ranching here is primitive, highly inefficient, seldom profitable. Little other economic activity was visible: with only vestiges of the timber remaining, sawmill operators and furniture makers had departed the region to move closer to the supply.

"Bem-vindo Boi na Brasa" ("Welcome from the Steak on the Grill") read one restaurant sign as I completed this depressing journey and approached Parauapebas. Along either side of the road now ranged an explosion of new commerce: the Hotel Pará, the Restaurante do Mineiro, auto repair shops, a three-story building housing the local branch

Citizens swim, play, and wash in the polluted Rio Parauapebas,
which flows past their community.

of a chain store called Casa Goiás. Trucks, cars, and even municipal
buses could be seen pitching along rutted streets of red clay leading
away from the highway. During nighttime hours, I was to discover,
streetlights using electricity from the huge new hydroelectric power
station at nearby Tucuruí bathed this scene in a lurid glow of greenish
white. The town pulsed with people.

A focal point of Parauapebas remains the tightly guarded gate at the
entrance to the CVRD property. Beyond, across the bridge over the
Rio Parauapebas, which winds gently past one side of town, the road
begins its ascent through dense, well-maintained forest into one of the
world's most beautiful and most ecologically successful mines. It is a
place where scarlet macaws fly freely over the open ore pits, where
brilliantly blue *Morpho* butterflies flash and flutter among the low
bushes at roadside, where on a previous trip I had had an enjoyable
birdwatching session at the terminus of the railway that carries CVRD's
iron-ore pellets to the Atlantic port of São Luís, 890 kilometers away.
Since the ore lies right on the surface, little deforestation was required
to begin digging. A larger area was, in fact, removed in order to create

the tidy "urban nucleus" where 6,800 CVRD people reside. Even in this tropical Levittown, the damage has been in some part repaired through a program of plantings from the company's carefully maintained tree and shrub nursery.

The question was whether, at least to some degree, CVRD's trim paramilitary values (many of the company people wear tan uniforms) had benefited life outside the closely guarded gate. The answer is resoundingly negative, for the new size and bustle of Parauapebas cannot disguise its essential disarray. Though city authorities have installed and tried to maintain drainage ditches, streets flood and become all but impassable during the frequent downpours that afflict the region. Everything, including litter and untreated human waste, flows into the Rio Parauapebas, which is also the town's principal source of drinking water, its bathtub, and its laundry. Amoebic dysentery and other water-related ailments have not surprisingly become the number-one health problem here. Close behind is venereal disease, easily traceable to the busy red-light street that was blaring and getting to work even at 11:30 a.m., when I drove its length. I pointed a camera at two girls in their mid-teens, dressed in tightly fitting shirts and shorts, sitting in the doorway of the Midnight Mystery bar. They hastily decamped. Though private doctors exist here, their fees are too high for most residents. No doctor serves the town "hospital"; most medicine is dispensed by means of the many pharmacies that line the streets. In this setting women suckle naked babies in front of their makeshift houses, older children swarm on the streets, men and adolescent boys play pool in dark corner bars. Violent crime, one portly young storeowner told me, is a daily occurrence here. "This place is one big slum," he said.

Its residents are the human flotsam of Amazonia. The first to arrive found construction work at the mine. A few commute up the hill to menial jobs for subcontractors (all of CVRD's own employees live inside the gates). Gold lured many to Serra Pelada, but enriched only a few; when production there slowed to a dribble a few years ago, many of the former miners retreated to Parauapebas. Some cut wood until all the wood was cut. Most of them were migrant farmers from the arid, poor northeast of Brazil and from the overcrowded south, young people in search of escape from the unpromising lives they knew they

Prostitutes take a break from work at a club in Parauapebas.

faced at home. They came with the expectation of owning land and being able to work it at a profit.

Such a man is Milton Fiuza de Almeida, a handsome, brush-mustached former resident of the coffee-growing countryside of southern São Paulo state. He arrived in Parauapebas back in 1977, when it hardly existed, and soon became resigned to something less than the new life he had come for. "It was just a workers' camp then," he told me in the strong, hard tones of southern Brazilian Portuguese. "Then came the whores, and then came everything else—the destruction of the trees, the violence to the landscape, the beginning of all our urban and social problems. I did get some land, but I never tried to work it. Only fifty hectares—hardly enough to raise a flock of chickens on. I ended up taking a job as a public functionary here in town, and here I still am."

Irineu dal Santo did not succumb so easily to the allure of Parauapebas. Early in the 1980s, when still living in his native state of Santa Catarina on the coast of southern Brazil, he heard that the government was giving away land near Parauapebas. You could grow cacao there, they said, and coffee, and other profitable commercial crops, and the government would provide all the necessary support. So Irineu packed

Irineu dal Santo in his house at Cedere I colony near Parauapebas

up his young family and collected his fifty hectares at an agricultural colonization site called Cedere I (after the Latin verb "to grant") twenty kilometers outside Parauapebas. In addition to his land, Irineu was given a sturdy wooden house with a cement floor, and a start-up supply of food. These blessings came from an agency called Executive Group of Araguaia-Tocantins Lands (GETAT), a creation of the military government that then ran Brazil. GETAT was widely believed to have been more interested in controlling subversion (there was a minor rebellion in the region in the 1970s), and in helping large landowners evict squatters as land conflicts grew increasingly violent, than in fulfilling its stated mission of settling landless peasants. All went well for a couple of years, when the newly cleared land was fresh and when GETAT's field staff remained on hand in tidy quarters equipped with a diesel generator for electricity. GETAT even ran a small hospital for the Cedere colonists. But in 1986, with little prior notice, GETAT closed the hospital, shut down the generator, and departed. With no assistance available from Parauapebas, the people of Cedere I were suddenly on their own.

After seven years of hard work, Irineu and his family (a wife and four children) were still living frugally when I came to call. In their immaculately clean house, its wooden floor waxed and highly polished, were beds with bedclothing, wooden benches and a table, a small propane gas stove, a freshwater filter, one standing alcohol lamp, and a few tools. Nothing more. Irineu was not bitter, and he cast no blame on GETAT. If any factor was responsible for his inability to make economic headway, he said calmly as we sat in his house one hot afternoon, it was the basic Amazonian paradox: that the soil, on which the magnificent trees of the rainforest are able to flourish because they recycle their own nutrients, tends itself to be barren. "The first thing we learned here," Irineu continued, "is that you can't mess around with this soil. It is only fertile for one year after you cut down the trees and then burn them; after that you can only do so much. I planted cacao but after two years the trees fell over and died. The soil was no good for coffee either. About all that we *can* raise here are a few pigs and chickens, and fruits and some vegetables. Even if we had fertilizer, which we cannot afford, it would do us no good because our heavy rains would just wash it away. We have some things to be thankful for. We have enough to eat, and our water is still clean— though I worry about poisoning from the mercury that spills into the rivers near here after gold prospectors have used it to separate out gold dust in their pans. We don't have malaria or any other serious health problems. But we don't have any money. And there is no way for us to get any."

What little cash Irineu could generate he was spending to buy bottled gas, alcohol for his lamp, cooking oil, rice, and other foods he could not grow. Until 1989 either he sold produce to people from Parauapebas who made the journey to Cedere I to take advantage of the low prices by buying directly from the farmers, or he carried his goods into town to sell them there. But sales were irregular and a better system was needed. In 1989, with encouragement from a young Italian who happened upon the colony, Irineu and seven neighbors formed a cooperative. "We charged fifty cruzados[3] per member," said Maria de Fatima Souza, who arrived as a newlywed about the same time as Irineu. "We had a little party and used the money to buy a large bag

---

3. About $2.00 U.S. at the exchange rate at the time.

of rice and a kilo of coffee." Soon after, even though it had no obligation to the community, CVRD made a deal with it. "It's good for us," said Irineu. "They only pay us half price. But they buy as much as we can grow. And their truck comes around regularly every Monday. That saves us the cost of transport."

Even with CVRD's support and the new vitality of the cooperative, Cedere I was on the wane at the time of my visit. The school's student body, once 144 in number, was down to 52 and dropping. The figures reflect the increasing rate at which, following a pattern that has become classic in Amazonia, Cedere's small landholders were selling out to cattle ranchers with slightly larger plots of 100, 200, or 300 hectares, and moving along. João, a jaunty young man who owned a motorbike bought with money he had earned in the States, rode it up to the entrance to the cooperative's small *cantina* (store). He had come to Cedere six months before, he explained, after encountering U.S. visa problems. He bought land, animals, and equipment. "But this is ridiculous," he said. "You can only make two dollars a day here. I've sold almost everything and am leaving in a few days." As soon as he could arrange it, João added, he would return to work he much preferred: a job as a busboy at a restaurant in Brookline, Massachusetts. Even the stalwart and cheerful Irineu said that he too was thinking of packing up and heading, not home (where it has become too crowded), but to the well-mechanized wheat fields of southern Mato Grosso state.

Cedere I, which according to the original GETAT plan was to be followed by Cederes II and III, was the region's *only* farming cooperative. If there were others, a CVRD ecologist had informed me, the company would gladly be working with them. Individual farmers, such as those in a festering nearby colony called Jader Barbalho, which was squeezed between large spreads and the edge of CVRD's primeval forest, had it much worse. Nor do even the ranchers make it, Irineu explained: "You need a lot of land, and you have to hire men to help you. It takes four years to fatten a calf to market weight. That's far longer than the five months it takes to raise a pig or just a few weeks for chickens. Few of the cattlemen I know around here are making any money." Many of those who abandon the countryside, Irineu continued, end up in Parauapebas. With nothing to do there, they add to the misery of that swelling, already wretched place. Thus, in microcosm, the untidy story of Brazil's misguided and ecologically unsound effort to colonize Amazonia. What was dense forest and home to small numbers of Indians only a decade ago has become bared and barren land, emptying of failed colonists who are crowding into foul raw towns that should never have taken root.

The dramatic differences between the development of unfortunate Parauapebas and what is currently being attempted in northwest Ecuador constitute the essence of this book. Parauapebas represents a dead end for the many common people who were the pawns of traditional top-down planning dominated by economists, engineers, and, in this instance, politico-military strategists. Those in charge, who believed that Brazil would gain power and security by taming the wild Amazon, were interested more in controlling subversion than in bringing about even ecologically unsound forms of development. Although major aid donors had been involved, no national or international environmental agency participated. Few anthropologists, sociologists, ecologists, or even agronomists advised the regime on the program. No one talked to the aboriginal forest dwellers or the Irineus or Miltons about their hopes and needs, or even to citizens of Belém, capital of the Brazilian Amazon for centuries, about development priorities. "The major enterprises come as parachutes," wrote Jean Hebette, professor-researcher at the Federal University of Pará.[4] "They are applied from the top to the bottom, not in accordance with the local social reality and not to address the needs of the region but for the benefit of external interests." Totally ignored were such fundamental ecological factors, already well known in some quarters when the Amazonian development schemes were being concocted, as the infertility of the soils underlying most humid tropical forest regions.

What is happening in northwest Ecuador, on the other hand, illustrates what could become a profoundly important revolution in the thought and practice of aid givers and of conservation agencies at work in rural parts of the developing world. Both the federal government in Quito and official foreign aid donors made clear their respect for the emerging new science of applied ecology. They were pleased to join

4. In a paper entitled *The Social Impact of the Amazonic Major Enterprises*, 1985.

forces with nongovernmental groups that the development mainstream had long considered irrelevant or even counterproductive. Aid officials also defied the canons of development orthodoxy by recognizing the need for both the Awá and the FETANE members to be integrally involved in considering the future of their region. This sort of bottom-up planning—and many eclectic new partnerships for rural microvelopment have convincingly demonstrated it elsewhere—is a principal key to achieving ecological balance.

Conservationists, too, wore new stripes. A previous generation of them, approaching the biological treasures of northwest Ecuador (or the Brazilian Amazon), would first have seen an opportunity to wall off a section of forest and to perfect conditions for the nonhuman species inside. Experience with UTEPA and FETANE brought the World Wildlife Fund, their principal private donor from abroad, toward understanding a new paradigm: while environmental degradation in the industrial world results from affluence and neglect, in developing countries the principal culprit is poverty; therefore, a highly effective way to protect nonhuman species as well as to help people is to provide economically viable alternatives to human assaults on the environment. While official aid agencies were uncustomarily thinking bottom-up and small, a traditional wildlife conservation group was helping to launch a community-based antipoverty program.

In part, the new working partnerships between environmentalists and economic developers have come about because their separate efforts were not sufficiently successful. During the years immediately following World War II, the quick revival of the Japanese and Western European economies seemed to prove the validity of classical economic-development ideas. But during the four decades from 1950 to 1990 a similar transformation failed to take place in the Third World. Billions of dollars in aid brought about significant advances in health and education, but per capita income disparities also increased, along with the total numbers of absolutely poor people; concurrently, development was doing profound ecological harm. Large dams that were meant to make deserts bloom also disrupted traditional fisheries, caused siltation, and spread infectious diseases. The introduction of agricultural machines did grave damage to fragile soils, and chemicals poisoned them. People in the aid agencies saw only progress in the act of felling forests to build highways or dams or to make cattle pastures. All these effects were known in the industrial and postindustrial nations, too, of course, but they were worst and most acute in the vulnerable ecosystems of the tropics.

The international conservation movement, meanwhile, was likewise falling far short of its goals. For twenty years after its establishment in 1962, the World Wildlife Fund (now known in some places as the World Wide Fund for Nature, and globally as WWF) concentrated on measures to protect "charismatic megafauna"—tigers, elephants, rhinos, large primates. Support came in fast-growing amounts from safari hunters, game viewers, and others who appreciated the movement's efforts to help hard-pressed, underfunded government wildlife departments to create game parks and nature reserves and to combat poaching within them. But as neglected human populations in areas adjacent to the parks rapidly increased, the numbers of many of the most popular species continued their downward slide despite good salaries and equipment for rangers, despite vehicles and planes and even expensive helicopters that the international sources provided. Particularly when conservationists became more broadly concerned about accelerating overall losses of biological diversity on the planet—about what was happening to the least as well as to the most visible species—evidence mounted that the movement could more effectively do the job it had assigned for itself if it paid greater heed to *human* needs beyond the borders of the national parks and protected areas. Without such a shift of attention, the most thoughtful conservationists began to fear, the planet would become a series of idyllic dots, devoid of people, scattered upon vast expanses of densely populated wasteland.

In this last decade of the century, both sides thus have ample reason to try new approaches. This convergence—the development community's belated discovery of environmental factors and the conservationists' new concern for human needs—would be an important trend even in the context of a kinder, more stable planet. But for most rural people in the Third World, the world has been neither static nor sympathetic. Rapid population growth is one reason. In 1750 the world's population was less than one billion, and in 1930 it had reached only 2 billion. Between 1930 and 1975 it doubled again. It added a fifth billion by 1990, and is expected to peak at somewhere between 10 and

14 billion during the coming century. Almost all of this increase is expected to take place in developing regions.[5] Already 4.1 billion people live in this Third World, with annual per capita incomes of $370 or less, and have taken up all but vestiges of the earth's usable land for farming and grazing. By 2000, according to the United Nations, the nations of the South (as the less developed world is often called) will have added 900 million more people while the population in the developed nations of the North remains relatively stable. Recently, the population specialist Michael S. Teitelbaum, of the Alfred P. Sloan Foundation, assembled a set of United Nations Population Division figures showing "low" and "high" projections for the population in seventeen large developing countries in the year 2025. At the least, the populations of these countries would grow by 2.2 billion, at most by 3.8 billion. Just the difference in this projected *increase* represents more people than the total current population of the entire industrialized world.

Despite the AIDS epidemic and other Malthusian factors, Africa's population is still expected to quadruple between 1975 and 2025. In that year Nigeria, hardly able to manage its current population of just over 120 million, will have at least 100 million more people. On the basis of current projections, reported Dr. Sharon Camp of the Population Crisis Committee in a pamphlet published in 1989, that wobbly nation "would attain a population by the year 2100 which will approximate that of present-day Latin America or Europe."

Third World cities, already greatly overstrained, will, of course, have to absorb much of this immense new human burden. Between 1990 and 2025, it is estimated, cities in developing countries will grow by 71 percent, adding 2.66 billion people.[6] In 2025, half of all the world's population of 8.2 billion may reside in cities in developing countries;[7] by 2000, ten Third World cities are expected to have populations of 10 million or more, with Mexico City and São Paulo topping the list

5. See Robert Repetto, "Population, Resources, Environment: An Uncertain Future," *Population Bulletin*, Vol. 42, No. 2 (July 1987).
6. According to data published in the World Resources Institute's *World Resources, 1990–91*.
7. Figure cited in Repetto, op. cit.

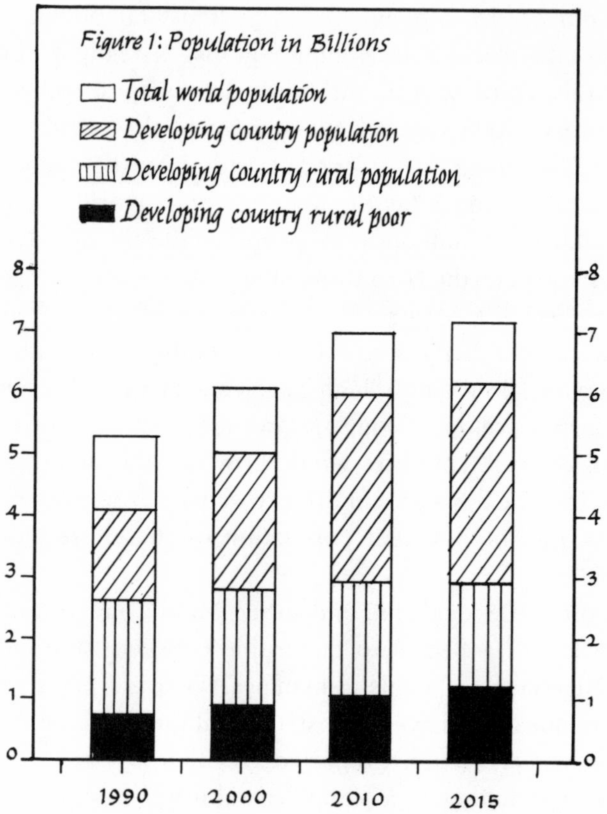
Figure 1: Population in Billions
Total world population
Developing country population
Developing country rural population
Developing country rural poor
0
1
2
3
4
5
6
7
8
1990
2000
2010
2015

at 17 million and 24 million, respectively.[8] Parauapebas manifests the surprising reality that even Amazonia is becoming an urban problem. But rapid urban growth will hardly cause the developing world's hard-pressed rural population to dwindle. The poorest and most needy of the world's poor, as H. Jeffrey Leonard, then of the World Wildlife Fund and the Conservation Foundation noted in a recent article, will often be pocketed in the least accessible places. "Instead of being ubiquitous across the landscape," he wrote, "poverty is in many developing countries more and more concentrated into definable geographical

8. Ibid.

areas." While perhaps one-quarter of the world's poorest people live in "flat lowlands, alluvial valleys, and other areas with good agricultural potential," Leonard continued, some 470 million, or 60 percent of them, live on steep hillsides, arid or very poor lands from which escape is difficult if not impossible.[9] The rest, while marginally better off, still count among the four-fifths of the world's 1.2 billion absolutely poor people who still live in rural areas despite rapid urbanization.[10] By 2015, according to the United Nations Development Program's *Human Development Report 1990* and other sources, the South's rural poor may number as many as 1.25 billion.

When the planet was more sparsely occupied, a migrant family could slash, burn, farm, and exhaust a piece of land, then move on to a virgin site and begin again. In tropical-forest regions, trees for fuel wood and clean fresh water tended to be close at hand. Shifting cultivation, as widely practiced in the rural tropics, was an environmentally sound way for people to subsist. Misery was not poverty's constant companion. Poverty itself was hard to define, since people in many "primitive" lands had little or no need for money. Today, in all but a few places such as the northwestern Amazon and parts of Central Africa, rural frontiers and empty spaces have already given way to patchwork human occupancy and depletion of natural resources. Deforestation and inequitable land-tenure arrangements have crowded the shifting cultivators, and the shorter fallow periods imposed upon them soon exhaust their usually poor-quality land. Lacking frontiers to escape to, they become mired in tangles of unpromising alternatives such as those faced in the eastern Amazon by Irineu dal Santo. For millions of the Third World's rural poor, flight from advancing desertification, or heightening levels of water pollution, is no longer an option.

Increasingly it is not only the degradation of the earth's surface but a befouled atmosphere that affects or further threatens people's lives.

9. In an overview essay to *Environment and the Poor: Development Strategies for a Common Agenda* (Washington, D.C.: Overseas Development Council, 1989), pp. 19, 22.
10. See Alan B. Durning, "Ending Poverty," in *State of the World 1990* (New York and London: Worldwatch Institute, 1990), p. 139.

Acid rain, which forms in clouds when smokestack gases mix with moisture and often travels long distances before it falls to the ground, kills trees in forests far from the source of the problem. The loss of the atmosphere's protective ozone shield (to emissions of such man-made ozone-eating chemicals as chlorofluorocarbons) brings new threats to plant as well as to human health: increases in skin cancer and other diseases are expected as the ozone, which protects the earth's surface from harmful ultraviolet rays that emanate from the sun, becomes ever more depleted. If global warming occurs even at the minimum end of current predictions, many species of plants and animals will not be able to adapt to climate changes—or migrate away from them—fast enough to prevent their extinction. As the sea level rises due to thermal expansion of the oceans and melting glaciers, many important coastal nursery areas—mangroves, sea-grass wetlands, coral reefs—will die or disappear. Health hazards and the prospect of food shortages are linked to all of these phenomena.

These environmental pressures impose severe strains on the poor in the backlands of the rural tropics. So do the security, political, and economic policies and practices of their national leaders. Military expenditures, which nearly doubled as a percentage of poor countries' gross national products between the 1960s and the 1980s, ran well ahead of outlays for social purposes in more than twenty-five of them. Far from helping the rural poor, the soldiers thus enhanced often oppose social objectives, or consume the financial resources needed to achieve them. Centralist or authoritarian political structures, more commonplace than democracies in Third World nations, inhibit the formation of effective community groups working in villages for sound rural development. To remain as popular as possible, or at least to dampen the potential for riots, Third World governments bestow a disproportionate share of benefits on their urban citizens.

Unrealistically low food prices—a subsidy for city dwellers—help to maintain absolute levels of rural poverty and to increase pressure on marginal lands. Inequitable land-tenure arrangements and low land values reduce landholders' incentives to husband their resources. Women, who in Asia and sub-Saharan Africa perform most of the farm labor, receive little of the formal training that the aid agencies provide in techniques of rural development. This form of discrimination against them inhibits the spread of urgently needed knowledge about sustainable means of growing crops. Devices that the governments of the South use to offset the general bias against agriculture usually take the form of subsidies for such "inputs" as water, credit, and fertilizers. But the powerful agricultural chemicals thus deployed, often banned from use in their countries of origin, do grave environmental harm in the countries to which they are legally exported,[11] and these subsidies usually benefit only small numbers of large landholders, while neighboring peasants are forced onto poor, hilly, and uneconomic sites. These are lands that often should not be farmed at all, but allowed to remain covered with perennial grasses or in forest in order to prevent erosion and maintain the natural balance of watershed systems.

The distorted way the world trades its farm goods helps to prolong these inequities. Nations of the North protect domestic farmers by paying some $300 billion a year in price subsidies at home and by "dumping" excess production on the South. The availability of cheap imported food makes it easier for the governments of developing countries to keep on discriminating, as they wish to, against the rural sector. Export taxes and overvalued exchange rates that make their own farm goods less competitive abroad fill coffers in the capitals. What remains marketable internationally, over and above all the policy constraints, often imposes ecologically unwise choices upon the South's small farmers. Many Thais kill their land by cultivating not tree or food crops for domestic consumption but large stands of cassava, or manioc, to send to Western Europe as animal feed. In other countries, forests have been unwisely sacrificed for the sake of beef cattle, bananas, or other commodities that are wanted on the global market.

In part because of imbalances in the trade system, developing countries have taken on ever greater debt loads. Between 1982 and 1991 the total debt of developing countries doubled to the unmanageable level of well over $1.3 trillion. This burden, of course, discourages environmental stability. When defaults occur or threaten, the World Bank

11. See G. Edward Schuh, "International Economic Policies and Sustainable Development," background paper for the Workshop on the Economics of Sustainable Development, Washington, D.C., January 23–26, 1990.

(sometimes in partnership with the austere International Monetary Fund) takes the lead in orchestrating "structural adjustment assistance" programs, in which debt relief is offered in return for reform commitments. One such "reform" is often an increased emphasis on exports, leading to predatory use of ecologically vital resources. As more fully described in Chapter 10, actions designed by economists to encourage economic stabilization all too often result in environmental destabilization.

The customary ways in which the international community has calculated national income and gross national product fail totally to take environmental costs, and a high proportion of human misery, into account. What mattered, stated the neoclassical economists who dominated the profession for much of this century, were invested capital and labor. Were environmental degradation to be factored in as an additional cost, the economist Robert Repetto of the World Resources Institute has figured, Indonesia's average GNP growth rate from 1971 to 1984 would, for example, decrease from 7.1 to 4 percent. This is but one example of how conventional economics discourages the maintenance of a sound environment.

Powerful barriers, then, obstruct the path toward enlightened economic and industrial activity everywhere, and therefore also toward development in the rural Third World. Rich governments and consumers in industrial nations, as well as autocrats in the poorer ones, compound the problems. Under these unfavorable circumstances, peasants the world over cling to the edge of nature. I have chosen to write about these people, and where they live, because of the striking and dramatic way their future represents everyone's. Not only will the needs of the poor in the rural tropics have to be met in any successful global "war" on poverty; they will have to be met in an ecologically sound way. The alternative is for these same people to become urban poor, living in equal or worse misery at a far greater cost to society and more tempted then to emigrate to industrial nations. No less than the welfare of all the world's people is involved.

Where the rural poor of the Third World live is also where biological diversity is heavily concentrated. In recent years, scientists' calculations of how many plant and animal species exist have zoomed upward. From 5 to 10 million was a frequent guess during the 1970s. Then

Terry Erwin of the Smithsonian Institution posited 30 million. Others bumped the number far higher. Said Edward O. Wilson: "Remarkably, we do not know the true number of species on Earth, even to the nearest order of magnitude. My own guess, based on the described flora and fauna and many discussions with entomologists and other specialists, is that the absolute number falls somewhere between 5 and 30 million."[12] Whatever the correct figure (who will ever know?), 90 percent or more of them occupy tropical forests—far and away the places on earth with the greatest biological wealth, where 200 million people also live. Right behind them are coral reefs. As many as half of all species may be concentrated upon only 2 percent of the planet— almost all of it in the rural tropics.

With every increase in scientists' estimates of how many species exist comes grim news about accelerating rates of extinction resulting from humans' careless occupancy and use of the planet. People depend in many ways on the properties of wild species—for food, medicine, and industrial products. Even in today's high-technology world, while these values can sometimes be replicated in laboratories, they often cannot be *created* there. Since the population is growing far faster than the amount of land that can be cultivated, crop yields must increase. A principal means of bringing about such increases in yields of the crops on which we largely depend—wheat, rice, corn—is genetic refreshment from wild sources, which creates new hybrids that resist blight and insects. Resistance to two of the four major diseases that affect rice, for example, comes from wild species of rice. "The case for crop genetic diversity is unassailable," says the ecologist Walter V. Reid of the World Resources Institute. Some medicines, such as a compound drawn from the Pacific yew that is used to combat ovarian cancer, cannot be made in the lab. An extract from the rosy periwinkle, a wildflower found in Madagascar, is used to treat leukemia and Hodgkin's disease; it can be made synthetically only at a prohibitive cost. Understandably, drug companies are fast increasing their investments in natural-products research. The overwhelmingly strong case for preserving the world's diversity of species, which often means preserving

---

12. From *Biodiversity*, the proceedings of a Smithsonian forum on the subject (Washington, D.C.: National Academy Press, 1988), p. 5.

Third World rural development in progress

their habitats, is thus based on very practical as well as on moral and aesthetic considerations.

The point is obvious: the fate of the rural poor in the Third World, and the pressures on already mushrooming cities in developing countries, and on the nations of the North as well, and the outlook for wild plants and animals, are all inseparably linked to each other. More than any other kinds of people, those who are the heroes of this book have learned and suffered the limits of sustainability. They have watched in despair as productive ecosystems have collapsed, often being forced by sheer need to participate in the devastation. If these same people, given a few breaks, cannot subsist in harmony with nature, no one can; if they fail, the planet will have suffered a crushing and perhaps even lethal defeat. All the world's security is at stake.

CHAPTER 2

Stages of Development

Boundless optimism about potential new ways for society to grow and prosper marked the era that followed World War II. Futuristic technologies would help people "conquer" and occupy the remaining frontiers. In Africa, fulfilling the old colonial dream of eliminating the tsetse fly would open new lands for domesticated herds, making the savanna the planet's great provider of beef. Britain began to implement, in Tanganyika, Northern Rhodesia, and Kenya, a giant program to "develop" 1.3 million hectares of land for the mechanized production of peanuts. The much-heralded purpose of the vaunted "groundnut scheme" was to alleviate the global shortage of edible oils and fats. The empty Amazon Basin would likewise fulfill its long-awaited destiny: once the forests had been stripped away, agricultural development would turn the region into the bountiful breadbasket that, even during the war, had been forecast by the economists C. P. Kindleberger and Alvin H. Hansen.[1] The influential American macro-planner Herman Kahn, who dismissed environmentalism as "an issue that has been in the past part of a broad anti-bourgeois, anti-industrial platform," later con-

---

1. "The Economic Tasks of the Postwar World," *Foreign Affairs,* April 1942.

tributed to the heedless Amazonian dream with his bizarre proposal that the region be dammed for hydroelectric power and to create a huge inland sea. Similar technologies would bring a burst of progress to Asian nations now liberated from Japanese oppression.

Such woozy utilitarianism marked the general uncertainty, rampant at the time, about the forms and purposes of economic development in poor countries. In his book *Economic Development: The History of an Idea,* the economist H. W. Arndt proposed several strands of "prehistory" leading toward the idea's post-1945 evolution. The Chinese leader Sun Yat-sen, Arndt stated, was "a generation ahead of his times" in advocating, in the 1920s, a program of Western-style modernization for his then feudal country. During World War II, while a few pioneering thinkers, such as Alva Myrdal of Sweden, were envisioning a postwar world in which wealth and power would be more equitably shared among industrial and developing nations, other voices from the past were still being heard. When they wrote of "advancement," Western thinkers from Adam Smith to Marx and Lenin had really meant further progress for already advanced societies. Neither John Maynard Keynes nor Joseph Schumpeter, who remain among the most admired economists of the early twentieth century, was greatly interested in addressing questions of poverty beyond Europe's borders. Following such strands of thought, midcentury colonialists still expressed their concern for "natives' " well-being in white-man's-burden code phrases such as *"la mission civilisatrice"* that thinly disguised the self-interest of the powerful in their relations with the periphery.

What colonies were good for, it was still widely believed, was the steady and inexpensive supply of primary products: rubber, coffee, cacao, timber. After exhausting the domestic supply of trees to fashion into masts for sailing ships during the eighteenth century, British entrepreneurs had invaded the pinewoods of North Carolina. To satisfy European cravings, planters of many nations had unhesitatingly turned the tropical forests of the Caribbean and northeast Brazil (as well as lands better suited for plantation agriculture) into sugar fields. Kindleberger and Hansen saw U.S. consumers as the postwar beneficiaries of their Amazonian deforestation scheme; the British would devour the lion's share of the African groundnuts. "Western dominance was advanced by force and superior technology," wrote Francis X. Sutton of the Ford Foundation, "but sustained by the prestige and deference that followed from power."[2]

With no empire to speak of, the United States disregarded the Third World's welfare for a different reason: the anticolonialism that was as much a part of the Marshall Plan's ideology as its altruism and its anticommunism. The program "was intended to restore the economies of the metropoles, not to sustain empires that in American eyes were anachronistic and even immoral," wrote Lincoln Gordon.[3] Some $65 billion (about $350 billion in 1990 dollars) was spent on the Marshall Plan effort over three years. (In 1989 only 15 percent of a meager $14 billion "foreign aid" budget was allocated to development assistance for Third World nations.)

This was the muddy playing field upon which the practice of development assistance for Third World nations was launched. There is some question about where exactly the idea came from. In his memoirs Harry S. Truman stated that he had begun to think about extending aid to such countries at the time the Marshall Plan was launched in 1947. Other sources claim that the idea, embodied in Franklin D. Roosevelt's Good Neighbor Policy toward Latin America, was later picked up by the indefatigable White House adviser Clark Clifford. A third version suggests that it was smuggled into the White House by a middle-ranking State Department official after it had been rejected within the State Department itself. Regardless of the origin, the announcement of what became known as the "Point Four Program" to provide technical help for developing countries was regarded as an innovative highlight of Truman's January 1949 inaugural address. He proposed a radical new international order. "The old imperialism . . . has no place in our plans," he said. "What we envisage is a program of development based on the concepts of democratic fair-dealing . . . a bold new program for making the benefits of our scientific advances and industrial progress available for the improvement and growth of underdeveloped areas."

2. In "Development Ideology: Its Emergence and Decline," *Daedalus*, Vol. 118, No. 1 (Winter 1989), pp. 35–58.
3. See "Recollections of a Marshall Planner," *Journal of International Affairs*, Summer 1988, p. 236.

Some of those commissioned to put the Point Four idea into practice came to regard development as a process in which "modernization," industrialization and GNP growth, achieved largely by means of public investments and comprehensive national planning, would lead to increasingly prosperous and contented free societies. In the North, an unprecedented network of governmental and multilateral institutions was created to equip poorer neighbors with financial and technical assistance to help them achieve these results. Yet from the outset, purist views were also tempered by voices suggesting something less than a clean break from the past. In his memoirs, Truman himself said he had been looking for something along the lines of "the Greece and Turkey proposition" to contain the spread of communism. Point Four was based, John Kenneth Galbraith later contended, on inadequate assumptions: that what was good for the United States was good for a developing country, that the problem was a shortage of capital rather than a lack of social justice or good government. The hidden agenda of development assistance, he complained, in spite of Truman's declaration of a new world, seemed to be to "pick up where colonialism left off."

Point Four's mixed set of motives was but one of many difficulties the proposal encountered. In Congress, Republican opponents reduced appropriations for it to a token level. Some believed that even with proper funding, inadequate knowledge and experience would inhibit the program's ability to bring about the social and economic transformations that enthusiasts envisioned. Prior to 1950, wrote the economic historian David Morawetz, there was no such thing as a university course on economic development or a scholarly journal addressing the subject.[4] The Third World remained far more the province of anthropologists than of economists.

Yet if Point Four itself accomplished little and the times were not yet right for a fully focused effort, the program led directly to a burst of institutional activity that gave the first structure to the development idea. During the late 1940s the World Bank and the International Monetary Fund came into existence; so did the United Nations technical assistance group that was to become the United Nations Development Program (UNDP), and United Nations dependencies such as the Food

4. David Morawetz, *Twenty-five Years of Economic Development, 1950 to 1975* (Washington, D.C.: The World Bank, 1977), Chapter 2.

and Agriculture Organization (FAO) and the World Health Organization (WHO). Its Economic Commission for Latin America (ECLA) was one of several regional bodies established to support the United Nations' development efforts. In the United States, as a direct consequence of Point Four, bilateral aid to developing countries became institutionalized as an instrument of foreign policy (though the development assistance component, as well as the total dollar commitment, declined sharply as the years went by, and though it was not until the 1980s that aid donors turned their attention to the environmental problems that they were exacerbating).

The very first World Bank mission, to Colombia in 1950, stressed the importance of meeting people's basic needs. For the most part, however, the development community was preoccupied more by technical achievement than by human welfare. The conventional wisdom of the time called for comprehensive economic plans to be supported by capital-intensive investments in large projects—dams, roads, power stations, industrial installations. The realization of these public works would reduce poor countries' need to spend hard currency reserves to buy manufactured goods abroad. It would also help to accelerate economic growth. As was Kennedy-era economics in the United States, the early World Bank model is often described as "neo-Keynesian" in recognition of its emphasis on government planning and job creation in the context of a free economy. Keynes, however, took little interest in the characteristic Third World problem of *under*employment: to him a job was a job. He also assumed that GNP growth would automatically lead to improvements in income distribution. For these and other reasons, applying his ideas to Third World needs proved to be less than fully effective.

During the 1950s GNP in developing countries did indeed grow at double the rate that had prevailed in the advanced world. New and impressive urban agglomerations, such as Caracas, Mexico City, and São Paulo, gave the appearance of progress. Yet within a decade the problems of poverty in prominent developing countries such as India were becoming ever more acute and visible. The per capita income gap continued to widen, both between rich and poor nations and between rich and poor people within the latter. The literature of development is replete with explanations for the general failure of the effort. Maybe the problems were truly intractable, some argued: the success of the

Marshall Plan in Western Europe had simply made it seem too easy. Complications ranging from trade-union power in industrial nations to chronic underemployment elsewhere rendered the center-periphery relationship far more complex.[5] Accelerating population growth, balance-of-payments difficulties, and an overemphasis on capital were among the other reasons cited. Domestic political strife often rendered economic progress difficult to achieve. Value systems diverged. "Expected to perform like wind-up toys and to 'lumber through' the various stages of development single-mindedly," as the peripatetic economist Albert Hirschman put it, referring to the economist Walt W. Rostow's scenario in which acceleration would lead to economic "takeoff," the countries of the periphery were "discovered to have passions as well as interests."[6]

These "passions" began in the 1960s to erupt into outright opposition to the established dogmas of development economics. Industrialization had not curbed poor nations' appetite for imports; what was needed was a new approach in which increased exports of manufactured goods would help them to balance their trade accounts. Led by the charismatic Argentine economist Raúl Prebisch, who had long contended that worsening terms of trade were chiefly responsible for keeping poor nations poor, the nations of the South now demanded trade concessions as well as support to build the factories where the goods to be traded would be made. Since they also needed greater flexibility in their use of aid funds, they came to prefer "program" loans that supported broad sectors of the economy, rather than financing for specific projects. Agriculture, previously ignored, would receive greater attention. A more market-oriented approach gained favor. Heralded as the core of the United Nations' "Decade of Development," loudly debated at the 1964 United Nations Conference on Trade and Development (UNCTAD), the new ideas gave hope for meaningful change in North-South economic relationships.

For all these procedural shifts, thinking about development re-

5. For a full analysis of these points, see "The Rise and Decline of Development Economics," the opening essay in Albert O. Hirschman's *Essays in Trespassing: Economics to Politics and Beyond* (Cambridge, Eng.: Cambridge University Press, 1981), pp. 1–24.
6. Ibid., p. 24.

mained largely bound within older orthodoxies and contradictions. Aid was still proffered almost entirely on a government-to-government basis, too often linked tightly to donor-country exports. It was assumed that positive benefits would "trickle down" from the top to a broader citizenry, and results were still measured in terms of overall "growth." Many of the foremost spokesmen for foreign aid perceived the alleviation of poverty not as an end in itself but as a means of reducing world tensions for the benefit of the aid donors. Paul Hoffman, the former automobile executive (Studebaker Corporation) who was a dominant figure from the time of the Marshall Plan until he left the United Nations Secretariat in 1971, had little doubt as to the purpose of his mission. As his biographer Alan R. Raucher put it, Hoffman "regarded foreign aid as an instrument to preserve democracy and capitalism by providing stability and the foundation for economic growth."[7]

In Brazil in 1964, after the United States helped its army to depose the leftist president João Goulart, a crash USAID program began. The streets of Recife, capital of the poor and drought-ridden northeast, suddenly filled with unprecedented processions of black Chevrolet sedans belonging to U.S. government officials. Central Intelligence Agency operatives worked the countryside, trying to build democratic counterparts to Marxist peasant institutions that had been formed during the Goulart era. No more than in Guatemala in the 1950s, or later in Vietnam, was the well-being of the people a central concern of the United States or its development and security agencies. In all three instances, the rationale for a U.S.-led economic development effort related directly to U.S. interests as defined by officials with short-term mind-sets.

In recipient countries, meanwhile, corruption inhibited the flow of donated funds from government offices to the programs for which they were intended, giving rise to accusations that the principal effect of development assistance was the transfer of funds from the poor in rich countries to the rich in poor countries. The appearance in their capitals of grandiose palaces, cathedrals, and other showy public works provided visual evidence. Added to the already long list of development

---

7. *Paul G. Hoffman: Architect of Foreign Aid* (Lexington, Ky.: University Press of Kentucky, 1985), p. 79.

failures, these manifestations were bound to alienate important segments of the donor public. In 1965 Barbara Ward (Lady Jackson), the inspired leader of the International Institute for Environment and Development (IIED), complained that with the exception of Taiwan, Israel, and a few other special places, the world had made no progress in lessening the North-South gap. Within fast-growing individual nations such as Nigeria, Brazil, and Pakistan, disparities among regions were increasing as well. In 1969, one year after his inauguration as World Bank president, another recycled automobile executive, Robert McNamara, noted telling examples of the development dilemma in his address to the annual meetings of the Bank and the International Monetary Fund. From 1950 to 1960, he noted, Venezuela and Jamaica had enjoyed average economic growth rates of 8 percent a year. Yet at the end of the period, unemployment in Venezuela was *higher* than it had been at the outset; in Jamaica it was just as high despite the emigration of 11 percent of the labor force. In 1968, McNamara added, the total of all development assistance spending was $9 billion; donor countries, while still growing proportionally richer, were spending $120 billion on arms. The Decade of Development, Barbara Ward concluded, was becoming "a study in frustration."

Some observers advised against rejecting the old theories out of hand. Since both slow-growing and fast-growing nations had large numbers of absolutely poor people, Morawetz noted, growth itself was not necessarily the problem. It was often suggested that while inequality would increase during early stages of growth, the curve would flatten later on. Yet for all such justifications, wrote Sutton, the "old doctrines of development" that had "flowered" early in the 1960s "fell away with remarkable speed as the decade came to an end." At the World Bank and International Monetary Fund's annual meetings, support for the development idea gave way to angry protests. "There was a desperate need to build a new alliance structure," said James P. Grant, then head of the Overseas Development Council, a business-supported private group in Washington, D.C. Out of it all came yet another new thought: that effective development should incorporate principles of equity as well as growth. During the 1970s, the second development decade, basic human needs were advanced as the central concern, and aid donors at last began to "take poverty seriously," as the authors Tom Dale

and Vernon Carter had long before advocated in their remarkable book
Topsoil and Civilization.[8]

"Unless life in the hinterland can be made tolerable," Dale and Carter
added, "the problem of world poverty is insoluble and will inevitably
get worse." In 1973, at the Bank/IMF annual meetings in Nairobi,
McNamara followed this prescription in announcing a series of Bank
programs to aid the developing world's small farmers, who then num-
bered 100 million, with the goal of achieving a 5 percent growth rate
in their productivity by 1985. The concept of "integrated rural development" (IRD) became fashionable, though some later wondered what
they had seen as its redeeming features.[9] The powerful Bank's leadership prompted many other large-scale development agencies to redirect
their attention from the capitals to the rural sector.

Others went further, embracing the view that markedly smaller-scale,
community-based approaches would work best in the rural Third
World. An early example was provided by the Inter-American Foundation, established in 1969 by the U.S. Congress as an experimental
agency to "chart new paths in development assistance."[10] In the wake
of the IAF's pioneer grant-making in the rural sector as well as in
towns and cities, mainstream aid donors undertook projects to mobilize local resources and decentralize authority, emphasize the productivity of poor people and enhance the value of this "human capital."
Now expatriate social workers as well as anthropologists fanned out
to rural areas at the ends of the world. They came from public entities
such as the Peace Corps or as church volunteers, or through programs
organized by private nongovernmental organizations (NGOs) with
names like ACCION International, Volunteers in Asia, the Pan American Development Foundation. Some worked at the most basic end of
the spectrum, supporting community health or education efforts, digging wells and ditches for sewage. Others, such as the IAF, worked

8. Norman, OK.: University of Oklahoma Press, 1955.
9. For an example of a meddlesome, overblown IRD scheme failing to interact posi-
tively with another, better-designed project, see the description of the ADMADE program in Zambia in Chapter 7.
10. From *They Know How: An Experiment in Development Assistance* (Rosslyn, Va.:
Inter-American Foundation, 1977), p. 1.

out more comprehensive ideas on how to bring about rural development. Most were fervent believers in the idea that a bottom-up, people-to-people orientation would in the long run be more effective than the trickle-down methodology that still dominated the practice of development assistance. Poor people were the best judges of their own needs, it was argued, and they lacked neither the intelligence nor the energy to help themselves if they received the right forms of support—as acknowledged in the title of the Inter-American Foundation's *They Know How.*

Far from all of the basic-needs initiatives were successful. Many of them, said the development economist John P. Lewis,[11] suffered from a lack of experience, excessive ambition, impatience, and a tendency to create artificial new management structures rather than reinforce what was already there. While growth was never the whole answer, he continued, the extent to which it had now been traded in for "village worship" was "overdone." Criticizing the aid community's performance from a different perspective, Barbara Ward in 1981 concluded bleakly that, despite the new approaches, the industrial democracies still had "no strategy and no vision in dealing with the developing 'south.' "[12] That same year Mahbub ul-Haq, a former Finance Minister of Pakistan and then director of policy planning at the World Bank, expressed the guardedly positive view that during the 1970s a "gradual shift" had taken place from "a mindless pursuit of economic growth" to "a better understanding of the problems of poverty and the urgency of meeting basic human needs."[13] None of these comments reached the heart of the matter: that project design and conceptual shortcomings were only minor contributors to the problems of the basic-needs approach. For far broader reasons, the concept never stood a chance.

The breaking point was the oil shock of 1973, which set off inflationary disruptions that deeply wounded the world economy. As debt problems began to surface in the nations of the South, McNamara delivered increasingly shrill exhortations to aid donors. Pleas for heav-

11. In his Introduction to John P. Lewis, ed., *Strengthening the Poor: What Have We Learned?* (Washington, D.C.: Overseas Development Council, 1988).
12. From "Another Chance in the North?" *Foreign Affairs,* Winter 1980–81, p. 386.
13. The Mahbub ul-Haq comment also appeared in "Negotiating the Future," *Foreign Affairs,* Winter 1980–81, p. 400.

ier aid flows also came from two blue-ribbon commissions that he appointed. The first was chaired by former Canadian Prime Minister Lester Pearson, the second by former West German Chancellor Willy Brandt. Beset at home, however, the donor nations hitched their belts ever tighter. The objective set for the first Decade of Development had been for the advanced nations to contribute 1 percent of their GNPs to the aid effort. But by 1978 the average was down to .031 percent, and it sank even lower before the end of the Second Development Decade. Within the club of rich nations—the Development Assistance Committee (DAC) of the Paris-based Organization for Economic Co-operation and Development—the worst record of all was being compiled by the United States. In 1979 its contribution had dwindled to what McNamara, by now a fervent champion of more generosity in development assistance, called a "disgraceful" level of .022 percent.

Increasingly, development support came now to consist not so much of aid for the poorest as of "structural adjustment assistance" programs to help countries cope with growing debt burdens through domestic austerity and increased exports. The manner in which these agreements were negotiated, reported the development economist Richard Jolly, represented a sharp deviation from the modes of earlier decades. Instead of involving numerous development and social planning officials, negotiations were more often sequestered within "a small group in the ministry of finance and the central bank—often working in great confidentiality and relating primarily to a visiting group of experts from the World Bank and IMF."[14] Committees thus composed seldom worked out packages that addressed the worsening social situation in many beneficiary countries. Both growth and equity had become secondary to the grim adjustment process. They remained so late in the 1980s even after, in recognition of austerity's effects on the poor, aid donors had attempted to impose a "human face" on it. During the course of the once vaunted Third Development Decade, per capita incomes showed disastrous drops both in sub-Saharan Africa and in Latin America, and long-range development goals were widely sacrificed in favor of what has been called "the economics of survival."[15]

14. From "Poverty and Adjustment in the 1990s," in Lewis, ed., op. cit.
15. Ibid.

Summing up, Jolly could still find no more positive an expression than the phrase "a development disaster" to characterize the overall results achieved during the 1980s.

One continuing and paramount theme runs through all these phases: the failure of aid agencies, until very recently, to assess the environmental costs of their actions or explore the close links between rural poverty and environmental degradation. Just as biologists and wildlife managers narrowed global conservation's focus until very recent times, the traditional dominance of economists and engineers in development circles limited the discipline's perceptions. Such people often ignored environmental factors entirely, viewing those who considered them important as hostile enemies. Wrote Lewis: "We may have been into the 1980s before the environment was widely recognized as an important dimension not just of development but of anti-poverty policy."[16]

Yet at the very outset of the postwar era, scattered voices had been sounding alarms about what humans were doing to the planet. At a 1949 International Technical Conference held in Lake Success, New York, participants warned of the perils of using the powerful insecticide DDT (this was thirteen years before Rachel Carson's *Silent Spring,* appealing for a cleaner environment, called attention to the disastrous effects of DDT). The Belgian conservationist Jean-Paul Harroy noted that it had been shown to be "mortal to crayfish" and should not be applied "except where absolutely necessary." At the same meeting, African experts expressed fears that a rapid expansion of grazing lands would lead not toward prosperity but rather toward the tragic degradation that has befallen the Sahel's landscape. They questioned the desirability of eradicating the tsetse fly, carrier of the disease trypanosomiasis (sleeping sickness) that is fatal to cattle, and releasing vast new areas to them and to their herders. Correctly they predicted that overgrazing, desertification, and soil erosion would be likelier results than prosperity.

Other speakers reasoned that the introduction of exotic plant and animal species in places where they did not breed, an already familiar form of biological manipulation that soon became commonplace, might lead to unexpected and negative consequences. "Man must recognize

16. Ibid., Introduction.

the necessity of cooperating with nature," concluded the prominent American naturalist Fairfield Osborn in his 1948 book *Our Plundered Planet.*[17] "He must temper his demands and use and conserve the natural living resources of this earth in a manner that alone can provide for the continuation of his civilization." But it was hardly in the spirit of the times to believe that environmental obstacles lay in the path of full-throttle development.

One early warning signal was the fate of the East African groundnut scheme. Haste, mismanagement, poor planning, and the difficulty of getting machines to Africa all impeded the progress of this grand effort. But its principal problems were environmental. Not even a practical farmer, let alone an ecologist, had been in on the planning. So eager for results was the sponsoring United Africa Company, Ltd., that the project was abruptly initiated without the benefit of soil and climate tests. The difficulty of extracting the thornbush covering the initial planting site, selected for the lightness of its ground cover, was greatly underestimated. The effect of drought, euphemistically characterized in one early report as a "temporary cessation of rain," was accorded far too little importance. After five years of expensive effort and little accomplishment, what had been predicted would become "one of the acknowledged glories of the commonwealth," promising for African farmers "a revolution in agricultural technique" and serving as "an example of the bold economic planning which is necessary to raise the standard of living of the African peasant,"[18] was in 1951 reduced to the pilot status from which it never should have been elevated.

With the publication in 1962 of *Silent Spring,* Rachel Carson brought to the broad public the bad news about DDT that had been reported at the 1949 Lake Success gathering of experts. Environmentalism as a mass movement was born, and it did not take long for its leaders to challenge the methodology of development. At Airlie House in Virginia in 1968, Fairfield Osborn's Conservation Foundation (CF) convened a pivotal meeting of ecologists and economists to consider "how to halt the historically careless application of technology and begin to

17. Boston: Little, Brown, 1948, p. 201.
18. From J. K. Matheson and E. W. Bovill, eds., *East African Agriculture* (Oxford: Oxford University Press, 1950), p. 119.

create a new technology in equilibrium with the biosphere."[19] The Conservation Foundation had assembled a distinguished group: Gunnar Myrdal, the economist Michael Boulding, the ecologist Barry Commoner, Raymond Dasmann of the International Union for the Conservation of Nature and Natural Resources (IUCN),[20] S. Dillon Ripley (then an ornithologist at Yale, later the Smithsonian's secretary). For several days these and other scholars reviewed the environmental consequences of development as it had been practiced since World War II. Commoner summed it up as having been a "general failure" in which the introduction of new technologies caused new environmental hazards. Nearly every irrigation project, he claimed, resulted in new diseases or pest problems for farmers; some had even *reduced* agricultural potential in the region meant to be the beneficiary. Serious ecological hazards had accompanied "nearly every reported instance" involving the introduction of chemical control of agricultural pests in newly developed farming areas; similar results had been found in the case histories of technological improvements in animal husbandry and fisheries. "The rescue rope offered to developing nations by modern science and technology," Commoner concluded, "is basically unsound."

In working sessions of the meeting, experts provided telling detail. In Liberia, ill-fated for environmental as well as for political reasons, new roads helped to spread sleeping sickness. Modern perennial irrigation in Egypt raised the disease called schistosomiasis, or bilharzia, transferred to humans via a snail, from low levels to an almost universal one. Further problems in Egypt included the virtual elimination of the eastern Mediterranean sardine fishery as a result of the Aswan High Dam, and massive fish die-offs in the lakes of the Nile delta after heavy pesticide applications. While a dam built on the Zambezi River in 1963 had provided the electric power that was the only consideration in its sponsors' cost-benefit analysis, negative results included the dis-

---

19. From the Foreword to M. Taghi Farvar and John M. Milton, eds., *The Careless Technology: Ecology and International Development* (Washington, D.C.: The Conservation Foundation, 1969), p. xv.

20. In 1990, this conglomeration of public and private conservation and environmental agencies renamed itself the World Conservation Union.

placement of 57,000 people, the spread of an aquatic fern that depressed the river's traditional fisheries, and an irrigation program that proved unable to "produce ecologically acceptable systems of land use that were also acceptable to the farmers."[21] Water projects from the Indus Basin to the upper Rio Grande to the never completed Anchicaya hydroelectric power station in Colombia caused side effects including waterlogging, salinity, pollution, and sedimentation. The infertility of tropical soils generally and the particular unsuitability of the Amazonian lowland for human settlement were noted. One participant suggested that Amazonia be carefully studied in advance of the arrival of settlers in order to "establish sound and enforceable regulations before our old mistakes in tropical resource development return to haunt us."

An illuminating case study presented at the meeting involved farmers' exclusive usage, between 1949 and 1956 in Peru's Cañete Valley, of large doses of synthetic pesticides. Marketed aggressively by new-style merchants, these chemicals appeared to be the "modern" answer to agricultural pest problems. But yields kept decreasing until the crisis year of 1956, when farmers lost half their crop. In 1957 an "integrated ecological program" was introduced, in desperation, as a substitute. Measures taken included a ban on the chemicals that had previously been used, the reintroduction of useful insects that had disappeared during the earlier program, careful management practices, and greater reliance on organic chemicals and minerals. Within a few years yields had risen sharply and the insect problem had all but vanished. Few such examples could be found, however, and the conservation historian Lynton K. Caldwell could offer only a grim conclusion: "The destructive potential of development has become so great and the misapplications of science-based technology have become so common that better policies and procedures are urgently needed to reduce the extent of damage to the biosphere until a more adequate applied ecology can be provided." A science adviser to USAID who attended the meeting as an observer said that he had "enjoyed" it.

As we shall see in Chapter 4, it only went downhill from there. Flawed as the record has been, however, it would be a misleading

21. Thayer Scudder, "Ecological Bottlenecks and the Development of the Kariba Lake Basin," in Farvar and Milton, eds., op. cit., pp 206–7.

oversight not to note some of the achievements of the development assistance effort as well as its shortcomings. It has, advocates point out, helped bring facilities they wanted—improved transportation, electricity, health, education, and technical services—to countless millions in poor nations. Foreign aid has been a factor in enabling developing countries to outpace the ferocious population explosion of the years 1950–90. World population had increased by half a billion between 1930 and 1950, global warfare notwithstanding, but few forecasters had predicted that it would more than double between then and 1990—from 2.5 billion to 5.3 billion. In 1989, according to the Worldwatch Institute, the 1.2 billion people who were living in utter poverty represented a shocking "poverty rate" of 23.4 percent, but the equivalent figure for 1950 had been 30 percent or more. Despite a dip in the figure during the 1980s, in other words, a marginally lower *percentage* of the world's population (though a record *number* of people) now cling to the very edge of life than did so in 1945. Foreign aid represents the major share of the total economies in a few very poor African nations, but in most developing countries development assistance income represents no more than a small part of the total economic effort. Progress also depends on many other factors: domestic resources and how they are allocated, fiscal and macroeconomic policies, world market conditions. What foreign aid programs alone can accomplish can easily be exaggerated.

Yet if there are reasons to defend the theory and practice of foreign aid, the environmental and economic plight of poor countries also highlights the substantial and growing gap between the current situation and what development theorists hoped might be accomplished through direct transfers over more than four decades. The record hardly constititutes "one of mankind's major public-affairs achievements in this half-century," as Lewis heralded it in 1986.[22] By the end of the 1980s, some were even calling for an outright end to it. In his melancholy polemic *Lords of Poverty,* the British journalist Graham Hancock maintained that the entire field of official development assistance had become a "sacred cow," the product of a massive and sustained public relations campaign, and had done no good whatever for

22. Lewis, ed., op. cit., Introduction.

the target countries. Its only beneficiaries are swarms of perk-laden expense-account-padding functionaries and consultants within the aid agencies, he argued, and the world would be far better off if the whole thing was categorically abandoned. In his book *Tropical Gangsters,* the economist Robert Klitgaard strikes what is probably a sounder balance. Coming off a World Bank posting to steamy Equatorial Guinea, he evenhandedly concludes: "The harsh conditions of underdevelopment encourage tropical gangsters of every variety—government, business, and international aid giver."[23] His wry account and scores like it leave no doubt that major improvements are required if the aid business is to fulfill the aspirations of its founders.

23. New York: Basic Books, 1990, p. 12.

CHAPTER 3

❧

The Changing Conservation Ethic

Severe contradictions have always buffeted the idea of nature conservation, whose origins extend back to the morning of human life. In early times, animal worship and anthropocentrism competed for public attention. From the medieval era until the eighteenth century, when a few soft Western voices joined Asian animists in considering the natural world with reverence, human needs remained dominant. More recently, conservation's political and financial fortunes varied with the degree of utilitarianism expressed by its advocates. Purist concern for animals and wilderness, while often rewarding to its proponents for moral or ethical reasons, tended to be politically and economically ineffective. Late in the 1970s, the global movement's reach and influence began a period of quick growth when its far-flung point men began to incorporate poor villagers as well as endangered animals into their "management" programs.

From the totemism of early North Americans to the scarab in Egypt, animals achieved the status of gods in ancient cultures the world over. Cows, trees, insects, monkeys, goats, and elephants all became objects of worship because of fear of the unknown or out of admiration for sexual prowess. Among Hindus there was no real gap between animals and men; animals as well as men had souls, and souls were perpetually passing from men into animals, and back again; all these species were woven into one infinite web of *Karma* and reincarnation.[1]

Buddha spent forty-five years wandering in the forest, and individual trees that marked important moments in his life are still worshipped by his followers. Forest monasteries, and individual monks who express particular love for forests and trees, remain commonplace in the religion. The Bible too begins with a warm nod to the diversity of the earth's biota:

> And God said, Let the waters bring forth abundantly, the moving creature that hath life, and fowl that may fly above the earth in the open firmament of heaven. And God created great whales, and every living creature that moveth, which the waters brought forth abundantly, after their kind, and every winged fowl after his kind, and God saw that it was good. And God blessed them, saying, Be fruitful, and multiply, and fill the waters in the seas, and let fowl multiply in the earth.[2]

Almost the very next words in Genesis, in which God grants humans "dominion . . . over every creeping thing that creepeth upon the earth," form a basis for the anthropocentric view of the relationship that, ever since, has been a strong element in Western thought. Respect for animals might be tolerated in a slightly dippy St. Francis, Christianity seemed to suggest, but would hardly become a central component of human behavior. In Europe it was a thought pattern that led to the extinction of the right whale in the Bay of Biscay during the Middle Ages, at the hands of Basque and British harvesters, and to the animal protectionism of William the Conqueror, who founded game parks and lopped off poachers' hands in order to assure his own meat supply. Each in his own way, Adam Smith and Malthus justified exploitation. In his detailed exploration of the evolution of ecological ideas, Malthus "thoroughly agreed that the natural economy's sole function was

1. Will Durant, *Our Oriental Heritage* (New York: Simon & Schuster, 1954), p. 509.
2. Genesis 1:20–22.

St. Francis preaching to the birds

to provide for man's ambitions," wrote the historian Donald Worster. So did the distinguished Swedish botanist Carl von Linné (Linnaeus). In his orderly mind, Worster continues, "man must vigorously pursue his assigned work of utilizing his fellow species to his own advantage."[3]

Following the Linnaean principle and the long-standing practices of their Mediterranean neighbors, who had systematically deforested and desertified their lands, Northern Europeans from the eighteenth century forward almost exclusively emphasized human needs in their use of land and natural resources. Forests were felled to make way for man-made landscapes that bespoke human control of the fearsome natural world. Conservation, if you could call it that, consisted of

3. Donald Worster, *Nature's Economy: A History of Ecological Ideas* (San Francisco: Sierra Club Books, 1977), pp. 36, 53.

Carl von Linné (Linnaeus)

Gilbert White, Vicar of Selborne

measures to inhibit erosion, avalanches, and flooding. Parks were hunting preserves. Many lesser species followed the mammoth and the European bison into oblivion, and even the tiniest birds were shot, eaten, and driven to the brink of extinction. Random shooting of sea gulls was a popular sport. Populations of egrets, birds of paradise, even hummingbirds were severely reduced for the sake of the millinery trade. The world's first international covenant concerning wildlife, first discussed at a meeting held in Vienna in 1868 and finally signed by twelve countries in 1902, was quintessentially rationalist in its motivation: it specified measures to protect birds useful to forestry and agriculture.

Quiet voices offered a different vision. One such was that of the English curate Gilbert White, whose *Natural History of Selborne,* published in 1789, manifests a greater degree of humility in its approach to the relationship. "An apparent mutual tolerance between man and nature is perhaps Selborne's defining characteristic," as Worster put it.[4] White's modest arcadianism and careful observations of the natural world won him enduring status as one of ecology's principal god-

4. Ibid, p. 4.

fathers. Echoes of his thought resurface in the poetry of Wordsworth, Coleridge, and other Romantics. But if Romanticism glorified the European landscape, the movement failed to generate much interest in its protection. The notion of bucolic pastoralism was hardly a match for the dirty but immensely powerful Industrial Revolution. It was not in Europe but in the faraway and less mechanized United States that White's notions led more directly toward a new conservationist ethic manifesting greater concern for nonhuman species.

Early settlers along the New England coast predictably replicated European land-use patterns. They cut down forests, drained swamps, submitted wild land to the plow, replaced the wolf and the bear with the sheep, the pig, and the cow, recklessly harvested the coastal resources that were so conspicuously abundant when they arrived. Then pioneers began their march westward, cutting and planting along the way, beginning the process that reduced the great prairies of the Midwest to the dust bowl of the 1930s. They killed almost every American bison and managed entirely to do in the passenger pigeon (of which 3 to 5 billion had existed at the beginning of the nineteenth century).

When the reaction began, a number of justifications for wilderness preservation were advanced. In part the movement reflected an intellectual continuum from Ralph Waldo Emerson, who while essentially regarding nature as a material commodity also accorded it godlike status, to White's North American counterpart: Henry David Thoreau. The founding of "national preserves," he argued, would support human "inspiration" and even the preservation of civilization. Religious fervor, Romanticism, and great outpourings of aesthetic zeal combined to evoke the sweeping canvases of landscape painters from Thomas Cole to Frederick Edwin Church. These artists and philosophers, as well as political theorists of the nineteenth century, equated the destruction of American wilderness with the loss of the innocence that had made North America seem different. Primordial abandon, it was argued, had greater moral value than the effetely mannered European landscape. Far from being the captive of their environment, added George Perkins Marsh in his influential 1864 book, *Man and Nature,* humans could control it as they wished. Blaming the fall of the Roman Empire on neglect for forests and soils, Marsh urged Americans to be more careful in their use of resources. "It was the rudest kick in the

Big game hunting in Africa, early twentieth century

face that American initiative, optimism and carelessness had yet received," wrote the California novelist Wallace Stegner.[5]

Out of it all came a rising chorus of mixed voices calling for the creation of national parks and forest reserves. According to many accounts, the movement began with the establishment of Mount Auburn Cemetery outside Boston, a place still much frequented by birdwatchers during warbler migration seasons, as a park in 1831. Yosemite (founded in 1864) and Yellowstone (1872) became early components of the system, along with national forests and such disparate elements as Niagara Falls and Manhattan's Central Park. Those offering rationales for the existence and expansion of this ungainly conglomerate of protected areas often reverted to European models. Western land was approved for inclusion in the system only if it was deemed too isolated or otherwise "worthless" for other forms of use. Frederick Law Olm-

5. "It All Began with Conservation," *Smithsonian,* April 1990, p. 38.

sted designed Yosemite's original trails and pathways more in the spirit of rustic eastern urban parks than of wilderness-loving John Muir, the high priest of the Sierras. Adirondack Forest Preserve was founded in 1885 at least in part out of New Yorkers' fear that continuing defor-estation would disrupt the city's water supply. Animal welfare was linked tightly to the welfare of hunters, who practiced what Theodore Roosevelt termed "a sport for a vigorous and masterful people." Gif-ford Pinchot, the President's Chief Forester, remained Muir's devoted ally for some years. Their bitter break, which came over whether to dry up a free-flowing California river in order to build the Hetch Hetchy Dam for the sake of San Francisco's water supply, revealed the powerful Pinchot's underlying pragmatism.

Somehow, by the end of the nineteenth century, the loose coalition of advocates blended into a significant national commitment. It led to the formalization of the National Park System and its excellent uni-formed service, the network of national forests and wildlife refuges, clusters of state and county parks. Forged at a time when similar ideas were still only vaguely being expressed in the United Kingdom, the movement continued to surprise Max Nicholson, a seasoned British conservation leader, with its accomplishments. For the first time in any country, he wrote, conservation had become a "major concern" of leading public officials and placed "on the map as a serious public issue."[6] The next step was for Americans and the now laggard Euro-peans to join forces to initiate conservation elsewhere in the world.

"Libya [Africa] always bears something new," wrote Aristotle.[7] One of many examples is the continent's status as the cradle of international wildlife conservation. Late in the nineteenth century, British authori-ties in East Africa and the Sudan established reserves to assure game supplies for recreational hunting by colonial officers and administra-tors. For similar reasons several reserves were also set up in southern Africa, including President Kruger's designation, in 1898, of the Sabi Game Reserve in the Transvaal (in 1926, almost thirty years later, the reserve became the very large and important Kruger National Park).

6. *The Environmental Revolution* (Cambridge, Eng.: Cambridge University Press, 1970).

7. *Historia Animalium,* VII, 28, 7.

So intensive was hunting by locals as well as international sportsmen that a number of game species had already become extinct. The blaubok vanished from South Africa in about 1800. The once commonplace, zebralike South African quagga was particularly prized for its hide, widely used for shoes and luggage, and gone from the veld by 1867. Other animals were threatened as the carnage, much of it initiated by Great White Hunters with well-documented and prodigious appetites for the aimlessly violent slaughter of big game, continued unopposed. With encouragement from precursors such as the legendary Sir Stamford Raffles, who expressed heated early concern about the welfare of wild animals observed during his adventures in Southeast Asia, an antihunting counterculture finally emerged. "As the balance of population shifted to include more hunters and fewer animals," wrote Harriet Ritvo in her book *The Animal Estate: The English and Other Creatures,* "the code of sport altered correspondingly. By both rhetoric and example, sportsmen who considered themselves enlightened attempted to replace an ethic that celebrated unbridled violence with one that attempted discrimination and restraint."[8]

In 1903 a group of British sportsmen founded the Society for the Preservation of the Wild Fauna of the Empire (SPWFE)[9] with the initial mission of trying to persuade the Sudan not to abandon a designated reserve for wildlife protection and to establish others elsewhere "ere it be too late." The British, whose empire at the time covered one-quarter of the globe, took on much of the game-protection burden. But citizens of other European nations concurrently began to develop similar ideas and organizations; from across the Atlantic the safari-loving Theodore Roosevelt lobbed in encouraging noises and eventually became an honorary SPWFE member.

World War I abruptly ended these incipient European moves to sequester the megafauna of the sub-Saharan savanna. But soon after the war came a second round of activities in the new field of international wildlife conservation, many of them initiated by the tireless Dutchman P. J. van Tienhoven. In 1922, the first conservation organization with a specifically international mandate, the International Council for Bird

8. Cambridge, Mass.: Harvard University Press, 1987, p. 276.
9. Later renamed the Fauna Protection Society.

Preservation (ICBP), was formed in the United Kingdom. Its principal objectives were to protect migratory birds and to control the feather trade. At the urging of several prominent conservationists, King Albert of the Belgians in 1925 designated the important Parc National Albert (now Virunga National Park) as a sanctuary for the rare mountain gorilla and as a place not for hunting but for scientific research. The idea of creating parks not for hunters but to protect animals slowly gained currency in other African and Asian countries. A number of international agreements, many of them focused on protection for harassed species such as fur seals or migratory birds, came into effect during the period. In 1933, all colonial powers signed the comprehensive London Convention Relevant to the Preservation of Fauna and Flora in Their Natural State, which set forth a wide range of conservation activities for the African colonies. In 1928, the initial version of the International Office for the Protection of Nature (IOPN) was established in Brussels with a mandate to gather information. Under the leadership of Jean-Paul Harroy, a former colonial administrator with passionate feelings about the fate of Africa's wildlife, who later became the dominant figure at IOPN, its charter was broadened to encompass conservation action.

Lacking an empire of its own, the United States could not be as directly involved as the Europeans in hands-on conservation beyond its own borders. Nevertheless, a handful of concerned Americans were beginning discussions with counterparts in Europe. One such was the ornithologist T. Gilbert Pearson, a president of the respected National Audubon Society, who helped found ICBP. The explorer and taxidermist Carl Akeley of the American Museum of Natural History was an important advocate for the Parc National Albert. Of all early leaders in the field, none was more distinctive than Harold J. Coolidge, Jr. A bantam Bostonian with an unforgettably raspy voice and relentless determination, Coolidge was already a seasoned scientific fieldworker before he graduated from Harvard in 1927, having studied Alaskan brown bears in situ, tropical diseases in Brazil, and large mammals in Liberia and the Congo. From the late 1920s until shortly before his death in 1985, even though plagued by ill health, Coolidge organized, led, and supported zoological collecting and research expeditions. His involvement in conservation accelerated in 1930, when he joined the

Boone & Crockett Club, an old-line hunters' group whose lineage went back to Theodore Roosevelt in the 1880s. Under the auspices of this club and with assistance from its well-connected members, Coolidge founded a research, fund-raising, and monitoring organization called the American Committee for International Wildlife Protection (in 1976, changed to the American Committee for International Conservation, or ACIC). With this as his institutional base, Coolidge went on, according to the political scientist Robert Boardman in his *International Organization and the Conservation of Nature,*[10] to become "the foremost internationalist in the conservation movement."

With the underfunded but influential ACIC in place on the U.S. side and European participation from IOPN and from SPWFE's "penitent butchers" (as they termed themselves in a notable publication) in the United Kingdom, the stage was set for an upswing in global conservation activity. Concern for extinct and vanishing animals was paramount in the value system of all three organizations, and each figured in the creation of the 1933 London Convention. This agreement, often referred to as the "magna carta" for international conservation, also served as a model for the first major inter-American effort in the field: the Pan-American Convention for the Protection of Wild Life in the Western Hemisphere, signed in Washington in 1940. Implementation of these covenants was, however, hampered by a shortage of money during the Depression years as well as by the prewar buildup of international political tension.

Though IOPN staggered on in Nazi-occupied Brussels until 1946, when the organization shut down completely, World War II almost totally disrupted the institutional and legal infrastructures of international conservation. Oblivion was avoided thanks largely to the efforts of the British biologist Julian Huxley, who in 1947–48 served as UNESCO's first director-general and provided leadership in enlarging the old IOPN and transforming it into what is still the world's premier international conservation institution, the International Union for the Protection of Nature, whose first secretary-general was Harroy. Its expanded membership would include governments and scientific bodies as well as private conservation organizations. "Protection of Nature,"

10. Bloomington: Indiana University Press, 1982.

as envisioned by its constitution, meant "the preservation of the entire world biotic community, or man's natural environment, which includes the earth's renewable natural resources of which it is composed, and on which rests the foundation of human civilization." The addition of the phrase "renewable natural resources," on which Hal Coolidge had foresightedly insisted at the organizing meetings, led to a significant 1956 change in its title, to the International Union for the *Conservation* of Nature *and Natural Resources*. From the outset, the objectives of the union were to promote public-private cooperation in preserving species and their habitats, encourage increases in scientific research and public knowledge, and work toward refining and expanding the worldwide system of laws and agreements that protect the natural world.

As collective efforts failed to raise even small fractions of the unprecedented sums that had suddenly become available for development efforts, conservation remained a marginal idea at the zenith of the Cold War. The movement required a low-cost niche. It was compelled to remain within the boundaries of its traditional domain: scientific research, saving animals from extinction, shoring up their habitats. At IUCN, emphasis was placed on compiling information about rare species and the threats that confronted them, and classifying these according to the degree of their gravity. There was plenty to think about. Some animals, such as Père David's deer and Przewalski's horse, were already gone from the wild and could be maintained only in zoos where captive breeding programs (with the objective of eventual reintroduction into their original habitats) could be attempted. The Indian and Javan rhinos, the Arabian oryx, and the Indian lion were among the "charismatic megafauna" that were in imminent danger of losing their last footholds in the wild. Many other species were in serious trouble.

Over and above its work with individual species IUCN pressed for a larger and more effective global system of parks and protected areas. According to classifications established by IUCN and adopted by many nations, Category I parks would be "strict nature reserves" where no human activity of any sort would be permitted. In Category II "national parks," tourism would be allowed—but no hunting or extractive activity of any sort. Although lesser designations provided for more extensive human use, including forestry, the top two categories of parks contained the highest levels of biological diversity and of endemism[11]—the presence of plant and animal species found nowhere else—and attracted the most attention. Pushing for a larger and more orderly park system was not only realistic but expressed the prevailing view among conservationists that the only hope for disappearing species was to wall them off from the earth's unruly people. Man and beast could hardly coexist in Africa, it was widely believed. To be saved the animals had to be protected from the natives, as many a colonialist might have put it. (This prejudice came to haunt conservationists all over the world—for example, when indigenous peoples in the Amazon and elsewhere opposed Westerners' efforts to use debt-for-nature swaps and other new devices to establish or consolidate new parkland in the 1980s. A coalition of Amazonian Indians maintained that the alliances forged between national governments and international conservationists served only to deprive those who had always lived within the forest of their rightful homelands.)

Even though its needs were quite modest, IUCN's finances were extremely precarious during the otherwise booming 1950s. Wrote Boardman:

> One IUCN Executive Board member of the late 1950s has commented that discussion of endangered species could revolve around the issue of whether or not the budget could stand the cost of contacting experts by mail. The cycle was difficult to break out of: sparse funds affected performance; lack of effectiveness deterred potential funders. Meetings of executive and scientific bodies were irregular, and often poorly attended; the secretariat was unable to develop as a base of scientific competence . . . the union seemed headed in the direction of being a loose association of members exchanging hopes, fears, and postage stamps.

"They were very well focused on the real issues," Nicholson recalled when I met him late in 1989 at his cozy house in London's Chelsea.

---

11. "Endemic" diseases are those permanently present in a given area. But when biologists apply the same word to plants and animal species, it takes on a positive connotation. For birdwatchers in the field, sighting an "endemic" is a particularly important goal.

"But they had *no* contact with heads of government or with important ministers. And they had *no* money. A lot of them were quite hopeless about anything practical. You couldn't leave everything to these poor scientists and missionaries. Nor could you just take a science-based movement and put businessmen or politicians at the top of it. You needed something separate, a different kind of an animal, a down-to-earth body with bankers and industrialists and others who live in the world of money." At the urging of IUCN's executive board, Nicholson convened a group of Europeans to design a parallel organization whose principal purpose would be to shore up the flagging union. Among the committee members were Huxley and Sir Peter Scott, a versatile naturalist, yachtsman, and artist, as well as several leading conservationists, royalty, and "several influential ladies." What emerged was the World Wildlife Fund (WWF), whose mission would be to handle fundraising and educational chores while the union concentrated on the scientific side. Prince Bernhard of the Netherlands became WWF's first president, to be succeeded later by another Dutchman, John Loudon, who had been managing director of Royal Dutch/Shell, and still later by Prince Philip of Great Britain. IUCN closed its headquarters in Brussels, where it had been from the outset, and in 1961 joined WWF in Morges, Switzerland.[12]

WWF's most prominent initial strategy was to seek support from individual and corporate donors by focusing sharply on the welfare of attractive and highly visible animal species. Among the organization's early successes were the rescue of a Spanish "wildlife paradise," as Nicholson termed it, called Coto Donana, and a determined campaign to control white rhino poaching in Uganda and save the animal from extinction. Operation Tiger in India was not far behind. Declining populations of other prominent species—the African elephant, whales, the mountain gorilla—were vividly brought to the public's attention. For several decades IUCN and WWF also worked, with growing success, to make these animals' habitats more secure. A major effort was made to persuade the new regimes of postcolonial Africa to maintain and improve the game parks that had been established during colonial

12. Late in 1979, both organizations moved to Gland, another town near Geneva, and into joint headquarters entitled the World Conservation Centre.

times. One notable event was the Symposium on the Conservation of Nature and Natural Resources in Modern African States that was held in Arusha, Tanganyika (now Tanzania), in 1961. Nicholson, who participated, later wrote with a touch of sarcasm about the sense of this meeting:

> Greeted warmly as partners, at a time when the ending of colonial regimes was being taken with an ill grace and with bitter forebodings in many quarters, the African participants responded keenly and contributed much to the success of the Arusha meeting, not least through their sense of humour. It was understandable, one of them remarked, that Europeans should be smitten with anxiety over the future of Africa's large animals; after all they knew what they themselves had done to the large mammals of Europe. Have no fear, however. For Africans their wild neighbors were a welcome and essential part of their peculiar heritage, and they would no more be destroyed than Europe would knock down its cathedrals.[13]

The resulting Arusha Declaration, in which African leaders formally accepted "the trusteeship of our wildlife," led to a major expansion of the African parks system.

Asian and Latin American governments expressed less enthusiasm, but global conservationists knew that they had dedicated allies in several biologically significant countries: Felipe Benavides in Peru, William Phelps in Venezuela, Dr. Boonsong in Thailand, and (a little later) the remarkable Brazilian Maria Teresa Jorge Pádua. Thirty years of intercontinental shuttlecock resulted, in 1962, in the establishment (by Europeans) of the Charles Darwin Research Station to study and help protect the biologically priceless Galápagos Islands off the coast of Ecuador. In Costa Rica, which was to become the Third World's model for environmentally sensitive development, formal conservation efforts began with the creation of the Cabo Blanco nature reserve in 1963. Similar Asian initiatives had some bizarre side effects. In Thailand, a minister felled large amounts of tropical forest to build a golf course

13. Nicholson, op. cit., p. 202.

in the middle of Khao Yai National Park, which was founded in 1962 and meant to protect elephants and tigers that range there. Overall, according to United Nations statistics, the worldwide parks system enjoyed explosive growth: from 400 units covering 10 million hectares in 1940 to 900 covering 230 million hectares in 1960, and 1,600 covering 400 million hectares by 1970.

Managing the parks was more difficult than declaring them. It was one thing for Third World government agencies to draw lines on maps, something else for them to administer remote areas effectively when poaching, hunting, and other forms of now illegal extraction had long been freely practiced there. National budgets were stretched tight, and corruption in the capitals often skimmed off the scanty available resources before they reached the field stations where they were needed. And foreign-aid donor nations were not yet supporting conservation. Wildlife officials were seldom equipped with surveillance aircraft. Ground vehicles, walkie-talkies, even boots and camping gear for park rangers were in grievously short supply. Many areas remained parks in name only. At least they were gazetted. Having the legal work done was in itself a plus.

Beyond species and habitat protection, the movement scored advances elsewhere. Scientists conducted pioneer research. Each increment of new data helped in its own way to define the areas most needing protection and the kinds of management technique that would be most effective for each. New communications channels connected isolated researchers living deep in the bush. IUCN worked hard for UNESCO's Man and the Biosphere program, a scientific endeavor that addresses the question of endangered species, and also for the unsung but useful World Heritage mechanism to safeguard important cultural sites. IUCN and other conservation groups lobbied for several important international agreements, including the Ramsar Convention on international wetlands and the Convention on International Trade in Endangered Species (CITES), to which more than a hundred nations currently adhere. The private-sector movement grew as well. WWF affiliates were founded in more than twenty countries during the 1960s and 1970s. National nongovernmental organizations (NGOs), including some that have since become very strong, were established in a number of key countries. Public information programs spread the conservation message.

Through all this, the contest between conservationists and developers remained unequal. Not even the most effective advocates for conservation could offset, with talk of adverse environmental consequences, the appeal of big contracts for dams, roads, and other large-scale development projects. The prospect of quick financial return from these activities made conservation appear to be the deadly enemy of economic progress. "The only view rich and poor countries seemed to share," wrote Peter Barthelmus, "was the conviction that environmental conscience and economic development are in conflict with each other."[14] In planning the 1972 Stockholm Conference on the Human Environment, the Canadian businessman Maurice Strong and other organizers faced the principal challenge of narrowing the gap. One event that helped to do so was a meeting of twenty-seven specialists that took place in 1971 in the village of Founex, Switzerland. After a fortnight of intensive discussion, the group issued a statement that tidily dealt with precisely that issue.

Economic development is often the cause of environmental woes in advanced nations, the report said, but in poor countries it is often the *cure* for them. One way to enable poor nations to improve their environmental condition, therefore, is for rich nations to increase their support for development. At the same time, the second set of environmental problems, which arise in development itself, can be addressed by means of "incorporation" of environmental concerns into the economic plans. In following ecological principles, the Founex report warily continued, "the extent to which developing countries pursue a style of development that is more responsive to social and environmental goals must be determined by the resources available to them." Much would therefore depend upon responses from the North: trade concessions, aid, the transfer of technology, and a general willingness to address the poverty issue. Developing countries might have apprehensions about the goodwill of industrial nations—fears about "neo-protectionism" and the threat that tougher environmental standards might shut down markets for their agricultural products—but, the conferees agreed, these "legitimate fears . . . should not be exaggerated." There were far greater threats implicit in ignoring the environment.

Founex was the crispest articulation yet made of how to use the

14. *Environment and Development* (Boston: Allen & Unwin, 1986), p. 11.

development process to overcome environmental problems and reduce poverty. At the ensuing meeting in Stockholm, not everyone agreed. Speech after speech reaffirmed the Third World's older fears that environmentalism would divert attention from poverty. Industrial nations, including the United States, refused to endorse the principle of "additionality," which would have imposed increases in aid budgets to cover environmental damage. Environment and development were nowhere nearly so "integrated" in the Stockholm debate as they had been at Founex. Much of the talk addressed questions of what individual nations might do to manage their pollution problems. Nonetheless, according to the conservation historian Lynton K. Caldwell, Stockholm's general result was "an enlarged and reinforced concept of environmental responsibility." Specific outcomes included the identification of the biosphere as "an object of national and international policy" and the resolution leading to the creation, in 1973, of the United Nations Environment Program (UNEP).

In a way, Stockholm reaffirmed the spirit of the moving statement that Adlai Stevenson had made on July 9, 1965, in his last speech before his death:

> We travel together, passengers on a little space ship, dependent on a vulnerable reserve of air and soil; all committed for our safety to its security and peace; preserved from annihilation only by the care, the work, and I will say, the love we give our fragile craft. We cannot maintain it half fortunate, half despairing, half slave— to the ancient enemies of man—half free in the liberation of resources undreamed of until this day. No craft, no crew, can travel safely with such vast contradictions. On their resolution depends the survival of us all.

At Stockholm, Robert McNamara invoked the "space ship earth" image, but, he added, one-fourth in first class and three-quarters in steerage "does not make for a happy ship." He suggested that global arrangements were needed to produce not an "idyllic environment peopled by the poor" but "a decent environment peopled by the proud." In Stockholm, Strong coined the phrase "ecodevelopment" to summarize the new approach.

In 1973 the ecologist Raymond F. Dasmann, of IUCN, provided

ecodevelopment with a road map in a benchmark book.[15] Almost two decades later, this work is still solid. The body of the text includes many rules that aid donors had seldom obeyed: beware of the hazards of simplifying biotic communities; build new roads into forested areas only on the basis of careful advance planning; use underutilized or inefficiently used land rather than open up new areas; consider harvesting wild game rather than introducing domestic livestock onto fragile rangelands; observe the "carrying capacity" for tourism as for other forms of land use; do the most careful possible scientific research before launching river-basin development projects, since, while they are often necessary, they are disaster-prone as well.

Modest project size was now advocated not only because it would enhance participatory and "bottom-up" development but also because it promoted environmental stability. In his hugely successful *Small Is Beautiful,* the unorthodox British economist E. F. Schumacher built upon earlier work in suggesting that "small-scale operations, no matter how numerous, are always less likely to be harmful to the natural environment than large-scale ones, simply because the individual force is small in relation to the recuperative forces of nature. . . . Men organized in small units will take better care of *their* bit of land or other natural resources than anonymous companies or megalomanic governments."[16]

Conservationists began to realize that they would have to reach well beyond the developers in getting people to follow sound environmental guidelines. Their increasingly vehement contention was that conservation is the very basis for sustainable development, that environmental and economic objectives are in fact inseparable—especially so in rural parts of the tropics where the planet's biological diversity reaches its maximum. Conservation would therefore have to get into the development act. Anthropologists and sociologists, biologists and ecologists would have to share knowledge and experience with the dominant economists and engineers. Working together, such multidis-

15. Raymond F. Dasmann, John P. Milton, and Peter H. Freeman, eds., *Ecological Principles for Economic Development* (London: John Wiley & Sons, 1973).
16. *Small Is Beautiful: Economics As If People Mattered* (New York: Harper & Row, 1973).

ciplinary teams might shape a new kind of world. Conservationists would have to become involved in the unfamiliar business of managing people as well as wildlife. Single-species and habitat strategies would have to give way to ecosystem approaches.

As early as the 1950s, his experiences in Africa had led IUCN's first staff ecologist, Lee Talbot,[17] to foresee this position. "I'm continually amazed at how little there ever is that's really new," he sighed recently. During the late 1960s and the 1970s, he, Dasmann, and a few other pioneers began to field-test the new concepts. The New York Zoological Society's David ("Jonah") Western in Africa and the American educator Kenton Miller[18] in Latin America were among other conservationists who began to think in terms of watershed management, of ecosystems encompassing human as well as nonhuman inhabitants. They incorporated resource utilization into their integrated conservation and development schemes, and included foresters and agronomists as well as biologists and protected-areas managers as participants in the elaboration of regional plans. The United Nations' Food and Agriculture Organization (FAO) underwrote several of these comprehensive programs—in Colombia, Chile, Botswana—with limited but important financial help from the United Nations Development Program (UNDP).

For the most part, however, the practice of global conservation remained mired within the rigid and elitist confines that had been set at the turn of the century. Biologists, wildlife managers, and other field practitioners were still largely carrying out traditional activities, ambling down the Franciscan byways, self-limited to the orthodoxies of species preservation and habitat management. They were no readier than specialized cameramen, dutifully filming animal behavior for the BBC's Natural History Unit and the faithful audiences attracted to the Public Broadcasting Service's *Nature* series, to embrace *Homo sapiens*

---

17. The son and grandson of distinguished conservationists, Talbot spent eight years conducting pioneer fieldwork in Africa during the 1950s. After later service at the Smithsonian Institution and the Council on Environmental Quality, Talbot returned to IUCN in 1978 and served as its director-general until 1983. Since then he has been doing consulting work, largely for the World Bank's African section.
18. Later he succeeded Talbot as IUCN's director-general.

in their fields of vision. All too frequently, their reaction to pressures on the wilderness was a categorical no: no people in the parks, no resource use of any sort, zero tolerance. At IUCN, those concerned about the welfare of fauna usually prevailed over others equally interested in plants or in human beings. North Americans, still "exporting an endangered-species mentality," as Miller puts it, were particularly rigid. Aid donors, meanwhile, largely ignored the lessons of Founex and Stockholm, continuing and even intensifying the severity of their assaults on the global environment.

It then became more generally clear that unless the conservation movement took urgent remedial actions, the reserves it had helped to create would become small and insignificant blots upon the prevailing wreckage of the landscapes around them. As W. A. Fitter put it in *The Penitent Butchers,* a book published to celebrate the seventy-fifth anniversary of the founding of Britain's Fauna Protection Society:

Today, while some wild animals and plants still have to be protected from direct human depredation—the great whales, for instance, and the many animals involved in the pet and curio trades—by far the greatest threat to the world's wildlife comes from habitat destruction. Tropical rain forests, for example, are being felled, for short-term gains, at a rate which ensures that they will almost be all gone by the end of the century. By that time also it seems unlikely that there will be any substantial natural ecosystems outside national parks and other protected areas throughout the tropics. Perhaps only parts of the northern hemisphere taiga and tundra, the Antarctic and a few very remote oceanic islands will by the year 2000 remain in anything approaching their pristine condition. At the time of writing, although the international wildlife conservation movement is moving in the right direction, it is moving so slowly that it cannot possibly rectify this unbalance unaided. A sharp change of gear is urgent . . .

Major institutions began to respond to these sorts of exhortation. WWF, for example, started fund-raising to save wetlands, then tropical forests. Under the joint auspices of WWF, IUCN, and UNEP, painstaking work also began on a comprehensive World Conservation

Strategy. The first of four working drafts emphasized traditional methods, but what was approved and published in 1980 called for radical change in the movement's mission. Like development, conservation is "for people," said the final report, and anything but the "harmful and anti-social" force it had long been accused of being. Its new goals would be not only the "maintenance of essential ecological processes and life-support systems" and the "preservation of genetic diversity," but also the "sustainable utilization of species and ecosystems." Harvesting wild plants and animals should be encouraged, not just tolerated, as one means to a revolutionary new end: "the integration of conservation and development to ensure that modifications to the planet do indeed secure the survival and wellbeing of all people."

Only development, conservationists now argued, would break the "vicious circle" in which poverty caused ecological degradation, which in turn caused more poverty. This was a dramatic shift. For most of a century conservation's principal practitioners had been arguing their case on ethical and moral grounds and winning support by asking people to remember the appeal of attractive animals. Now a more pragmatic approach, more in the style of Linnaeus and Pinchot than of White or Muir, more attentive to pressing human needs in poor countries, was gaining favor.

The change was precipitated in part by dismay at the mess that development was making of things, in part by a recognition that conservation had failed to respond to the new realities. In limited respects, it had performed effectively, at times even splendidly: species had been saved, parks created and managed, important science accomplished, and international agreements reached. But critical habitats were being surrendered to the chain saw, and the appeal of cold cash for elephant tusk or rhino horn was stronger to poor villagers than moral arguments or even the opposition of armed rangers. In any case, the fate of the megafauna was only one part of a huge and complex global problem. Propinquity, as the zoologist Larry Harris of the University of Florida put it, would now "carry the day."[19]

19. At a New York Zoological Society conference held at Rockefeller University, New York, 1986.

While pragmatism came to prevail among global environmentalists, the development agencies—sometimes under public pressure to do so—were gradually incorporating environmental concepts into their operations. In Washington early in the 1970s, when he served as director of the newly created White House Council on Environmental Quality, the lawyer and conservationist Russell E. Train repeatedly wrote letters to the State Department and to USAID asking why the latter had not filed environmental impact statements, as called for by the 1969 National Environmental Policy Act (NEPA), in connection with its exports of toxic agricultural chemicals. Though these resulted in no change, a mid-1970s lawsuit filed by the Environmental Defense Fund (EDF) was successful with regard to the specific question of toxics, and it raised broader issues as well. "This was the trigger," says Albert J. Printz, Jr., who for many years served as USAID's environmental spokesman. In response, USAID made cautious moves to join forces with such conservation-minded government entities as the U.S. National Park Service's tiny but doughty international program. In 1978 USAID, which then had but one forester on its staff, took the initiative in co-hosting a "strategy conference" on tropical deforestation. The development unit soon issued a policy statement on pesticides and created a new Forestry, Environment, and Natural Resource Office in Washington. Environmental assessment procedures "for any USAID project significantly affecting the environment"[20] became mandatory in 1981. Two years later a section on endangered species was added to the Foreign Assistance Act. Subsequent changes establish the conservation and sustainable management of tropical forests "as a priority development goal,"[21] single out biodiversity as a specific area for program activity, and require the agency to monitor the multilateral development banks (MDBs) and "compile a list of MDB projects which may have adverse impacts on the environment, natural resources, or indigenous peoples." As tighter laws imposed new obligations on USAID, the decentralized (sprawling, some might call it) agency ac-

20. Per listing in a USAID policy paper, "Environment and Natural Resources," published in April 1988.
21. From USAID's 1988–89 report to Congress, "Conserving Tropical Forests and Biological Diversity."

companied the new legal language with a blizzard of new policy papers and declarations about how to respond. Though its performance was hardly perfect, as we shall see in the next chapter, USAID had willy-nilly become the environmental leader among bilateral aid agencies.

Elsewhere, indications of progress could also be found. During the decade after the 1972 Stockholm meeting, the number of countries with environment and natural resource management agencies increased from 26 to 144.[22] Jointly with UNEP, the World Bank in 1980 published a Declaration of Environmental Policies and Procedures Relating to Economic Development and created a committee to implement it and to foster sound environmental practice in development lending. Plans to enact the United Nations' benchmark World Charter for Nature were initiated. At the USAID conference on tropical forests the environmental writer Erik Eckholm, then of the Worldwatch Institute, spoke bravely of a "significant convergence" between the environment and development communities.

Overall, though, the 1980s became less a decade of further movement toward integration than one of disappointment and hostility. In the United States, an unexpected obstacle was the dismal environmental performance of Ronald Reagan's presidency, personified by the swaggering antagonism of Interior Secretary James Watt. The worldwide economic downturn of 1981–82 caused developing countries' debt problems to balloon and limited all nations' ability to move forward on environmental matters. Financial and management setbacks hampered the efforts of IUCN (which in 1990 became the World Conservation Union) to promote the cause. With UNEP's budget also remaining at a bare-bones level, the environment lacked strong official voices. Of all the foot-draggers, none was more conspicuous than the ponderous World Bank. For all the murmurings about ecology that had begun to emanate from its Washington portals, the Bank too often still seemed willing to wink at environmental consequences in its eagerness to dole out big loans. Lending officers were judged not so much for the quality as for the volume of their programs. Male staff members with backgrounds in unleavened economics or engineering almost invariably held the key senior management positions.

---

22. Information included in USAID policy paper, "Environment and Natural Resources."

These shortcomings, on the other hand, were just what was required to invigorate the nongovernmental environmental movement. The polarization did much to increase its size, competence, and influence dramatically. As they expanded and as environmental issues became more international, a number of U.S. organizations that had concentrated on domestic affairs turned their attention to global needs and problems, including those of the rural tropics. Green parties flowered in Europe, approaching the peak of their influence, and environmental NGOs emerged there and in developing countries as well.

The next chapter traces the course of the infighting between the two sides that took place during the 1980s, and how it led at last to the current climate, which more securely supports the quest for a sustainable economic life.

❧

CHAPTER 4

The Delayed Connection

My return to the Brazilian Amazon in 1990 enabled me to survey Parauapebas as a specific example of the heedless occupation of the basin. It also gave me a chance to review the broader results of the massive development effort that Brazil, with generous support from international lenders, has been attempting there for several decades. Leaving shoddy Parauapebas at the end of my visit, I recrossed a stream with the unfortunate name of Coco II. Depending on accent marks the word in Portuguese can mean either coconut *(côco)* or excrement *(cocó);* the word on the roadside bridge sign ambiguously bore neither marking. Along the road back toward sprawling Marabá, on another sunny morning at the height of what is supposed to be the rainy season (was deforestation causing a drying and warming tendency in the microclimate here as elsewhere in Amazonia?), mounted cowboys were driving small herds of cattle. Passing trucks carried logs and lumber, and the coils of hoses and other paraphernalia that gold prospectors use to blast high-pressure water at the riverbanks.

The small city of Marabá, capital of the "Brazil-nut polygon," in southeast Pará state, once thrived on harvesting the protein-rich crop. During the 1980s Marabá enjoyed a boom from construction, forest

An older Amazonia

products, ranching, and mining that lifted its population to 300,000. Currently, its economic hopes center on the introduction of plants to make pig iron from CVRD iron-ore pellets. Carloads of these pass by every day on the railway from the Carajás mine to the exporting port at São Luís; the company and government planners shared positive views about including pig-iron manufacturing in the overall economic development program along the railroad line. In Marabá at the time of my visit two pig-iron plants, representing a combined total of $350 million in investment capital, were beginning operations, and two more were under construction.

Environmentally, the problem with these plants is the energy they require. According to industry calculations, making pig iron in Amazonia is economic only if the fuel used in the process is not mineral coal brought in from far away, but charcoal made more cheaply from the trees of the nearby forest (and then economic only if environmental damage is not factored in as a cost). Each plant would require an average of 40,000 tons of vegetable charcoal per year—an amount requiring the destruction of between 3,000 and 6,600 hectares of nat-

Modern development in Amazonia: pig-iron plant near Marabá

ural forest.[1] In all, the thirty pig-iron projects that the government once planned for the region would involve a total forest loss of 200,000 hectares or more per year.

As vendor of ore to the pig-iron processors and rail carrier of the finished product to its coastal port facility, the bottom-line-oriented (and highly profitable) CVRD, to which the World Bank made $405 million in loans to launch the iron-ore project early in the 1980s, was hardly a disinterested party. Still, in view of the exemplary effort that the mining company had made to maintain high environmental quality and conserve forest within the mining area, some thought it might oppose the pig-iron scheme. The company's own in-house environmental adviser, Maria de Lourdes Davies de Freitas, objected vigorously. But when the matter came up for decision at the interministerial council then managing the region's development, CVRD voted *sim*.

1. These numbers are based on calculations made by Dennis J. Mahar, an economist at the World Bank.

"There was nothing I could do about the decision," Freitas told me at luncheon in Rio de Janeiro. "The top people at CVRD were in favor, most of the ministers in Brasília were in favor, the World Bank was in favor. The pig-iron people are very powerful and very well connected."

"I'm very optimistic," said Juvenil, a bright and fast-moving young Marabá entrepreneur who owned buses to transport pig-iron workers to and from their jobs; he also imported window glass from São Paulo (five days on the truck) and had just bought the local auto-rental business. "There's not much social life here, not even a club. It's just a place to make money. Even though I haven't been here long, I've put some away." I could not blame Juvenil, a native of crime-ridden Rio de Janeiro, for wanting to cash in on the boom while some of it lasted. But I could hardly share his view of the future. The region's Brazil-nut industry is already the victim of an ecological disaster. With no forest left to speak of—500,000 hectares have been cleared from an area that was virtually untouched only twenty years ago—the single species of bee that pollinates the trees can no longer survive in most of the region, and nut production has plummeted. Sawmills are moving closer to the timber supply. The cattle ranches around Marabá, like those near Parauapebas, are marginal or uneconomic without lavish subsidies, which the national government is gradually removing. The positive short-term effect of jobs at the pig-iron plants is far outweighed by the amount of environmental destruction they cause. The Amazonian ecologist Philip M. Fearnside wrote:

> Once the investment has been made in an expensive installation such as a pig-iron plant, the plant will play a role similar to a cuckoo in the nest. When a cuckoo lays an egg in another bird's nest, the unfortunate host soon finds itself diverting all of its efforts to providing food for the enormous cuckoo chick. In the same way, the forests and the entire economy of the areas around the pig-iron plants will be irresistibly drawn into feeding the plants with charcoal, regardless of the local population's own interests.[2]

2. "Deforestation and International Development Projects in Brazilian Amazonia," *Conservation Biology*, Vol. 1, No. 3 (October 1987), p. 219.

Panning for gold in Amazonia

Every increment of forest loss for charcoal production will involve more human misery and further threats to countless nonhuman species. As charcoal ovens move nearer to the remaining supplies of timber, moreover, the rising cost of the fuel will cause financial difficulties for Marabá's pig-iron plants—and perhaps even their relocation to points closer to the energy source. Prospectively, Marabá has become a maxi-Parauapebas.

During my visit I began also to gather information about what was happening to Indians living not inside CVRD's mining compound but in settlements close to the ore export corridor and in other nearby areas affected by mining exploration. In the Brazilian Amazon generally, indigenous populations were, up to the 1960s, relatively well protected by law, a sympathetic federal agency, and the sheer distance between them and others in the sparsely peopled basin. But the military regime that took power in 1964 viewed the Indians as an obstacle to development, and took a much harsher position: assimilate or die. The government remained passive while gold miners and others invaded Indian lands; protection services became corrupt, neglectful, and plainly hostile to Indian needs. The overall consequences of what one observer called a policy of "unstated genocide" have been dreadful. Once robust and self-sufficient millions were by 1990 reduced to some 220,000 people clustered in small and often weak settlements. CVRD was doing better than this around Carajás by supplying medical services to some groups that had never before had them. Two nurses living with the Xikrín in their spacious reserve (almost 1,000 hectares per capita) near the mine had helped them grow from a low of under 300 to more than 400. Although they hardly sought out the mercury poisoning that nearby gold prospecting has given them (gold panners use the metal to separate gold dust from sand, then discard the residues into rivers), their health problems have also resulted from their own decision to mingle freely with a hostile outside world. A serious flu epidemic afflicted scores of Xikrín, for example, after several of them went on a trading trip to Marabá. But even the relatively benevolent CVRD puts on a hard face when a choice must be made between Indian welfare and achieving corporate objectives. A group of native Amazonians called the Guaja, isolated hunter-gatherers little more than a decade ago, have suffered great hardship as a direct consequence of deforestation for the pig-iron program and their first contacts with white society. According to David Treece, a consultant to a British organization called Survival International, the "devastating epidemics of infectious diseases" will almost certainly lead to the group's extinction.[3]

Flying northward from Parauapebas and Marabá, my plane dodged low clouds and rain showers as it passed over the mighty, 8 million-kilowatt Tucuruí dam. Even as seen from the height of a jetliner, the giant plume of foamy white spray flung skyward by the turbines dominated a broad panorama of nature jerked around by engineers. When completed in the mid-1980s, Tucuruí was the world's fourth-largest hydroelectric power station. Its construction required the inundation of 250,000 hectares of virgin forest. Even now the gray canopies of tall trees, few of them harvested before the floodgates opened, pro-

3. See the article by Treece that was originally published in the February 1988 issue of *Multinational Monitor,* a magazine published in Washington, D.C., by Essential Information, Inc.

truded above the lake's surface as forlorn reminders of the former forest.[4] Tucuruí, as well as the iron mine and the pig-iron plants, the cattle ranches and the stillborn colonization efforts, all form part of the $62 billion eastern Amazon development scheme called Projeto Grande Carajás (PGC), which Brazilian officials cooked up in the late 1970s and peddled to public and private investors around the world. Its ambitious objectives were to "occupy" what was perceived as a largely empty and therefore exploitable region, and bring on a new Brazilian boom based on mineral exports. The World Bank and other public lenders supported many components of this grand design.

In itself, not even PGC was enough to satisfy the grandiose ambitions for Amazonia that the Brazilian government entertained at the time. Within the basin, many other areas were slated for hydropower development, oil or minerals exploration, or road building and colonization. One major program was called Polonoroeste, or the Northwest Regional Development Pole. At a cost of $2.25 billion between 1981 and 1986, of which about one-third was provided by the World Bank, Polonoroeste was supposed to organize the human settlement of a large tropical-forest region in the remote northwestern territory (later state) of Rondônia. More and more "economic refugees" from elsewhere in Brazil were crowding into Rondônia, whose politicians were issuing warm welcomes, hoping, of course, for ever-larger pork-barrel allocations from Brasília. Polonoroeste involved paving BR-364, a 1,400-kilometer highway between the city of Cuiabá and Rondônia's capital of Pôrto Velho, and providing supporting services for the mounting torrent of landless immigrants. Dennis J. Mahar, who did extensive advance fieldwork on the project, wrote that a principal objective was "to reduce forest clearing on land with little long-term agricultural potential and to promote, instead, sustainable farming

---

4. In August 1990, James Brooke of *The New York Times* reported the installation of an "underwater logging" business whereby divers operating waterproof chain saws began to harvest these submerged trees to make charcoal for the pig-iron plants and lumber for housing. This program might temporarily relieve the pressures on the remaining forest. It is forecast, however, that 1.5 million hectares of forest would be required to provide charcoal for all the pig-iron plants that have been proposed for the Carajás–São Luís railway corridor. If this estimate proves to be correct, underwater logging will provide no more than short-term mitigation.

systems based on tree crops."[5] Others, as we shall see, believed that things had been less clearly thought out.

Similar macro-projects were being elaborated elsewhere in the world. One such was Indonesia's long-running effort to resettle landless people living the very densely populated island of Java—where, in the early 1980s, 65 percent of the sprawling nation's 150 million people managed to subsist—to less crowded parts of the archipelago. Since many of the transmigration sites selected by the government were located in ecologically sensitive tropical-forest or wetlands regions, colonization risked provoking severe environmental stress while frequently not bringing people the prosperity they sought. In 1982 I visited a six-thousand-family transmigration site called P2W Pilot Project, in the Tulang Bawang district of southern Sumatra's Lampung province. Little was to be seen but listless farming and degraded forest in a region that, not long before, had provided habitat for a rich diversity of tropical species. Agricultural research, insofar as we could identify it, consisted of a scraggly small plot adjacent to a modest administration building.

No one better personifies the environmentalists' opposition to these sorts of projects than Bruce Rich, a quietly obstinate Washington-based attorney. From a mid-level position at the Natural Resources Defense Council (he later transferred to the Environmental Defense Fund), and with minimal financial support, Rich in 1983 launched an almost single-handed attack on the World Bank's environmental performance. Rather than attempting a broadside campaign, he chose initially to focus sharply on the Polonoroeste road-building and colonization effort. As the Bank officially saw it, the question was whether, as Brazilians would put it, to *deixar as coisas como estão p'ra ver como vão ficar*—leave things as they are in order to see how they'll turn out—or to step in and try to give structure to the disorderly mass migration. Internally, the Bank debated long and hard about the wisdom of intervening. Copies of internal memoranda, which Rich acquired "in the middle of the night," informed him of strong objections registered by consul-

5. The Mahar monograph, entitled "Government Policies and Deforestation in Brazil's Amazon Region," was published by the World Bank, in cooperation with the World Wildlife Fund and the Conservation Foundation, in 1989.

tants and staff reviewers. But, he told me when we met in his cluttered office in an offbeat corner of Washington, these were ignored or suppressed when the project came up for approval at higher levels. After getting promises from various Brazilian agencies that Rondônia's environment and indigenous populations would be protected, the Bank decided to take the gamble.

But skeptics were right. Polonoroeste may have appeared feasible on paper in faraway Washington, but putting its theory into practice in a remote and loosely governed Brazilian territory was another matter. Before it had even begun, much of the good land in the region had already been devoted to growing coffee or cacao. Few of the newcomers, however enthusiastic and energetic, fared better than the colonists of Parauapebas—clearing precious forest to create farms on which they could barely subsist, awaiting promised government assistance that usually failed to materialize. Virtually irreplaceable woodlands were being lost at a rate so rapid that, according to one exaggerated scientific forecast frequently cited at the time, Rondônia would be totally bereft of its forest by 1990. (In fact, partially because immigration slowed, only about one-fourth of its forest had been destroyed by 1990. But what had already been sacrificed opened the way for more destruction, and at little long-term benefit to the region's new occupants. Rondônia's forest is indeed doomed unless a miracle occurs; the error that the scientists made in the heat of the moment was only one of timing.) Seldom protected as pledged, Indians suffered severely, contracting diseases brought by the immigrants, dying from gunmen's bullets, facing extinction. In a crescendo of articles and appearances before congressional committees during 1983 and 1984, Rich pressed home his argument that Polonoroeste was "the Bank's biggest . . . and most disastrous involvement in forest colonization in the tropics"[6] and called for its withdrawal.

Many recruits joined Rich's Polonoroeste crusade. The biologist Thomas Lovejoy, who then represented the World Wildlife Fund, pressed both in Brasília and in Washington for more attention and less damage. On Capitol Hill, demands for U.S. actions against the Bank, many of them made by Senator Robert Kasten of Wisconsin, then

6. Article in *The Ecologist,* Vol. 15, No. 1/2 (1985), p. 59.

chairman of the Senate Appropriations Subcommittee on Foreign Operations, came ever more frequently. Tropical-forest protection became a broader concern by means of the Rainforest Action Network, a nongovernmental coalition of environmental activists. During the course of the 1985 annual meetings of the Bank and the International Monetary Fund, its representatives attracted plenty of public attention by picketing and by decorating the outside of one of the Bank's downtown Washington office buildings with a large banner reading "World Bank Destroys Tropical Rainforests." The CBS public-affairs program *60 Minutes* denounced the Bank in a strong piece during which the anchorwoman Diane Sawyer, waving Rich's pirated documents at the hapless José Botafogo, the Bank's vice president for external relations, defied him to defend the Polonoroeste loans. A Boston-based organization called Cultural Survival, concerned about the well-being of threatened indigenous populations, brought an additional constituency to the struggle.

As the Polonoroeste fracas continued, Rich and others began to question other large Bank projects on environmental grounds. One prominent target was Indonesia's transmigration scheme. According to its president, the World Bank's support for this was "intended to assure sustainable and environmentally and socially sound resettlement."[7] But the many instances of the program's failure to achieve these goals— Tulang Bawang was hardly an isolated example—brought it fusillades of criticism. Representatives of fifty-one nongovernmental organizations from fourteen nations co-signed one of Rich's tirades. The Polonoroeste and transmigration campaigns led to broadside challenges to the Bank's ideas about rural development. An entire 1985 issue of *The Ecologist,* a British publication, was devoted to attacks against its "global financing of impoverishment and famine." In the United States a coalition of environmental organizations issued a strong attack, entitled "Financing Ecological Destruction," that accused the Bank and its less public sister agency, the International Monetary Fund, of being negligent about the environmental consequences of "five fatal" large projects.

7. Letter to Rich from A. W. Clausen, then president of the World Bank, dated June 13, 1986.

The Bank's support for cattle-raising ventures also came under closer scrutiny. Until the late 1980s, when its government at last renounced the subsidies that had caused much of the problem, Brazil was widely accused of heedlessly sacrificing virgin tropical forest to create ranches that would soon become unproductive because of the underlying in-capacity of Amazonian soils to support even pasture grasses, let alone food crops.[8] Since its loans to Projeto Grande Carajás helped cattle ranchers as well as miners, the Bank came under criticism as well for not raising its voice against these subsidies. Cattle ranching (if not the eating habits of North Americans) became the paramount reason for Brazilian Amazon rainforest destruction. In Central America, regimes and ranchers did ravish forests in large part for the sake of United States beef consumers. Cattle ventures in Botswana, which enjoyed privileged access to Western European markets for prime beef, re-sulted in overgrazing, rangeland degradation, and stress upon wildlife populations.

The World Bank, which extended several cattle loans to Botswana during the 1970s and 1980s and has supported the sector as sound development policy, is a principal reason for these trends. In an un-repentant 1990 report, the Bank suggested no policy to counter its forecast of a continuation, in Amazonia, of the grim cycle: after a few years during which crops can be raised on the region's typically defi-cient soils, small-scale farmers then cultivate less demanding pasture grasses and sell their land to ranchers; they, in turn, run cattle until weeds crowd out the pasture, eventually abandon the land and move along, leaving behind a new stretch of moonscape.

Hydroelectric projects as well as tropical-forest degradation at-tracted the attention of environmental groups such as the Sierra Club, which in 1984 issued *The Social and Environmental Effects of*

8. Often, those complaining incorrectly added the allegation that Brazilian beef was being exported to the United States to form part of the celebrated "hamburger con-nection." So keen is Brazilian enthusiasm for beef, in fact, that the country usually consumes all that it produces; little of the beef raised in the Brazilian Amazon even reaches the major markets of southern Brazil. Even if Brazil had surpluses, U.S. restrictions to control the spread of hoof-and-mouth disease would prevent the entry of any Brazilian beef except in "cooked" form. Brazil's beef exports to the United States, then, consist entirely of small quantities of corned beef.

Large Dams. It is a catalogue of negative consequences, including siltation, spreading disease, forest destruction, and the forced resettlement of large numbers of people because of dam-related flooding. The Bank, citing the positive benefits of clean hydropower and irrigation for agriculture, continued its support for several massive projects of this sort: the Nam Choan Dam in Thailand, the Narmada River Development Program in India, China's Three Gorges Dam, the Xingu River development program in the heart of Indian lands in central Brazil. But opposition to traditional activities was growing broader and stronger, and these schemes faced increasingly vehement challenges from local tree-huggers as well as international environmentalists.

On the other hand, the World Bank met resistance from two key sectors in trying to come to terms with environmental criticisms. Wall Street financiers, whose bond issues had from the outset been vitally important to the Bank, expressed more concern for profitability than for environmental consequences, which, they believed, were the responsibility of the borrowers. At the opposite end of the spectrum, the borrowers themselves had reservations about the Bank's imposing environmental or human-rights conditionalities; from their point of view, such constraints violated sovereign rights and were an unwelcome form of interventionism. Many of the Bank's own directors and senior officials tacitly agreed with these views.

Still, the climate was changing. While in 1984 the World Bank was still defending Polonoroeste as "a carefully planned regional development program," World Bank president A. W. Clausen admitted in a March 1985 letter to Senator Kasten that the accusations had helped to prompt a "mid-term review" of the project. The following month the Bank suspended payments on a portion of its loans, alleging Brazilian inattention to the program's Indian and wildlife components. In 1986, the Bank gave up completely and, taking Rich's advice, canceled the loan. It was the first time it had taken such a step on environmental grounds. Speaking at a World Resources Institute gathering the following year, incoming president Barber Conable admitted that the Bank had "stumbled" on Polonoroeste. He called the experience "a sobering example of an environmentally sound effort which went wrong" because the Bank had "misread the human, institutional, and physical realities of the jungle and the frontier." In a section of the speech less frequently cited by environmentalists, Conable added that the affair was hardly going to cause the Bank to retreat. "Where development is taking place," he said, "it cannot be halted, only directed. The Bank cannot influence progress from the sidelines. It must be part of the action. With the developing nations, we must go on learning by doing." Conable thus also reiterated a line of reasoning that the Bank often followed: think how much worse things would be if it had refused to become involved.

The qualifiers notwithstanding, Conable had made a forthright admission of environmental failure, and actions followed his words in the form of further encouraging change in the Bank's Amazonian strategy. In 1989 it withdrew a $500 million construction loan for a vast network of 147 dams in the Brazilian Amazon that would cause the inundation of vast areas of forest. That year it also announced an innovative $117 million loan to Brazil for "environmental" projects in the Amazon from which no economic return was anticipated, and stated that the future would hold more of the same.

The Inter-American Development Bank (IDB) also reacted to criticism directed at the $58.5 million it committed (in spite of official U.S. objections expressed at the outset) to extending the infamous BR-364 highway from Rondônia to Acre territory on the Brazil-Peru border. At Rich's instigation, Senators Kasten and Daniel Inouye, and U.S. Treasury officials, continued to address heated correspondence to IDB. In 1987 the celebrated rubber-tapper Chico Mendes, who was later assassinated by opponents of his efforts to protect the forests of Acre (he wanted to establish special reserves for traditional harvesters of such goods as natural rubber and Brazil nuts), made a widely publicized trip to the United States to press the case. In August 1987 the IDB told Brazil that payments under the loan agreements would be suspended pending evidence of compliance with their environmental provisions. Though the payments were later made, the unprecedented ultimatum compelled Brazil to pay greater heed.

While complaints about Indonesia's transmigration effort did not interrupt the flow of World Bank support, which surpassed $1 billion, what did result was a reallocation of funds to parts of the program that would do little harm to the remaining intact rainforest. Whereas

World Bank loans made during the 1970s had enabled Indonesia to clear forest for new transmigrants, subsequent funds were earmarked for improvements in site selection and for assistance on already established sites. Beyond these modifications, opponents of transmigration welcomed the 1980s decline in oil prices, for it severely curtailed the Indonesian government's ability to carry forward the resettlement effort at the previous pace. Drastically reducing its earlier goal of moving 100,000 official transmigrants a year, the ministry in 1987 actually transferred only 3,000.

In short, these recent shifts in lending strategy express the slowly increasing environmental awareness within the Bank. In 1970, at the urging of Barbara Ward, McNamara had hired the Bank's first environmental adviser, James Lee, who was supposed to influence Bank decisions by means of internal seminars and publications. In 1972 the Bank established the Office of Environmental and Scientific Affairs (OESA), which the following year issued the first of many Bank publications on the environment. An initial round of "environmental" projects was funded in 1974, and that year the Bank's first booklet on the symmetry between environment and development also appeared. The 1978 forestry paper, which created a precedent by drawing attention to community or "social" as opposed to strictly commercial projects, led to further "sector" and policy declarations. In 1984 the Bank made its first overall statement about environmental criteria for its loans; in 1986 came an operational policy on wildlands conservation that showed interest in biodiversity. While none of these steps was significant by itself, the Bank alleged steady progress. The big ship, it often claimed, could not begin to turn the minute the wheel was spun.

In his 1987 World Resources Institute speech Conable gave the helm a more abrupt wrench by announcing, among other things, the creation of a new "top level" Environment Department to be manned by thirty professional staff members; it would support the efforts of the smaller environmental units within geographically oriented operational departments and help to develop "strategies to integrate environmental considerations into our overall lending and policy activities." The Bank, Conable added, would also undertake "an urgent, country-by-country assessment of the most severely threatened environments in developing nations"; participate actively in a multi-agency tropical-forest action plan; and launch a program of technical studies. Late in 1989 the Bank issued "Operational Directive 4.00, Annex A": a full deck of flexible but mandatory environmental assessment procedures governing most kinds of Bank lending. The 1990 announcement of a $1.15 billion Global Environment Facility, by means of which money would be loaned to countries addressing environmental problems, was a notably adventuresome departure.

The easing of the mother ship's helm did not relieve all within the community of regional MDBs. The Inter-American Development Bank, first bloodied in the battle over the road-building project in Brazil, has taken some internal steps to promote environmentalism. Its current president, the Uruguayan economist Enrique Iglesias, is far more concerned about the issue than was his longtime predecessor, the orthodox Antonio Ortiz Mena of Mexico. Iglesias brought in Marc Dourojeanni, an experienced Peruvian with strong views about conservation matters and North-South relations (he favors the South), as the bank's principal environmentalist. After only a few months on the job, Dourojeanni in mid-1990 claimed rapid progress in building up his department, extending the range of projects requiring environmental assessments, and increasing the magnitude of strictly environmental lending. Still, the conservative attitudes of its Latin American customers, many of whom are little concerned by environmental matters, inhibit IDB's ability to change. The Asian Development Bank in Manila is given higher marks for flexibility and responsiveness. It has a longstanding interest in social forestry, has been doing environmental impact assessments for some time, and gets credit for the quality of its analysis. The African Development Bank has yet to mount a significant environmental effort.

The United Nations Development Program (UNDP) has come a long way since the days of Paul Hoffman, its first head. A small agency that makes only some $1 billion in grants a year, it considers itself a testing ground for innovative ideas that can then be passed along to the World Bank or other larger-scale development lenders. William H. Draper III, the gregarious California businessman who is its current administrator, attaches a high priority to the environment. "I gave my very first speech on the subject," he told me early in 1990. Though the rank and file remain unsure of how deep Draper's commitment extends, the beginnings of an environmental program are under way. The point man in 1990 was Erik Helland-Hansen, a pleasant, salt-and-pepper-bearded Norwegian engineer who took on the job after twenty years of working on water projects in Africa. His objective, he said when we met in his small office at UN headquarters on New York's First Avenue, was not to separate the environment from operations, as the World Bank in large measure does, but to integrate it into general operations. "You don't have to be an environmentalist to do this work," he said. "What's required is no more than broad understanding." Though this approach seems somewhat reminiscent of James Lee's early World Bank years of seminars and memoranda, Helland-Hansen said he is equipping UNDP with an important new tool: a comprehensive set of "environmental guidelines for sustainable development." These are being developed in full partnership with the agency's field offices; it will take several years and the outcome depends in large measure on how much of an environmentalist Draper, in fact, turns out to be. "We're far from making anything operational," Helland-Hansen said. "But we're starting, and for now this is the important thing." UNDP has also worked hard to improve its relations with non-governmental organizations (NGOs) in developing countries. Under a program established in 1988, UNDP allocated $25,000 to each of sixty-two countries for distribution to one small NGO, or more, in each. An extension of the same principle is the UNDP-led Africa 2000 Network, which seeks local partnerships to "promote ecologically sustainable development."

For all the new concern at USAID (described in the previous chapter), its critics are quick to note that the agency, which has suffered from weak leadership in recent years, failed to produce a comprehensive environmental policy document until 1988, though it had been conducting studies and creating policy for more than a decade. The foot-dragging may not have been entirely accidental, for many influential people—including President Bush and Senator Claiborne Pell, chairman of the Senate Foreign Relations Committee and a principal godfather of the U.S. foreign assistance effort—preferred giving greater weight to security and political objectives than to sustainable development. The emphasis in the Reagan years on private-sector business participation was another distraction. In 1988, members of the House of Representatives Committee on Foreign Affairs, led by Congressman Lee Hamilton, conducted a deep review of U.S. foreign aid. In a speech to the Overseas Development Council and a subsequent article in *Foreign Service Journal,* Hamilton highlighted many criticisms of the agency's workings and advocated radical change. "Our current program," he said, "suffers from too great a concentration on the Middle East, too much emphasis on military sales . . . and too great an emphasis on immediate political objectives. . . . The purpose of the U.S. development program should be sustainable, broad-based economic growth in developing countries." But the House has gotten nowhere with USAID reform, because of reluctance on the Senate side, and Hamilton remains frustrated. Among others who are unsatisfied by USAID's environmental performance is the retired diplomat Robert Blake, founder of a group that reviews USAID's agricultural and rural-development programs. He and his associates concluded that it would take much to transform "a somewhat dispirited agency with declining resources into a proactive, aggressive force for needed change," and suggested that one useful step would be to "institutionalize" the principles of sustainability within the agency.[9] Within USAID, environmental coordinator Larry Hausman worried in mid-1990 that with change in progress at the World Bank, Rich and his coalition would shift their attention back to the environmental quality of U.S. bilateral assistance.

USAID's size and diversity make it difficult to assess the agency's overall performance. It is even hard to analyze the numbers, which show impressive growth in the size of grants for such matters as forestry and biodiversity but may include agricultural projects that degrade the environment. "A lot of what they call biodiversity boils down to sorghum," huffs Rob Milne, the seasoned director of the International Program at the National Park Service. Still, the progress suggested by USAID's reports to Congress is encouraging. By 1989 the agency could document healthy and growing levels of support for en-

9. From "The Transition to Sustainable Agriculture: A Two Year Review of AID's Agricultural and Rural Development Programs and an Agenda for the 1990s," published by the Committee on Agricultural Sustainability for Developing Countries, December 1989.

vironmentally sound forestry activities, the congressionally mandated biodiversity sector, and other innovations.

USAID has also increased its support for experimental efforts designed by private environmental agencies that reflect its new interest in human development. In 1985 R. Michael Wright of the World Wildlife Fund, a fervent attorney who then already had more than a decade of experience in international conservation work, expressed his dissatisfaction with traditional methods and designed an innovative program called Wildlands and Human Needs (WLHN). Its purpose, he wrote, is "to improve the quality of life of rural people through practical field projects that integrate the management of natural resources with grassroots economic development."[10] USAID began to assist these ventures, some of which are described in the next three chapters. Subsequently it completed broader agreements with WWF, the World Resources Institute, and the Nature Conservancy to work with local institutions to preserve biological diversity using techniques as varied as agroforestry, land preservation, and debt-for-nature swaps. During the 1990s, USAID seems destined to become schizoid, with Congress and environmental groups continuing to insist that the agency underwrite sustainable development and equally powerful voices demanding that it simply support U.S. trade interests (such was the thrust of an ominous bill presented to Congress, though not voted on, in 1990). Still, it seems likely to maintain a shaky lead as the foremost environmentalist among the bilateral aid donors.

The activities of other aid givers tend to be more closely tied to host-country exports and commercial interests. Japan's 1990 program included a $1.4 billion "environmental" allocation to be spread over three years (substantially larger than the $300 million in the 1990 U.S. budget for all forms of environmental aid), but Japan's aid tends to be conservative, linked to trade, and little connected with sustainability. The Western European nations have shown great (but, according to some observers, imprecise) enthusiasm for achieving sustainability and controlling domestic pollution of all sorts. As a percentage of per capita gross national product, their bilateral foreign-aid allocations dwarf

---

10. Statement contained in a WWF leaflet entitled "Wildlands and Human Needs—A Program of the World Wildlife Fund."

those of the United States, which since the glory days of the Marshall Plan has sunk to the bottom, but the quality is surprisingly varied. At Britain's uptight Overseas Development Administration (ODA), which barely gave me a civil welcome and was delighted to see me off its modest London premises, traditional commercial forestry is far more prominently supported than what the World Bank calls "social forestry."

As for regional assistance programs, the European Community (EC) has made progress in establishing environmental rules to govern trade and aid relations with its Lomé Convention partners in Africa, the Caribbean, and the Pacific. Hazardous-waste exports have been banned, and environmental assessment guidelines are being drawn up. Stanley Johnson, a seasoned EC bureaucrat and as of 1990 the Brussels-based chief of its energy division, admits that the Community has a long way to go. "As a result of colonial guilt, over the years we've passed along $14 billion in development assistance to the Lomé nations," he said. "But conditionality is anathema around here, and green conditionality even more so. Our environmental awakening will be rather slower than it is at the multilateral banks."

Even today, all is far from well in the relationship between the aid donors and the NGO community. Bruce Rich's fangs are still bared. Larry Williams, head of the international affairs program at the Sierra Club, continues to be skeptical about the World Bank. "Dealing with them is like housebreaking a puppy," he told me. "Every time they make a mistake with an individual project, we have to spank them to teach them a lesson in hopes they'll eventually learn to behave better. They have a long way to go. They're still pushing that big Narmada dam project in India, for example." The primatologist Russell Mittermeier, formerly vice president for science at the World Wildlife Fund and now president of Conservation International,[11] no longer pays much attention to the World Bank even though he once worked there as a consultant. "Lip service, just lip service," he snorted when I visited his office. "They don't really want us involved. I've given up on them."

11. A highly visible global conservation group founded in 1987 and currently staffed by Mittermeier and a number of other World Wildlife Fund and Nature Conservancy alumni.

But if confrontation is still often the manner, cooperation is not impossible. At USAID, the WLHN program is one operational field partnership. In Washington, NGO representatives are newly being invited in to help USAID design its natural resources program. UNDP is far from the only aid donor that has deliberately set out to improve working relations with NGOs. The shift has much to do with the strengthening, and internationalization, of the NGO community itself. Ten years ago, the principal private U.S. agencies working internationally were the World Wildlife Fund, with a program staff of three people and a grants budget of some $2 million, and the Nature Conservancy, whose overseas program was a tiny replica of its hugely successful land preservation efforts within the United States. The size and professionalism of these two organizations have grown mightily: as of 1990 WWF's total budget was up to $49 million. Many among its professional staff of 150 people have developed their skills within an entity whose senior alumni now are able to claim such positions as U.S. Environmental Protection Agency administrator (William K. Reilly) and Assistant Secretary of State for Oceans, Environment, and Space (E. U. Curtis Bohlen). Not only has the Nature Conservancy (TNC) enjoyed similar growth; it has spawned the lively splinter group Conservation International. Founded only in 1982 by James Gustave Speth, a Yale-trained lawyer who served as head of President Jimmy Carter's Council on Environmental Quality, the World Resources Institute has become a highly respected and well-funded environmental think tank. The Sierra Club, the National Audubon Society, the National Wildlife Federation, and an enlarged Friends of the Earth have initiated or expanded their international activities. The influence of Greenpeace, which in 1989 collected $14 million simply by ringing doorbells and far more using other fund-raising methods, has grown remarkably.

Equally impressive has been the explosion of the NGO movement in developing countries. In 1980 the number of these was minuscule—in Latin America, only dedicated individuals, not organizations—and their influence was insignificant. Today, many developing countries have dozens of environmental NGOs, including some partially funded by public and private international donors. Eighty-seven of them somehow existed, in 1990, in the chaotic political and economic climate of Peru. Guatemala had fifteen, most of them two years old or newer. Worldwide, some thirty thousand environmental NGOs were in operation. Many, though independent, are forming mutually useful ties with official organizations. The big donors, who remained skeptical about the little ones' ability to handle large amounts of money and "scale up," also began to show admiration for their skill in the field. Sometimes naïvely, NGOs shed their fear of Big Brother control for the sake of greater security and influence.

The concept of sustainability, as articulated in the Brundtland report, is now widely accepted even if uncertainties remain about how to define or achieve it. In calling for current actions that do not place the planet in jeopardy for future generations, the influential statement also recommends a development strategy that Joseph C. Wheeler, chairman from 1986 to 1991 of the Development Assistance Committee of the Organization for Economic Cooperation and Development, has called a "basic paradox." It is that, "although development is resource-utilizing and therefore puts pressure on the sustainability of our forests, our soils, our water and our air, yet it is only through a process of development that we can achieve the balance which will save us."[12]

Attention is also being paid to the 1992 United Nations Conference on Environment and Development (UNCED), the Rio de Janeiro "Earth Summit" with Maurice Strong back in the chair. In preparing for this watershed event, aid donors and environmentalists were better equipped than ever before to address the challenge of Wheeler's paradox. Redefining the nature of development has begun. Much has been learned as a result of the antagonisms generated ten years ago and the changes that took place because of them. From village-level experiments, launched late in the 1980s by partnerships between environmentalists and aid donors, came important clues about how development can best be accomplished in the context of sustainability. The next three chapters contain descriptions of several of these delicate examples.

12. In the Chairman's Overview, 1989 report of the OECD: "Development Cooperation in the 1990s."

PART II

AT WORK
IN THE FIELD

CHAPTER 5

The Asian Miracle

One image that Westerners have of tropical Asia has to do with its urban poverty: the endless millions jammed into Manila, Bangkok, Jakarta. You think of shanty houses built out over fetid pools of inky, garbage-strewn water, overcrowded buses and overloaded trucks belching black smoke, cultures wavering between flower-decked temple and garish pseudo-Hollywood. Contrary visions accentuate the go-go sleekness of Hong Kong and Singapore ("McCity," the travel writer Pico Iyer called it) with their tall office towers and teeth-gnashing business drive, or the stolid pace of peasant life in pollution-choked China. None of these eye-bites gets at the lingering beauty of Asia's natural world, seen and appreciated by fewer and fewer Asians, let alone foreign visitors.

On the banks of the Alas River in northern Sumatra, as the light faded one evening a decade ago, I sat transfixed while two troops of monkeys waged a cautious little war over a large tree in whose lofty canopy both wanted to spend the night. On the same visit, to Gunung Leuser National Park, we saw many hornbills and other remarkable birds, the world's largest flower (the rafflesia, with its three-foot di-

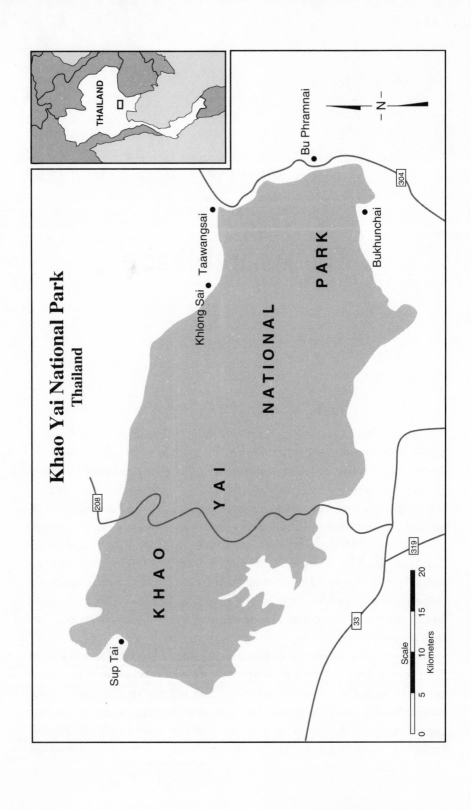

Khao Yai National Park
Thailand

ameter), the wonders of a dense dipterocarp[1] forest occupied by unseen elephants, rhinos, and tigers and all but devoid of humans. It is not so elsewhere on this crowded island, at the western end of the 3,200-mile-wide Indonesian archipelago, an entrepôt long frequented by explorers, traders, and conquerors from the Asian mainland, Arabia, and Europe. On its southern tip, across the narrow straits from densely populated Java, what was lately a velvet blanket of tropical forest has been largely reduced to unproductive farmland for government-sponsored Javanese transmigrants. Wild elephants making last stands near the new towns and villages trample the sugar crops at night, and occasionally kill a passerby. Even in the north, around Gunung Leuser, a USAID-funded highway bisects the Alas Valley and increases pressures on the region's dwindling biological resources. Throughout Southeast Asia, destruction like this has become dramatically commonplace. But in Asia as elsewhere, evidence of hopeful little counter-thrusts back toward a decent environmental and economic balance can also be found.

Thailand provides one example. There, late in 1988 when the monsoon season crested, floods of unprecedented severity swept the southern part of the country. More than three hundred people were killed and large tracts of rich farmland devastated. The government correctly placed much of the blame on erosion and instability caused by the nation's grievous loss of forest cover, by then down to less than 20 percent of what it once was. The heartening official response, decreed just as 1989 began, was the abrogation of all three hundred timber concessions awarded to logging companies to fell trees on public lands.

As the crackdown loomed, the loggers made haste to cut while they still could. One set up a camp at the village of Taawangsai, on the edge of Khao Yai National Park, two hundred kilometers northeast of Bangkok. Khao Yai itself, founded in 1962 and Thailand's oldest, remains cool and green in its biological richness even during the region's

---

1. Dipterocarps are a family of some five hundred species of woody plants found only in certain parts of Asia, of which some grow to as high as sixty meters and of which many species have great commercial value. Dipterocarp forests, "unique in the world," according to the botanist T. C. Whitmore, are the most magnificent of all tropical rainforests.

Landscape bordering Thailand's Khao Yai National Park

pronounced dry months, when the surrounding areas become brown and dusty. On its borderlands, almost fully transformed into fields and farmland after previous logging and slash-and-burn agriculture, occasional tall trees still dot the stark landscape. These the logging company's thirty-man crew, equipped with ten chain saws and a small fleet of trucks, now began to attack at a frenzied pace. Not even the thick forest within the park boundary remained safe. On the open fields, the remains of freshly cut trees lay like giant jackstraws. But the local villagers are learning through experience about the importance of forest cover to the well-being of watersheds, and the crew's arrival prompted them to take quick action. Lacking telephones, they used a telex machine to reach the nearby village of Khlong Sai with a message to Nikhom Putta, a field representative for a private organization called Wildlife Fund Thailand (WFT).

Nikhom reacted to the news of a possibly illegal logging blitz in the neighborhood by inviting a Bangkok journalist into the region to report on what happened next. Then, impulsively and at considerable risk in a sometimes trigger-happy rural area, he loaded ten village

Nikhom Putta, field representative of Wildlife Fund Thailand,
in Khlong Sai village

leaders onto the back of his small Toyota pickup. Following an old if not always productive national tradition, Nikhom then drove to Bangkok (where many in the group had never been) so that the delegation could discuss the matter face-to-face with the Minister of Agriculture. A day later Nikhom returned to his Khlong Sai headquarters, a well-built structure with a dramatic unobstructed view across open corn and cassava fields to the abrupt slopes and green trees of Khao Yai. Tightly bunched on the spotless floor of the office room were yet more village leaders keen to know how the trip had gone. Not only had the minister received the delegation, Nikhom told them; he had suggested moving the park's boundary outward to remove all doubt about the illegality of the assault on the trees. The minister also pledged to send an associate to look into the matter, and thanked the group for acting as the government's eyes and ears. Media coverage of the event, which took place at a time of student demonstrations and national concern about forest policy, was extensive.

The incident marked a pivotal moment for local villagers who, for

want of organization or funds until very recent times, had seldom before been able to air their concerns at the provincial level, let alone in
the capital. It also served to demonstrate, yet again, the importance of
nongovernmental intermediaries to sustainable development strategies.
The Thai government's encouraging shift from apathy about logging
to a far more protective approach, in a booming country long accustomed to squandering natural resources for the sake of a quick economic return, highlighted the degree of leadership that Wildlife Fund
Thailand has achieved.

Founded in 1983 by a former IBM executive named Pisit na Patalung,
WFT has its head office in Bangkok and an all-Thai staff of more than
thirty people; it has received financial support from various Thai
sources and from several Western governmental organizations, including USAID and the World Wildlife Fund. The assortment of programs
it conducts includes environmental education and nature tourism for
Thai citizens, media and lobbying campaigns, research, and field activities designed to protect national parks and highlight the effectiveness of rural development as a conservation method. Of these, the
most significant—and the most challenging—is a program called The
Environmental Awareness and Development Mobilization (TEAM).
Its objective is to protect Khao Yai National Park while at the same
time showing the villagers crowding against its borders how to improve their lives without depending, as the logging companies have,
on the shrinking forest as their principal nonrenewable asset. TEAM's
fieldworkers try to establish innovative and economically productive
ways of using the buffer lands adjacent to the park from which the
forest has already been stripped. A mobile education unit is improving
environmental awareness in thirty-seven villages near the park. In ten
of these, community organization, crop diversification, and credit extension activities have been launched.

One afternoon early in 1989, my wife, Flo, and I drove from Bangkok toward Khao Yai in the good company of Surapon Duangkhae,
WFT's projects manager and a wildlife biologist. After an hour en-
meshed in choked Bangkok traffic, we broke out into flat open farmland. Beside the road were canals where men cast fishnets and water
buffalo roamed. Soon we were within the borders of the park, which
is well staffed and trimly maintained and encompasses more than

300,000 hectares of almost entirely virgin tropical forest.[2] Its green hills jut sharply upward from the lowlands extending far inland from Thailand's southern coast, and form a boundary between that rich farming area and the grassy plains in the country's center.

Within Khao Yai's borders live 10 percent of all Thailand's wild elephants, along with tigers, wild pigs, large wild oxen called gaurs, and sambar and barking deer. Walking in the forest, we saw these odd little deer. We saw a snake eating a frog, and we stood still while a small troop of white-handed gibbons, their wailing vocalizations echoing hauntingly through the forest, crashed from tree to tree overhead. We saw several species of the impressive and highly visible hornbills that occupy top rank among Khao Yai's two hundred kinds of birds. Tall trees, notably the prized dipterocarp hardwoods with their attendant epiphytes and bromeliads, densely covered the sun-dappled ground. At dusk, birdwatching from an observation tower near the park headquarters, we also saw a monk meditating among low bushes, walking in steady rhythms back and forth along a set little route.

Beyond its importance as a habitat for valuable flora and fauna, Khao Yai is a critical watershed for the surrounding plains and lowlands. To migrants traveling past Khao Yai to the rich Bangkok area from the often arid Khmer lands of northeast Thailand, the area was known for centuries as "the dangerous place." Few humans have ever lived within what are now its boundaries. But beginning about a century ago, people established villages on its periphery. Previously experienced in basic agricultural techniques, these settlers—who sharply increased in number as Thailand's population soared and other rural areas became overcrowded during the 1960s and 1970s—raised what crops they could on farmland they created by cutting back the forest. As is often the case in tropical-forest regions, the soils they uncovered tended to be poor. What grew best on the barren land near many villages were the least glamorous but most practical of crops: corn and cassava for export to Europe as feed for livestock.

That these products fetched low prices was but one of the farmers'

---

2. The exception is the golf course, referred to in Chapter 2, which was sliced out of the forest by a government minister who believed that a park is not a park without golf.

Farmer in field near Khao Yai
National Park

problems. Another was that they occupied lands owned by the crown (Thailand is a constitutional monarchy), on which they had no right to live, let alone plant crops. Their ability to move beyond bare subsistence was, moreover, badly constrained by moneylenders and middlemen on whom they relied for plowing and trucking services and for high-interest loans to tide them over between crops. In areas where rice could be cultivated, the farmers even had to buy their own produce at the market at high prices, after others had milled and processed it, rather than consume directly what they had grown.

Under these conditions the easiest way for the region's residents to break out of the poverty trap was to harvest the forest's resources as intensively as they could. They tapped the dipterocarps for sticky sap that could be sold, raw, as a sealant for baskets and other containers. They felled rare sandalwood trees for their oil, used in perfume, and to make incense sticks from the sawdust. They cut the strong, slow-growing stalks of the rattan palm to sell to furniture makers. They hunted game for their own cooking pots, and caught baby myna birds to sell commercially. Most of all, they logged the once abundant hardwoods, and from these alone they could earn five- or sixfold the daily income to be derived from their traditional crops.

Back when the park was new and its management weaker, villagers and logging concessionaires alike could continue their incursions. Bribes sometimes persuaded enforcement officials to look the other way as the trees crashed down. But in recent years law enforcement techniques employed at the park have become far more sophisticated. Helicopter patrols, a scarce luxury in Third World park systems, are daily events at Khao Yai. The toughening vigilance made it ever harder for villagers and commercial loggers alike to harvest the forest as freely as before.

While authorities began to apply the stick more firmly, Wildlife Fund Thailand joined other agencies in experimenting with carrots. In 1985 and 1986, WFT and a private economic development agency called the Population and Community Development Association mounted a pilot effort to provide services—conservation education, low-interest loans—to residents of the village of Sup Tai on Khao Yai's northern boundary. "It became evident that conservation cannot enter such an area alone," WFT director Pisit told me in Bangkok at the end of our trip. "When people think the forest is there to be cut and its animals are to be eaten, you can only preach the conservation message when it comes packed in a bigger basket."

For WFT (if not for USAID, as it turned out) it seemed too big a jump from one village to a new program encompassing all 153,000 people in all of the 156 villages around the Khao Yai park. But its staff drew heavily on the pilot experience in designing the considerably larger TEAM model. The latter, too, features environmental education, community organization, agricultural diversification and innovation, and services branching as far afield as health and nutrition.

Most of all, it emphasizes low-interest credit, a feature that won the support of USAID's rural development program. In return for pledging to stop invading the forest and to adopt environmentally sound practices in their use of open spaces, villagers become entitled to receive loans at a 12 percent annual interest rate, a bargain in relation to the crippling 10 percent *a month* charged by local moneylenders. With money available to them at lower interest rates, villagers not only can survive between crops but can also contemplate making investments to improve their operations. More important, their dependence on Chinese intermediaries, anathema to ethnic Thais, lessens.

Despite the appeal of this pivotal sector of the program, WFT field-workers faced hostility when, early in 1987, they began to introduce the TEAM idea at village meetings. "We had to work hard to explain that the project would help people and not get them into trouble," said Surapon. At the village of Bu Phramnai, whose residents had grown accustomed to extracting easy profit from the forest, WFT fieldworker Nikhom was roundly booed at the conclusion of his initial slide presentation. "We have no use for you or your project," the villagers said threateningly. "Get out of here, and leave us alone." Elsewhere the reaction was more positive. This was particularly so in the rather new village of Khlong Sai, on the park's northeastern flank and in a critical watershed area. Here lived about seventy-five households of very poor families who had gathered from many different parts of Thailand. But over the twenty years of the village's existence very little community organization of any sort had been accomplished. "It's as if they hardly even knew each other," Surapon said. With little hesitation, the villagers came to see the TEAM idea as a way to gather collective strength and decrease their reliance on moneylenders and middlemen.

So receptive were Khlong Sai's citizens that it was decided to establish TEAM's field headquarters at this key location. Early in 1988 the training-center building was completed and Nikhom moved to the village. Over the course of its first year, Flo and I discovered when we left the cool green world of Khao Yai and drove the dusty dirt roads of its periphery to Khlong Sai, TEAM had already accomplished a lot. The project headquarters had become a focus for many community activities, ranging from business and conservation education across a spectrum that also included health, nutrition, and family planning. We spent several days there, sleeping on the floor of a large room along with the snoring, snorting driver of our car. During our visit a nurse who worked as the assistant health officer for the area borrowed the premises to hold a twenty-four-hour series of events, including a well-attended evening lecture and an open-house clinic for villagers who must normally travel ten miles by road to get first aid or more than two hours to reach the nearest hospital. "This is wonderful," said the nurse as she took a break on the patio outside the headquarters building. "I do not know of anything equal to this anywhere else in our district."

An Environmental Protection Society had also been established, with a ten-man governing committee to set rules, manage the expanding credit program, decide how to allocate the 40 percent of future loan repayments to be earmarked for community development (the remaining 60 percent would be reinvested in the loan fund), and help organize activities such as a cooperative store. The committee was gaining confidence in its ability to make independent decisions—not easy in a land whose intricate culture tends not to encourage assertive behavior.

A crop diversification program was well launched. Among the innovations introduced at Khlong Sai (some not new to the region) are the planting and harvesting of cashews, bamboo, coconut palms, mango and jackfruit trees, mung beans and other legumes such as peanuts, several green vegetables, "dry" rice that can be grown not in paddies but on hillsides and can endure the area's long rainless season. Several teams of villagers had been formed to cultivate these crops in flourishing, well-tended community gardens. Composting was effectively replacing the use of chemical fertilizers, which pollute watercourses, in these and other village gardens. Pigs, which once wandered freely in the village, causing pollution problems and damaging crops, were being enclosed in pens. A WFT contributor had supplied a small experimental herd of dairy cows, to be raised in the village and sold for profit. Rabbits had been introduced. During the wet season fish were being raised in the fields. Some were used as food; those left to die became natural fertilizer.

Since many children come to the village school hungry, project funds were allocated for a school lunch program. Early one morning, under a sun that was already bright and hot, I strolled in the schoolyard, watching the children as they tended the crops they were cultivating in a tidy hillside garden adjacent to the schoolhouse. Health and family-planning issues were being directly if not fully addressed. Since less than half of the households in Khlong Sai have gravity-flow flush toilets (and during the dry season these function only sporadically), a flexible approach to sanitation is required. TEAM encourages people to build toilets if they already own large jars to collect rainwater, and to purchase the jars if they don't already have them. Among the items for sale at the program's cooperative store, located at the center of the village near the headquarters building, were condoms and birth-control pills.

The TEAM effort was expanding beyond Khlong Sai. The ten villages slated for special attention had functioning conservation committees and low-interest loan programs. In the recalcitrant community of Bu Phramnai, where a mellower mood eventually replaced the initial friction, a project training center now stands at a prominent location on the main road. If only because the credit-extension program decreases villagers' dependence on the high-interest moneylenders, said Surapon, "almost everybody likes the project now."

Under the best of circumstances, those closest to TEAM believe, achieving its objectives will take longer than originally thought. "Just getting organized to bring about change requires a lot of time and effort," said the energetic Nikhom. Dr. Gary Suwannarat, an American consultant to USAID and a keen observer of TEAM's progress, thinks that three years of fieldwork is only the beginning. "Some of my colleagues are oriented toward quick results," she said in Bangkok. "My view is that, given the need for some initial time to get started, a three-year rural project probably means only two crop seasons. And suppose one of those years you have bad weather and a crop failure? Then you end up with no basis for evaluation. It's just not enough time." In fact, even though major increases in the WFT field staff would probably speed things up, Suwannarat tends to oppose them: a larger WFT presence, she fears, would inhibit villagers from achieving the self-reliance in decision-making abilities and economic welfare that is TEAM's ultimate goal. In Washington, however, Suwannarat lost out to a senior administrator well known among environmentalists for her lack of interest in anything but purely private-sector initiatives; when WFT balked at rapidly expanding TEAM, USAID withdrew from the project.

In many countries like Thailand, residents of areas adjacent to national parks are allowed to enter them to hunt for their own food and to harvest forest resources in other limited ways. But Thailand's firm laws, which are enthusiastically supported by public and private leaders, mandate a strict boundary between parks and people; a more lenient approach, it is widely believed, would have tragic results. This rigidity means that economic improvements must be wrested entirely from agricultural innovations in already degraded areas beyond the park borders. Since the quickest possible economic return would come from bamboo shoots, which can only be harvested three years after they have been planted, the patience of villagers and funders alike is sorely tried.

A related concern is whether the keystone credit facility can ever become self-perpetuating solely on the basis of loan repayments and net income from cooperative stores—and whether it can eventually be managed by villagers with no outside help. The question has been much debated, Dr. Suwannarat admitted. She hoped that, at the very least, commercial banks would join TEAM as lenders to the villagers, with interest rates lower than those commanded by the local usurers. If they do so, there would be marked economic improvement even if the TEAM lending program itself fails to cover all needs. Without such extra support, on the other hand, the danger remains that the subsidy the forest gave the villagers will be replaced only by an equally unsustainable subsidy in the form of artificially below-market credit from an outside source.

There is also the chance that, despite the Thai government's current expressions of commitment to conservation, a resumption of its negligence or a resurgence of corruption could undercut TEAM and other worthy grass-roots efforts. If the authorities do not enforce the cancellation of the logging concessions, one Thai general warned, the forest might be more relentlessly attacked than ever before. The final danger is that TEAM might ironically become a victim of its own success. The more the villagers prosper as a consequence of the program, the more likely it is that new people will overcrowd the area in search of the same unusual opportunities—and cancel out the gains achieved.

But for all the hazards and uncertainties, TEAM's accomplishments to date outweigh the inevitable questions surrounding its inventive structure. In a very short time, it has become a very appealing institution within its communities. "I welcome it," said a leader named Nut Ngodklang in Taawangsai village. "It is the only way I can become free from the moneylenders." Surapon put the issue more strongly. If the government maintains its will and its ability to police the forest, he said, the villagers will have no choice: "Either they join the program or they leave the region."

TEAM is also exercising a broader influence. Its basic principle of working to help villagers living in or near protected areas, rather than simply applying militaristic coercion to keep them outside the parks, has been applied to grass-roots conservation and development efforts elsewhere in Thailand. TEAM's ideas are "gaining ground all the time," said Dr. Suwannarat, "even though some sections of the bureaucracies are more advanced than others." At WFT, meanwhile, the patient and sometimes frustrating task of keeping TEAM on track moves steadily along. At the heart of it is the zeal and determination of the staff people, many of whom had no prior training for this sort of work. Before becoming WFT's projects manager Surapon had spent the better part of five years conducting field studies of the bumblebee bat, a species endemic to Thailand that, with a head-to-rump length of as little as three centimeters, has the distinction of being the world's smallest mammal. "They're small, but they are much easier to keep track of than people," he said. "Still, I am confident that we have made progress."

What WFT is attempting around Khao Yai is a rearguard action to achieve sustainability in what is already (except for the park itself) a badly degraded region. Too often, conservation planning gets started this way, at the eleventh hour. Not so in equatorial Irian Jaya, the western half of the island of New Guinea that forms the eastern terminus of the Indonesian archipelago, a lightly populated land of dense unbroken rainforest, girded by coral reefs and crystal waters. Here government officials, together with private-sector advisers, have de-

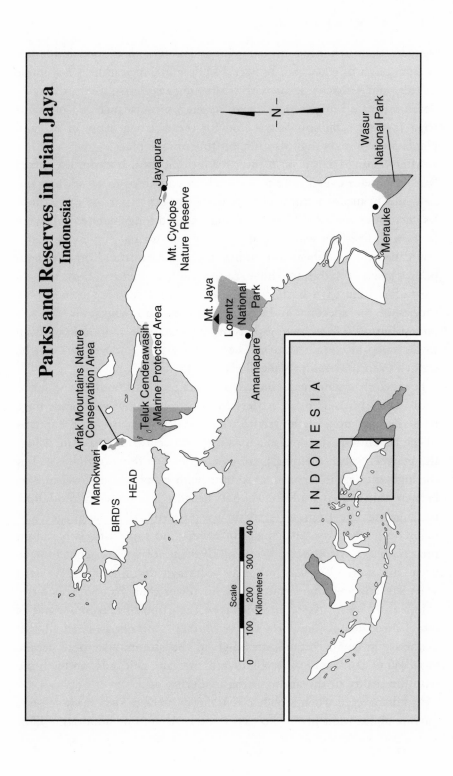

Parks and Reserves in Irian Jaya
Indonesia

N

Arfak Mountains Nature
Conservation Area

Manokwari

BIRD'S

HEAD

Teluk Cenderawasih
Marine Protected Area

Mt. Jaya

Lorentz
National
Park

Mt. Cyclops
Nature Reserve

Jayapura

Amamapare

Wasur
National Park

Merauke

Scale
100 200 300 400
0
Kilometers

INDONESIA

signed a comprehensive master plan in *advance* of the inevitable up-coming burst of economic activity. While implementation is no simple matter, and setbacks occur with frustrating regularity, the sustainable development strategies now being applied promise benefits both for Irian Jaya's 1.6 million people and for the dazzling array of unusual plants and animals that also inhabit this unique place.

After visiting Irian Jaya in 1858, the intrepid British naturalist Alfred Russel Wallace called it "a country which contained more strange and new and beautiful natural objects than any other part of the globe." Its curiosities include clams more than a yard long; bats called flying foxes with five-foot wingspreads; a furry, ant-eating, egg-laying mam-mal called the long-beaked echidna; tree kangaroos and other marsu-pials closely related to those found on the nearby continent of Australia. Irian Jaya harbors 852 different bird species, including 26 species of the spectacular bird of paradise. Bird wings, the world's largest butterflies, with wingspans of up to ten inches, abound on Irian Jaya's steep mountain slopes. Their vivid greens and yellows can be sighted even near the provincial capital, Jayapura.

Few people are more distinctive than the highland hunters and farm-ers of Irian Jaya. Though settlers from other Indonesian islands have made melting pots of the territory's coastal towns, the pure Papuans of the mountains still live much as they did centuries ago. Ritual bat-tles between spear-wielding factions are mostly a thing of the past. But the highland Irianese continue to hunt with bows and arrows, in part because this is their tradition, in part because Indonesia will not allow them guns. The Irianese speak many different tribal languages and maintain an intricate assortment of beliefs and superstitions based on their natural environment. While all of them are now thought to have been "discovered," it was only fifty years ago that a team of Western scientists and explorers ran across no fewer than 50,000 previously "hidden" Irianese. As recently as 1979, helicopter-borne missionaries established the outside world's "first contact" with one isolated village. Gathered in small communities high in the mountains, these people grow yams, corn, and vegetables, raise pigs and chickens, and grapple with the reality of the approaching modern world.

As I discovered when I made a visit during the late 1988 rainy season, moving about Irian Jaya is no easy matter. About one hundred million years ago, two large tectonic plates collided to form New Guinea, the world's second-largest island (after Greenland). The seismic activity shaped a tightly folded region of towering mountains. More than 16,000 feet in height, Mount Jaya is Southeast Asia's summit. Below it lies one of the world's few permanent glaciers in an equatorial zone. The mountains, punctuated by narrow valleys and interlaced with fast-flowing streams of cold clear water, tend to plunge almost directly into the sea. Motorways make little headway into this terrain from the narrow coastal plains. There are only a few short grass airstrips. The mere act of walking is hazardous and slow on the slippery, hilly mountain trails. Though the Irianese move along them with speed and agility, often carrying heavy loads on their backs, the rule of thumb remains that in the highlands it takes a day on foot to cover the same distance that can be spanned in no more than ten minutes of flight aboard a slow Cessna. Coastal travel is still accomplished largely by means of a *perahu* (an outboard-powered outrigger canoe).

While development has been slow to reach such a remote and difficult place, large-scale economic activity is accelerating. Logging and wood-chipping operations have cropped up here and there, and one region produces substantial amounts of oil. Beginning in the 1960s, a company called Freeport-McMoRan installed a major open-pit copper mine near the ice fields high in the central mountains. The company pipes the ore, mixed with water, down to the port of Amamapare, one hundred kilometers away on the southern coast. As part of an ambitious scheme to relieve pressure on overcrowded Java (and, some say, to weaken Irianese hostility by "Javanizing" Irian Jaya), the Jakarta government has established transmigrant settlements along the coast. The Scott Paper Company walked away from Irian Jaya after environmentalists protested its plans to install a pulp mill on the southern coast. The national government in 1990 remained determined to move the project forward, ironically negotiating with Taiwanese private-sector partners less likely than Scott to follow careful environmental guidelines.

Still, with a small population and the largest area (158,556 square miles, or almost 42 million hectares) of any Indonesian province, Irian Jaya at the end of the 1980s remained much as Wallace found it. In Papua New Guinea, the freestanding democracy that occupies the island's eastern half, large tracts of the original forest have been logged or cleared to make way for coffee, rubber, and palm-oil plantations. Virgin forest still covers 80 percent of Irian Jaya. Except for damage around the larger towns such as the provincial capital, Jayapura, and in a few heavily fished areas, coastal and marine resources remain intact. In Irian Jaya conservation's task is not to undo past errors, but to brace the region for the burst of development that, it is believed, lies just ahead as people begin to brave the hostile terrain to reach the province's minerals and other resources.

Among biologists and conservationists, interest in the region has continued steadily since Wallace's time. In the 1870s the Italian explorers Luigi d'Albertis and Odoardo Beccari brought the first extensive Irianese collections of plant and animal material back to Europe, thus initiating a prolonged period of attention to the species-rich Bird's Head area near the island's northwestern end, where they spent most of their time. In 1919, the Dutch, who governed Irian Jaya until 1963, established the province's first nature reserve in what is now the huge, 1,483,200-hectare Lorentz National Park. Soon after Indonesia assumed control of Irian Jaya in 1969, following a brief United Nations protectorate, conservation planning began anew. In 1980, Ronald Petocz, an American wildlife biologist, arrived in Jayapura under the auspices of the World Wildlife Fund and IUCN. His principal task was to map out a broad, preemptive conservation and development strategy for the region.

In a report presented to the Indonesian government in 1983, still the basic text for conservation in Irian Jaya, Petocz recommended adjustments and a dramatic expansion in the scope of Irian Jaya's system of nature reserves and protected areas. In total, he proposed that more than 83,000 square kilometers,[3] or some 20 percent of the entire province, be gazetted as nature reserve. Protection was also suggested for three extensive marine areas. Following the tenets of the then new doctrine of sustainable development for conservation, the proposal outlined a series of economic innovations to improve human lives without placing new stress upon forest or marine resources. His plan encompassed nearly 40 percent of all "programmed" conservation areas in Indonesia, Petocz commented later, and was when published "one of the most ambitious in the Pacific basin."

3. One square kilometer equals 1,000 hectares.

Once the overall strategy had been approved, the next and more difficult step was to begin active management of the reserves and border regions that were most exposed to destructive pressures. It is one thing to draw lines on a map. The tougher challenges are to mark boundaries and get people to respect them (sometimes addressing complex questions of land ownership and tenure along the way) and to reach fair and workable agreements with traditional users of protected lands who live near or even within them about such matters as subsistence farming, hunting, and logging rights. Corruption, accidents, illnesses, technical foul-ups, and other problems associated with a fast-growing staff doing experimental work (many of them more familiar with binoculars than with machines) are further impediments as the program moves from paper onto the ground.

My objective in 1988 was to see how things were going, five years after the publication of the Petocz report and at a moment when the ambitious plans to implement and extend it were being developed and financed. I flew to Jayapura from Los Angeles, via Honolulu and a scruffy island called Biak, the scene of major fighting during World War II. As the plane approached the airport at Jayapura, a considerable distance outside the town, an uninterrupted view of thick green forest gave way to bare hillside. Stephen Nash, a young Canadian who was serving as WWF's program manager for Irian Jaya, met me. The damage, he explained as we drove the busy, winding road into town, was largely local, attributable to the fact that 100,000 people, or almost a tenth of the province's total population, lived in or near Jayapura.

Nash installed me high on a hillside on the outskirts, in a guest house that had been built some years before by the Japan Development Foundation. Its front deck yielded a spacious view across Harcourt Bay, which contained many weirs and fishing vessels, to the northernmost points of Papua New Guinea along the far horizon. Silver, gray, and black rainsqualls scudded and swirled across the dark water behind a stiff northwest breeze. In the town, active until just after lunch, when it empties and a lethargic tropical afternoon sets in, traffic hummed and buzzed. The population seemed about half Asian, half black Irianese.

After I had obtained a police visa for internal travel, an unexpected requirement in a region not yet fully recovered from a guerrilla insurrection of the late 1960s and still tense with ethnic conflict, Nash drove me a short distance out of town to look briefly at a pioneer social forestry program that stems in part from the Petocz report and is, in structure, a Rube Goldberg collaboration involving Indonesia's Ministry of Forestry, the provincial government of Irian Jaya, the Irian Jaya Rural Development Foundation, the Ford Foundation, and WWF. The target areas are farming settlements along one side of the small and well-forested Mount Cyclops Nature Reserve on the northern coast near Jayapura and a series of fishing villages on Cyclops's seaside flank.

The Cyclops reserve, protected since 1978, a critical watershed for the provincial capital, was being penetrated by farmers, hunters, and loggers. Villagers' ancestral claims to nearby land conflicted with the boundaries that had been drawn on the map. To function properly, said Mark Poffenberger, then of the Ford Foundation staff in Jakarta, what the reserve urgently needed was "a viable management system" developed "through the mutual agreement of surrounding interest groups and communities." The project team that Ford assembled enlisted local people in all aspects of managing the region. Village representatives helped to establish land ownership and settle reserve boundaries. After completing a training course in social forestry (in which high environmental standards are maintained) fieldworkers drawn from the villages began negotiating with farmers and the management staff to develop new rules and methods to benefit the residents without harming the forest. Soil-conserving techniques, in which perennial tree crops are interspersed with beans, maize, and other annual staples, were introduced. To support these initiatives, villagers established tree-seedling nurseries. Community leaders helped to decide on ways to regulate hunting, fuel-wood collection, and hardwood logging for houses and boats. Since most tree crops take years to mature and yield income, patience is required.

The time lag is but one of many reasons, Nash said as we left the main road and entered a vividly green world of small farms, why the intricate Cyclops program was not ready for an A-to-Z evaluation. Like all such programs, it needs many different kinds of people and institutions, with widely differing habits and values, to cooperate and interact. Insects, shortages of seedlings and other critical supplies, and bureaucratic delays all impede progress, and early achievements are fragmented.

Still, some signals were already evident, and one was to be found in the hamlet of Sabrondosai, on the edge of the reserve and hard against the base of the 5,300-foot mountain range. Here, we walked into fields where healthy stands of mixed crops were growing. Yasong, a social forestry fieldworker, and Marcus, a farmer with land directly adjacent to the reserve, both accompanied us. Yasong had persuaded Marcus to work not independently but partially in partnership with Irianese and transmigrants from the community. While Marcus tended his healthy stands of corn, beans, and tomatoes, village volunteer teams would plant cocoa and various fruit trees on the same land. Eventually these trees will generate enough income for the villagers to dampen their interest in leapfrogging Marcus's land and invading the reserve to open new areas for traditional slash-and-burn agriculture. The twenty hectares he has allocated to the scheme is enough land to engage the entire village, which would also benefit from a more reliable water supply than it would have if forest cutting continued. Marcus himself would maintain a favored position at the forest edge.

Such are the combined results desired, on a far broader scale, for the Cyclops project, for the reserve, and for the 85,000 people who live on its borders. As of 1990, the project had become bogged down, just as similar efforts have in many other rural places where politics are the worst enemy of sustainable economic growth and conservation. But this hardly means that Marcus's and his neighbors' sturdier values will not prevail in the end.

After casting an eye on Cyclops, my next and eagerly awaited task was to visit the 650,000-hectare Arfak Mountains Nature Conservation Area in the Bird's Head region. In the cool damp heights of the Arfaks, part of a separate island before New Guinea's tectonic crunch, live many plants and animals found nowhere else, including endemic species of both the bird of paradise and the bird-wing butterfly. Here the Vogelkop bowerbird practices its amazing architecture, carefully constructing an expansive straw house with a pointed roof, then decorating its entryway with neat pyramids of fruit and fungi. Settlements in the Arfaks lie as high as four thousand feet above sea level and are accessible only by steep and narrow foot trails or by means of a few small missionary aircraft that, for a higher price than what you would put into the collection plate, will carry passengers and freight into and out of the region's few grass strips.

About ten thousand people of the Hatam tribe, many of them carrying bows and arrows, also live in these remote mountains. Some 35 percent of all Hatam children die as babies; a local bird called the western smoky honey eater enters villages and cries, the Hatam believe, when such a death takes place. Most of the Hatam are illiterate. Jakarta is a concept, not a place. Property ownership, the links between health and cleanliness, what distances mean—these are all shadowy notions in a society still dominated by traditions, superstitions, and animosities that often stem from disputes about the pigs that range freely in their villages.

Once the Hatam lived scattered through the forest in tiny settlements of one or two or three houses. They cleared small patches of land to grow crops for their families; long fallow periods regenerated the soil. The Hatam put little stress on their environment. Beginning in the 1960s, though, two factors caused them to congregate in larger groups and begin cutting deeper into the forest. For one thing, they joined the separatist rebellion that Irianese mounted against the 1969 Indonesian takeover of their land. One of the consequences of this unequal war, which lingers on, was government orders for the Hatam to move from their forest enclaves out into open villages where they could be watched more closely. Pushed toward them by the government, the Hatam were also attracted to the airstrips the missionaries had opened. Though inhibited from migrating down to coastal areas because of tribal rivalries and the lack of available land, they had long been in touch with the coastal people. When populations in such towns as Manokwari on the northern coast swelled with the arrival of transmigrants and detachments of Indonesian soldiers, the Hatam found expanding markets for potatoes and other crops and for their bird-wing butterflies and birds of paradise—alive or dead. While their backs continued to serve as the principal means of getting the goods to market, the Hatam also began to use the missionary airplanes. The planes brought in goods and ferried very sick villagers to the hospital in Manokwari. Inevitably, the new Hatam habits began to take their toll on forest lands around the larger villages, whose horizons began to bear the scars of deforestation. Bird-wing butterflies were so heavily netted around the Hatam communities that most are now found only on steep upper slopes, and the same goes for birds of paradise. Since the Hatam could quickly destroy a significant portion of the entire Arfak forest, conservation's challenge here was to guide the energies of these people along lucrative but less destructive tracks.

Nash and I flew to Manokwari, not an easy task given the uncertainties of commercial aviation in Irian Jaya, and paused there to snorkel the clean waters nearby, which are marred only by the hulk of a U.S. landing craft sunk in the bay during World War II. We looked at Warmare, a transmigration settlement at the foot of the Arfak range. Ian Craven, a British biologist who was serving as WWF's representative in the region, took time on the day of his wedding (to Mary Ann, a Canadian Mennonite schoolteacher) to explain his efforts to work with the Hatam. The first step, said this willowy, soft-spoken young man, was obviously to get to know them better, which he did by spending most of a year trekking the rough Arfak trails. From the experience, he drew one cardinal lesson: the need for Hatam participation in any broad planning for the region. Taking a cue from the stubborn Hatam involvement in the guerrilla war, he warned that "a coercive and strict approach to management will not succeed in these mountains."

Craven and his frequent hiking companion, the Irian Jaya–born conservationist Yance de Fretes, drew maps—often the most detailed ever produced of the region. They showed how important it was to avoid conflict by negotiating with the Hatam for equitable divisions between land for farming and land for the reserve. This in itself was a complicated matter since the fuzzy Hatam beliefs about land rights are based on ancestral occupancy and opinions vary about who was where. The Hatam did not understand that they could no longer use land once they had sold it. Craven and Fretes first addressed this issue in a slide show about forest conservation, popular entertainment in an area where electricity hardly exists outside the well-supplied missionary camps. Then they broached the subject of boundaries to a group of *gembala*—"shepherds" from various communities who had already received leadership training from the Evangelical Alliance Mission, an American Protestant group that had long been active in the Arfaks. Good relations with these people—"an interesting marriage between conservation and religion," as Nash put it—led to the formation of village committees to get the boundaries marked.

New boundaries, the Hatam discovered, would mean new rules: no gardening or house building inside the reserve, limitations on hunting and on catching protected species. Even so, the Hatam came to favor the new system, so as to protect their territory from claims by outsiders. Hatam have participated vigorously in boundary-marking expeditions and have shown great respect for the markers once placed. "If the village helped mark the boundary, it's there for good," said Craven. "We've had no problems at all with violations. If a marker is missing, they'll come and tell us." "We call this a conservation area," Nash added. "In the Hatam language, it is 'the place we guard.'" People from a tribe called the Sougb, who live on the western border of the Hatam lands, so badly want their own nature reserve that not long ago they caused trouble by stealing a number of the Hatam boundary-marking signs.

With boundaries and rules established, the WWF team could begin looking for new ways to generate Hatam income without causing further forest destruction. Here, Craven concluded, the principal hope lies in building up wild butterfly stocks while also selling the insects to avid buyers all over the world. Commonplace Irian Jaya butterflies fetch a dollar apiece on the international market; choice Arfak bird wings can bring five dollars or more. Tourists, collectors, museums, and educational institutions all buy dead butterflies. Trade in live insects is also fast growing to supply summertime "butterfly houses"—colonies nurtured in greenhouses that people pay to visit—which have become popular in the United Kingdom and are spreading across Europe. Since even healthy butterflies live only briefly, these exhibitors need monthly or even weekly infusions of fresh stock during their operating seasons.

Ranching butterflies in the wild is both legal and sustainable, and if conducted properly results in ever-larger wild populations and rising incomes for the ranchers. On selected areas of forest or grassland, ranchers cluster plants whose flowers or leaves are known to attract key butterfly species for nectar, pollen, or egg-laying. They regulate their harvests acccording to market demand and sustainable limits. From the Arfaks the easily transportable chrysalides, and some live specimens, can be flown in small planes to the nearby Biak airport, which offers, for instance, frequent one-stop jet service to Los Angeles.

*Hatam men pay Dave, pilot for American missionaries,
to fly their potatoes to market.*

During my visit, Craven was organizing the ranching program. To be launched with funds from USAID, it would, if all went well, be self-sufficient within three years. The first step toward trying to make butterfly ranching commonplace and profitable throughout Irian Jaya would be an experimental phase among the Hatam in the Arfaks. The very first model ranch was planned for the Hatam village of Mokwam. It was to this destination that Dave, an American missionary whose calling was to learn to fly, now took us in his shiny, beautifully maintained plane.

Only fourteen minutes in duration from Manokwari, the flight took us over land near the coast that is farmed by transmigrants from other Indonesian islands. We climbed over one crinkly green ridge to an altitude of about 4,500 feet, then dropped down toward a narrow airstrip. Dave added a strong burst of power after we landed so that the plane could taxi up the steep hill to the top of the strip. What appeared to be the village's entire population (about thirty houses' worth) was on hand to greet us. Men loaded sacks of potatoes, to be sold in Manokwari, onto the plane for its return flight. Women and children sat in clumps on the grass nearby. We walked the slippery terrain, through farmland that the Hatam had cleared near the village, toward a site that had been selected as a prospective butterfly ranch. A man wearing a safety pin in his ear, carrying a bow and several arrows, appointed himself as my special guardian and watched for any misstep as I negotiated the narrow and slippery path. We reached our destination, from which we could look over the narrow valley toward magnificent stretches of unbroken rainforest beyond. Craven pointed to a high ridge atop which he had slept. It had taken him several days to walk there from Manokwari.

Clouds gathered and swirled on the hillsides as we returned to the village. By the time we reached WWF's small bamboo house, rain was clattering onto its corrugated roof. A smoky wood fire warmed us. *Gembala,* or "shepherds," sat on their heels, listening patiently while Craven and Nash reviewed the status of the butterfly program. Then the men asked many questions, and a lively discussion ensued. "They are eager," Craven explained. "The younger men have plenty of time. But the old people are concerned that they won't see progress with the conservation area, or with the ranching program, before they die. We're just stalling them now. When we get the final go-ahead, they will start right away. They will get the job done, and they will do it well. The promise of butterflies was an economic incentive that generated enthusiasm to mark boundaries. The trade clearly links butterflies to the nature reserve. Lose your forest and you lose your money. Money talks!" Added Nash: "The hope and expectation is that the Hatam will put as much time into butterfly ranching as they have into cutting the forest in recent years. Already the Hatam strongly support conservation on the grounds that it gives them better control over their land. If the butterfly concept works and provides the anticipated economic benefits, they will be some of the most enthusiastic conservationists anywhere." Soil conservation measures, as well as small-scale chicken- and fish-raising activities, are also being introduced in the Arfaks.

The next day we walked the slippery trail in the company of several Hatam. They led us into the woods to show us two spectacular bowerbird houses. The "offerings" placed on their front verandas included

*Ian Craven of World Wildlife Fund (left), the author,
and Hatam guides hike in Arfak Mountains.*

bits of plastic that the male birds had gathered from the trail. According to Hatam legend, the cuscus, a small arboreal marsupial of this forest, helps the bird start its garden by dancing on a patch of spongy moss to flatten it down. If I squinted, I wanted to believe, I would see this dance. In midafternoon we neared the settlement of Minyambou, where 500 Hatam live, tending little gardens and livestock. We neared the airstrip, where I was astonished to see a motorbike in motion. It turned out to belong to Doug Miller, the resident missionary, who had lived among the Hatam for twenty-two years. He took us to his house, where a diesel generator supplied power and where beside a sofa and easy chairs a bookshelf contained copies of the *Reader's Digest* and *The Common Treasury of Knowledge*. Apologizing that his wife and children were away on home leave and that conditions would therefore be a little primitive, the hearty Miller invited us to take hot showers, have an American dinner, sleep over.

As we talked I discovered something of missionary values. Things among the Hatam were very different when he first arrived at the time of the insurrection and the Indonesian occupation, Miller explained. Hatam from Minyambou, fleeing from the soldiers, had melted into the bush. But he had formed a *gembala* corps and gradually the faithful had been gathered into Bible schools as slowly they came or were forced back to the village. I inquired about changes in their agriculture. "You'll have to ask my wife about that," Doug replied. I followed with a question about deforestation. Doug leafed through his stack of *Reader's Digest*s. "In here somewhere," he said, "there's an article about a tree that we can plant and get our jungle back. We need to do something about that." In the morning I walked the quiet paths of Minyambou and watched pigs. ("Pigs," Doug had said, "are at the root of most of the troubles we have around here. Not so long ago a wild pig bit one of our men in the leg, and he bled to death.") I saw a brilliant green-and-black bird-wing flapping ponderously across a meadow, shimmering in the sunlight. A giant colorful beetle nuzzled among yellow flowers. Dave arrived on schedule and whisked us back to Manokwari. He said goodbye and took off again, this time to fetch a decomposing body at a distant outpost and bring it back to town for a proper Hatam funeral. These missionaries seemed better equipped to deal with souls than with bodies. We bade Ian and Mary Ann farewell as they went off on their honeymoon to Canada and the United States. Then, miraculously without delay, Stephen and I caught the scheduled flight back to Jayapura.

Beyond Cyclops and the Arfaks, Irian Jaya offers other opportunities to blend conservation and development. The extensive 82,500-hectare Teluk Cenderawasih (Bird of Paradise Bay) Marine Protection Area on Irian Jaya's northern coast, between Jayapura and Manokwari, is a wonderland of coral reefs and atolls with a great wealth of life on and around them. The manatee-like dugong, sea turtles, and giant clams all inhabit these waters. In some places great walls of coral descend from near the ocean surface to depths of one hundred feet; swarms of small, brightly colored tropical fish cluster around the coral leaves and branches.

Some ten thousand people live in about forty small villages, and several more substantial towns, along this region's mainland seacoast and on the larger offshore islands. Almost all these people have access to fish; no one is starving. But few in the region have managed to rise above poverty. Though marine resources are ample, the markets in towns like Manokwari are far away, and the seas often too rough to reach them by outrigger canoe. Local fishermen also face cutthroat competition from better-equipped teams who travel from ports on far-away Sulawesi (Celebes) Island to harvest at Teluk Cenderawasih. They use scuba gear, which the locals cannot afford. They also stun fish by detonating small bombs of cordite packed into beer bottles which (to reduce noise) are wrapped inside papaya shells; sometimes they get their powder by sawing open unexploded shells from World War II dredged from the seafloor. They often disfigure themselves while attempting this tricky business, and the explosions cause grave damage to coral reefs. Desperate for income, the locals have used some resources way beyond sustainable limits. The giant clams, whose meat is tasty and whose shell is ground up to make floor tiles, are in jeopardy. So are sea turtle and pearl oyster populations.

Plans for the region include new rules to control the harvest of the Cenderawasih resources; the participation of community working groups in setting and enforcing these through the highly organized local religious structure; and the inauguration of "alternative income-generating activities" such as a cooperative to catch, salt, and market the reef fishes—a project that has gotten off to a balky start but shows long-term promise. For the near future, one economic hope lies in the sustainable harvest and marketing of the bay's ample stocks of aquarium fish. Beyond simply gathering them from the wild, there exists the further possibility of establishing aquarium fish "farms" in the bay. Tourism may eventually benefit Cenderawasih over the longer term as well, although time will be required to create the necessary transportation, lodging, and recreational facilities in an area still virtually devoid of hotels or restaurants. One alternative is to bring live-aboard dive boats into the bay from Biak.

For more additions to the total conservation effort in Irian Jaya, opportunities abound in such places as the Western Papuan Islands to the west of the Bird's Head, the islands of Supiori and Biak, and the Wasur National Park. Of all the areas to work in, the giant Lorentz Strict Nature Reserve, dominated by Mount Jaya is the greatest challenge. With its abundance of mineral resources, this area of extreme biological importance and extraordinary beauty is a prospective focal point for insensitive development.

After my visit, because USAID and WWF trusted a Belgian butterfly consultant who proved to be untrustworthy, the butterfly ranching project fell into disorder and required reorganization. Frustrations mounted elsewhere as well. As in Papua New Guinea, forest, mineral, and marine resources remain so plentiful around Irian Jaya that many businessmen, and some government officials, are constantly being drawn to them. As in developed countries, heedless schemes fueled by payoffs sometimes win the day. But if nothing else, Irian Jaya shows that foresightedness is essential. And all in all, what has been accomplished and planned there represents a remarkable record for a wilderness region that only yesterday had been explored by few outsiders other than soldiers and missionaries. People in the province are fast learning the sound economic reasons why they should defend their territory from the environmental degradation that rapid development has brought to many tropical-forest areas—without bringing financial rewards as well. On this half of a rich island, conservation has a good chance of joining the missionaries' Christianity as a militant article of faith.

CHAPTER 6

ꩡ

Latin America:
The Lost Continent

In Latin America and the Caribbean, lightly populated until the twentieth century, widespread environmental degradation is recent. In this large and diverse region of long coasts and coral reefs, high mountains and endless savanna and matchless tropical forest, small indigenous populations long enjoyed abundant resources and plenty of space. Faced with shortages, people could simply move on. When European colonists established the plantations, fincas, estancias, fazendas, and haciendas that sprawled inefficiently across the land, the casual use they made of it caused little direct environmental damage. During this century, however, even though rural population densities remain quite low, a combination of bad habits and overall population growth led to rapid deterioration. Inequitable land-tenure systems forced impoverished and powerless millions out onto the marginal lands of former forest regions, and unsustainable degradation began in many areas. In large measure, stress on the rural environment is what led to El Salvador's political quagmire. Peru overexploited its *anchoveta,* the small and once abundant fish used to make fish meal for animal feed, wiping out the resource—and the industry—for two decades.

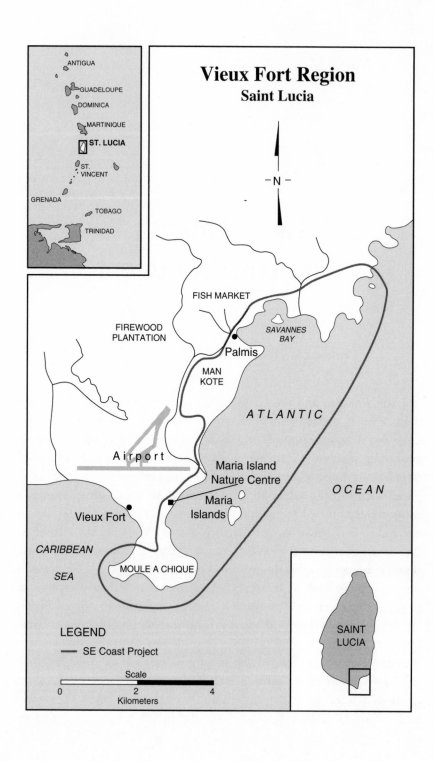

Vieux Fort Region
Saint Lucia

ANTIGUA

GUADELOUPE

DOMINICA

MARTINIQUE

ST. LUCIA

ST. VINCENT

GRENADA

TOBAGO

TRINIDAD

– N –

FISH MARKET

FIREWOOD PLANTATION

SAVANNES BAY

Palmis

MAN KOTE

ATLANTIC

Airport

Maria Island Nature Centre

OCEAN

Maria Islands

Vieux Fort

CARIBBEAN

SEA

MOULE A CHIQUE

LEGEND

— SE Coast Project

Scale

| 0 | 2 | | 4 |
Kilometers

SAINT LUCIA

Mexico's sloppy industrialization created one of the most severe air-pollution problems anywhere in the world.

Late in the 1970s a quiet reaction began to take shape. In tiny Costa Rica, with an abundance of biological resources and enlightened political leadership, commitment to the preservation of environmental quality became a national goal. During the 1980s the movement extended to many other nations. New nongovernmental organizations (there are now more than a thousand in the region) were born and became effective especially in Colombia, Venezuela, Ecuador, and many Caribbean islands. In 1990 the Venezuelan government, which had already placed sharp limits on resort development on the threatened Isla Margarita in the Caribbean, astonished foreign observers and its own upper class by simply bulldozing into oblivion a number of elegant and long-tolerated vacation homes that had been illegally built on another island near the coast.

In few of the many places I visited late in the 1980s and in 1990 did the new principles of employing conservation strategies for much-needed economic development, and of working in partnership with local people to achieve better conditions, stand out more vividly than in a neglected corner of the Caribbean island of St. Lucia. My destination on several occasions was the port of Vieux Fort, St. Lucia's second-largest town (pop. 12,000) on the hilly green island's southeast corner. Here the white banana boat makes a regular weekly call. Vans and pickups laden with field-boxed green fruit line up for more than a mile to unload their cargoes for a good price; the company guarantees the purchases, even though when sometimes burdened with too much supply it must dump the new fruit into the sea. Along one end of town is the island's principal airport, which each day welcomes several jetloads of tourists. Often it also serves as the departure point for goods from a dozen small assembly plants in the adjacent industrial complex. A busy Club Med occupies a prime spot on the golden three-mile beach flanking Vieux Fort, and for years there has been talk of an even larger hotel and casino. On Friday, payday, Vieux Fort's Clarke Street bustles with traffic; the banks and bars are busy. Tony Boreil, a local coconut-palm planter and real estate entrepreneur, keeps hoping for land values to go up. "I can smell the boom coming," he told me.

Despite the veneer of glitter and promise, prosperity remains elusive for most of the Vieux Fort region's 27,000 citizens. They live a world apart from the modern Caribbean of Puerto Rico, Barbados, or the French islands, and well removed even from the bustle to be found an hour's drive north in Castries, St. Lucia's capital. Vieux Fort's traditional sugar economy has disappeared, and the local boom that ignited when the airfield was built as a U.S. base lasted only as long as World War II. When postwar tourism unexpectedly concentrated at the very opposite corner of St. Lucia, most Vieux Fortiens were left with few options but fishing, farming, or odd jobs. Unemployment, 20 percent overall on the island, is even higher here.

When I first came to visit in 1988, the short drive from the airport to the funky Hotel Kimatrai on a hill above the town offered ample evidence of Vieux Fort's bad fortune. Cows, horses, pigs, sheep, and goats freely wandered the streets and grazed at an unsightly open garbage dump. Rusting derelict cars lined the bumpy roads. Urban planning was sporadic, with squatters in their third year of constructing an entire subdivision on public land along one side of town, unopposed by local authorities. But what I saw, I soon learned, represents great improvement from the past.

For many years, I heard, local residents used the region's ample biological resources as carelessly as they were still using its streets. In productive waters near town, fishermen dynamited reefs in search of lobsters for which tourist-hotel keepers paid high prices, devastating inshore stocks. Overfishing threatened the populations of the small reef fish, called potfish, that formed a staple of the local diet. Harvesters decimated the supply of wild sea moss (algae used to make a popular tonic thought to possess aphrodisiac qualities) and prized white sea urchins they call sea eggs. Local people plundered nesting bird colonies on the Maria Islands, two dots of land in the middle of the inshore fishing grounds, by gathering eggs for food. Human use of these islands jeopardized two species—a small snake and a ground lizard—found only there.

Within the region, special interests worked against each other. Having stripped many hillsides bare, local producers of charcoal—still most islanders' preferred fuel—turned to trees from the nearby Man Kote mangrove area, a critically important nursery for many marine species. To get access to the marina he proposed, one developer sought permission to slam a channel through a reef that teems with fish. Construction tradespeople, often acting on behalf of the government, "mined" sand from the very beaches on which the tourism industry' depended. Raw sewage from an open drainpipe flowed from the airport and the industrial zone into the heart of a prime beach used by fishermen, board sailors, and swimmers. Pollution and avarice, both rising throughout the region, helped neither people nor nature.

This was the scene that, in 1982, confronted a private agency then called the Eastern Caribbean Natural Areas Management Program. After an initial survey of the region, the program sought protection for the tiny Maria Islands and their endangered species. Now called CANARI (Caribbean Natural Resources Institute), the group soon concluded that any realistic attempt to cure the Vieux Fort region's long history of environmental abuse would involve far more than traditional conservation techniques. A far broader, radically different approach, tackling head-on the human development side of the equation, would be needed. CANARI therefore set up an office on Clarke Street and began to work with an assortment of groups and individuals within a region of surprising human diversity. CANARI's goals were both to raise the incomes of people in the region and to provide them with economic reasons to safeguard the natural resources they depended on.

The design of what became known as the Southeast Coast Project was done in full knowledge of a history of earlier failure. In 1983, Yves Renard, its originator and coordinator, a Creole-speaking Frenchman raised in Guadeloupe and educated there and in Bordeaux, began talking with the community, identifying goals, and patiently building coalitions to "initiate change that starts from what people already do." He and townspeople thought hard together about what could be done to make fishing more profitable without killing the resource; about how the Maria Islands could be made into a magnet for tourism and conservation education; about ways to produce fuel wood without stripping the mangroves; about how to place sea-moss cultivation on a commercial basis; and about how to improve the town's image simply by cleaning up. "We had an area representing a microcosm of the whole eastern Caribbean," he said. "Everything was here: sun and sand and coral reefs, great biological resources, a tradition of farming, a port town, an airport, tourism, industry. In the past, international agencies used this town as a testing place for their ideas. What actually happened on the ground was another story. Except for the industrial estates and the airport, I can hardly think of any real results. The top-down planning was not working. The question was what we could do to help the users get better control over their own resources and develop systematic plans for how to conserve and take advantage of them." By 1990, when I last visited Vieux Fort, the results of Renard's quietly effective approach to the problems of this odd hybrid community were coming clear.

The first stage of my work there was to become familiar with the project's original components. When I came to call, the shorefront Maria Islands Nature Center, a handsome building completed in 1985 and operated by the St. Lucia National Trust, was receiving vanloads of schoolchildren on field trips from Castries. Inside the building were displays attesting to the importance of the change that had come to the Maria Islands and the waters surrounding them: from the depletion of their resources to a new phase of protecting and sustaining them. Outside, a fieldworker named William "Fragile" Mathurin and a boatman, Ignatius Williams, hauled a Zodiac inflatable dinghy out from a shed, attached an outboard, and launched the boat through the surf to open water off the Anse des Sables beach. Spray flew as we bucked a stiff head wind, then nosed under the lee of the larger Maria's bluffs and landed on a small, quiet sandy beach. It was breeding season for several of the bird species that inhabit the Maria Islands, now declared a nature reserve with limited public access. Walking up the steep pathway to the narrow crown of the island, Mathurin spotted a female of the endemic species of ground lizard, *Cnemidophorus vanzoi*, scuffling on dry ground beneath dense vegetation. The species once existed all over St. Lucia, Mathurin explained, but vanished on the mainland due to predation from the mongoose, a small but ferocious Asian carnivore introduced during the nineteenth century in an effort to rid the island of mice and rats. Without natural enemies, protected from human invasion of its habitat, the lizard now suffers most from its own behavior: highly territorial, brightly hued males fight during the breeding season, sometimes lopping off each other's tails. Yet an estimated 1,500 of them continue to exist on the island, and they appear to be doing well despite their self-destructive tendencies.

On this ascent, as on almost every other, Mathurin failed to find one of the shy *couresse* grass snakes, *Dromicus ornatus,* the islands' other endemic species. Though about 115 of the snakes probably survive, thanks again to the lack of mongoose predation, Mathurin saw the animal only twice in eight years of research (late in 1989, he left the island to continue his education in the United States). Doves scrambled from secluded ground nests as Mathurin continued his climb, and bridled and sooty terns circled low overhead. Brown noddies roosted on the island's far corner. Members of a small but growing red-billed tropicbird colony cried shrilly as they flew offshore. Crossing to nearby Maria Minor, a hectare and a half in size, Mathurin walked carefully to its bare crest. There, pairs of brownish common-tern eggs lay in shallow open nests, almost directly on the volcanic rock. Screaming, the parent birds hovered and swooped low overhead. All the bird populations have increased since the islands were protected, said Mathurin.

Near the islands were flourishing patches of coral reef. Gone are the dynamiting days. "You'd go to prison for life if you got caught doing that now," Mathurin said. Oxygen-producing sea grasses also seemed in good health; fishermen generally were respecting the islands' protected status and using it carefully. Sea eggs, too, were on the rebound after a disastrous period of overharvesting. "It's easy to figure out the sustainable use of this species," Mathurin explained. "It's just a question of visual observation—how many you see on the bottom, and how big they are. Before the government enacted the total ban, the sea eggs were gone here. Overall, the ban is not adequately enforced. Even so, around the Maria Islands, the eggs are all over the place again."

The general public, once accustomed to picnicking freely on the islands, was now being allowed access only if accompanied by one of the half dozen CANARI-trained guides. These paid guides, who are Vieux Fortiens, lead expeditions to the islands no more than twice a week—the maximum frequency for the ecosystem's carrying capacity. None was there on this day. But as the Zodiac returned to St. Lucia's mainland, a few spearfishermen swam the waters near the islands and windsurfers from the Club Med's beach station skimmed about.

On several levels, then, the imposition of tighter controls on the Maria Islands and the addition of the Nature Center have been pluses for Vieux Fort. Protecting the islands helps in the recovery of threatened populations of harvestable marine species in the adjacent waters;

tours provide a new form of employment for local people and attract the kind of tourism that can be carefully controlled, which in turn offers collateral benefits for service industries. The Nature Center has become St. Lucia's principal museum as well as its chief source of environmental education; the handsome building attracts tourists as well as schoolchildren.

Important to Renard's success was gaining the cooperation of the traditionally unruly local fishermen. To show me this side of the story, he introduced me to the black-bearded Sebastian Daniel, a man with a somewhat shadowy past who now had a brighter future. In the mid-1980s, Daniel, an occasional fisherman and transport driver, made most of his money on periodic trips to Martinique to cut sugarcane. In 1990, Daniel owned a brightly painted wooden fishing *canot* (canoe) equipped with a shiny 55-horsepower outboard, as well as a share in a second boat. He could not join his crews on their triweekly fishing outings, for he was too busy elsewhere. Proprietor of a spanking new green van, he had a government contract to ferry groups of schoolchildren to and from a distant village. He was also driving other paying passengers and taking fish to market. In addition, he was a leading figure in the association of about thirty fishermen, operating seven working canoes, that CANARI helped to establish in the little port of Palmis on Savannes Bay.

Artisanal fishing is deeply rooted in these parts. During the first half of the year, fishermen aboard dugout canoes they make themselves do long-lines fishing for migratory deep-sea species such as tuna, dolphin-fish, and kingfish. Catches of these fish plummet when their migratory season ends at midyear. Then the fishermen set bamboo or chicken-wire "pots" to capture small schooling reef fish that will follow a leader into the trap. All year, except during the breeding season from May through August, the fishermen use pots or spear guns to pursue the lucrative spiny lobster, which in 1990 was fetching a price of six dollars a pound. Even though evidence exists of a gradual decline in St. Lucia's overall catch, lack of fish seems not to be a problem for these men, but marketing has been. While they have always been able to dispose of some of their harvest at the landing point, which is on the heavily used main road from Vieux Fort to Castries, the fishermen often had to load fresh fish into vehicles and "take it around" to local villages,

Savannes Bay fishermen prepare and sell fish in a building they built.

alerting customers to their arrival by blowing on conch horns as they passed through. Romantic as this practice might seem, it is also costly and time-consuming. "Sometimes you don't get back until midnight," one fisherman told a visiting researcher. A related shortcoming was the lack of any place at the landing site for the fishermen to store motors, nets, and other portable equipment. Every day of fishing included long periods at each end hauling the gear back and forth, to and from their houses, as much as several miles away, often on foot. Fishing around Vieux Fort was a marginal and poorly organized activity.

In 1984, Renard and the Savannes Bay fishermen began discussing the possibility of a storage and marketing facility at Palmis. After great efforts, permission to use the government-owned land for it was gained. A design for a building was drawn up and funds raised from several sources. Then the fishermen built the solid structure that now forms a central pillar of their entire operation. A carnival atmosphere prevails at the landing site when the boats begin to come in, usually late in the morning. Men unload the fish into baskets and plastic containers for weighing and selling to many eager consumers, some of whom wait for several hours for the catch to arrive. With improved marketing and operating techniques, and greater stability in the supply of fish in local waters, good times for the fishing community have in several senses replaced the marginality of a few years ago. Once they had lived in shacks; now they are able to expand their homes and afford luxuries like carpets. In 1985 their transportation capabilities consisted of two run-down vans; later they got five vehicles, including three that in 1990 were in top condition. Self-help and a simple fix had brought relative prosperity.

That the Savannes Bay fishermen had themselves become an active, well-organized community did not end their troubles. For many years, they had been accusing members of a nearby group of fishermen of the sin—considered cardinal in fishing villages the world over—of stealing from their pots. In 1989 the dispute boiled over. At sea, two boats from the rival group, carrying seven men, deliberately rammed one Savannes Bay boat with three men aboard. Although only the boat's remains and one body were found, the seven aggressors were accused of murder and jailed. The stealing abruptly stopped. During the calm that eventually returned, the Savannes Bay fishermen could redirect their attention to exercising discipline among themselves for the sake of sustainability. In 1990 they also had a new plan: to get permission to bolster their income by building a gas station, to fuel passing vehicles as well as their own outboard motors, at the fish landing site. Even without the benefits of this scheme, though, Sebastian Daniel may never again have to resort to cane-cutting in Martinique.

Additional pressure for environmental quality in Savannes Bay comes from those who need clean water to cultivate sea moss. For as long as anyone can remember, St. Lucians have been gathering these algae from the wild. They dry the seaweed, then blend it with milk and spices. In 1981 the Ministry of Agriculture's Fisheries Management Unit, with Canadian government support, launched a project to see if sea moss could be grown commercially. The marine biologist Allan Smith, manager of the project, had by 1984 inaugurated experimental cultivation of two sea-moss species. The following year, Smith joined Renard to continue his research into ways of maximizing produc-

*Sea-moss grower Marcellus Edwin
at work on his farm*

tion from sea-moss farms. He also sought to adapt the mariculture techniques he had developed to the needs of people around Vieux Fort.

Using methods that evolved from Smith's research, a grower can enter the business with a capital investment of under $100 in U.S. currency (or even less when the government's fisheries department provides assistance). Only plant stock, rope, bamboo, a bucket, a knife, and a cutlass (as St. Lucians call the machete) are required. After constructing the rafts and attaching the plants to rows of braided nylon lines strung lengthwise on them, the grower pulls the rigs out into water, anchors them to large rocks, and lets the algae grow. Periodic tending is needed to clear the lines of parasitic plants and make sure that the rafts are secure. Fertilizer and careful species selection can speed growth.

While opinions vary as to the exact level of profitability of sea-moss farming, the potential is undeniably considerable. "I see the profits in it," said Anthony Clarke, a young St. Lucian more commonly known as Ginger. "You must be patient. It takes six to eight months to get something out of it—the first crop you must plant it back. And you have to spend time, be out there once or twice a week. But I will never give up. Nothing will prevent me from doing it, and I will do it all my life." Simply by drying and bagging and marketing the raw material, grower Marcellus Edwin estimated, he might earn in excess of $200 per raft, or $5,000 a harvest from a twenty-five-raft operation—the maximum practical number of rafts for a single grower to manage. Clarke was planning to take his marketing program a step further by entering the bottling business. From each line of sea moss, he calculated, he could sustainably collect as much as fifteen pounds of wet moss—enough to produce ten gallons of the beverage. Since it can be sold for $3.70 a quart, the prospective return per line of moss (six to a raft) is $148. Gross profits from a twenty-five-raft operation under this formula could theoretically reach $22,000 per harvest. Another possible source of income is extracting the seaweed's agar, a thickening agent widely used in the processed food industry, as is already being done in Asia, Europe, and the United States.

No one has fully demonstrated the validity of these impressive figures. Nor has the size of the potential market for sea moss been established: it is by no means certain that Clarke's profits would withstand the pressure of rival farmers who by 1990 were entering the market. By then the original growers had already been reminded that, like all farming, sea-moss mariculture is neither effortless nor risk-free: all of them lost their rafts during a severe storm in 1989. Before that setback occurred, however, Clarke had repaid the loan that he took out to get started, and had cleared himself of business debts. And the storm hardly deterred him from beginning again, using improved stock and technologies that quicken the plants' growth rate (Smith's favorite varieties double in volume each ten days), make possible more frequent harvests, and increase profits. Cultivated sea moss, whose quality is higher than that of the wild variety, fetches double the price and is much in demand. The farmers' harvests are sold within a day.

Smith claims that what has already been achieved at Vieux Fort represents "the first profitable cultivation of seaweeds in the Caribbean or anywhere in the Atlantic." While hardly a triumph yet, the project's combination of soundly applied science and the hard work of community residents has produced a highly promising innovation, and the beginning of an economic return. Since sea moss cultivation requires clean water, moreover, it represents a case where economic progress and environmental conservation are inseparably linked.

To show me an equally "economic" approach to the conservation of resources ashore, Leslie Charles, a government extension officer who now also works part-time for CANARI, drove down a litter-strewn dirt road near Vieux Fort and parked by a narrow trail. He walked uphill through dense scrub to a grassy overlook, then peered out at the sixty-hectare Man Kote mangrove area. "Around here there are two ways for people to cook," he explained. "One way is with charcoal, the other is with gas. A coal pot costs about two dollars. The cost for a simple three-burner gas stove, with no oven, plus a regulator and the smallest-size bottle of gas, is almost eighty dollars. Each gas refill costs about eight dollars. It costs three times as much to cook with charcoal; nevertheless, many people simply cannot afford the initial investment in a gas stove. These considerations have led to a continuation of the traditional charcoal industry around here. Producers started cutting this mangrove back in the 1940s. When they started, the diameter of the average tree they cut was eight inches. At the time I entered the project in 1985, the diameter was three inches, and had been dropping fast. Now it is down to between one and two inches. Both the mangrove and the producers working here are in big trouble."

Charles introduced several measures to remedy the situation for the charcoal producers, who have long ranked among the most marginal of all workers in the Vieux Fort region. The new association he helped form adopted rules to control the cutting in Man Kote. At CANARI's urging the government's Forestry Division inaugurated a ten-hectare fuel-wood plantation near the charcoal producers' homes. The fast-growing species first planted there, *Leucaena leucocephala,* has not performed up to expectations because of poor soil conditions, erratic maintenance, and problems arising from land and tree tenure. Lessons drawn from agroforestry efforts conducted by international agencies elsewhere in the developing world might have helped in St. Lucia; yet, as is so often the case, information from these widely scattered projects is not readily available.

Although disappointed with the results achieved so far, CANARI has adapted and persevered, as all rural development projects must. A different species, *Gmelina,* has been introduced, and new groves are being added at the rate of two hectares a year. The sustainable harvest from the plantation, which is being monitored from aircraft, will soon begin to relieve pressure on the mangroves while enabling the charcoal producers to continue to make a living. Charcoal manufacturing from the plantation trees has been initiated. CANARI also persuaded the government to make nearby land available to the charcoal producers for agriculture. Three hectares—more than sufficient for each family to grow subsistence crops and also sell commercially in the market— had by 1990 been fenced and planted for a fourth year. The crops were doing well. Land clearing and planting were continuing, and many ideas for diversification had come forward. Among them: a plan to harvest fruit from the guava trees that abound on the property the association uses, make jelly, and sell it to the tourist hotels (many of which habitually serve their guests little plastic rectangles of U.S.-processed jellies sweetened with corn syrup).

Of the original six charcoal producers with whom Charles began working, three had by 1990 left for other occupations. The remainder were producing less charcoal and spending more time at farming and other, more lucrative and environmentally less destructive tasks. The most desirable end result—the cessation of all mangrove harvesting for charcoal—remains only a distant hope; even the short-term benefits achieved for the charcoal producers are still difficult to calculate. The prospects for at least one of them, however, have improved dramatically. Habitually this man depended, for much of his living, on seasonal trips to the United States to pick fruit. In 1988, he did not go.

Another indication of a more disciplined Vieux Fort is to be found in its waste-management practices. When he arrived in Vieux Fort late in 1987, a government health official named Edward Emmanuel told me, garbage was a big problem for the community. People had long been in the habit of dumping their trash at one or another of thirteen illegal sites on the edge of town. No communal garbage receptacles existed other than haphazardly located oil drums which were often knocked over by animals. Collection from these, by open-backed trucks subject to high winds that frequently returned litter to the streets, was only sporadic, and abandoned vehicles were strewn along the streets. Health hazards abounded. Renard's term for the situation was "horrible." After meeting with representatives of CANARI, a local youth group called ROUTES, and colleagues from the Ministry of Health, Emmanuel resolved to "involve the entire community" in the issue. His first step was to form a Group of Concerned Citizens. It successfully sought funding from the Organization of Eastern Caribbean States, then began to implement a remedial program.

Progress was rapid. From posters, flyers, videos, and even theater performances, Vieux Fortiens repeatedly got the message that proper waste management was important. A massive cleanup day, involving hundreds of town inhabitants, drove home the point. Illegal dump sites were shut down and the refuse removed from them. New receptacles were placed at strategic locations. A newly militant community petitioned the government in Castries for a long-promised modern garbage truck. Political pressure resulted in quick action. "Vieux Fort had never had this kind of community participation," Emmanuel continued. "Anyone trying to mobilize people was always assumed to have some kind of ulterior motive. People here had also had the experience of continuous failure with previous efforts. But this was a different approach. For the first time we had a real cross section involved, and the people came from both political parties. Now, vandalism is far less likely. The new bins are still there. ROUTES people put pressure on residents if they see a violation. There is a positive perception of the litter warden. The truck driver is so motivated that often he makes a voluntary collection if he sees a need."

With litter under better control, Emmanuel and others began thinking about further phases: dealing with effluents as well as trash from the industrial zone and the airport, tackling sewage treatment and disposal. Already, though, clear gains had been scored. A cleaner town is likely not only to attract tourists but also to lessen the danger of polluting the surrounding waters during heavy rainfall and runoff.

The tourist boom has yet to ignite. Garbage still swirls high in the air, caught by blustery trade winds at the poorly managed dump on Vieux Fort's outskirts. The risks of sea-moss cultivation have been experienced, and the charcoal producers' project lags behind expectations. The death of the three Savannes Bay fishermen represented a serious setback. But for all the problems, many citizens still feel that Vieux Fort is a stronger, healthier, more disciplined place. From garbage to sea-egg harvesting, citizens are exercising greater responsibility for the common good. "I see the change now," said William Mathurin. "Formerly, people were accustomed to doing anything. Any sort of restriction was viewed just as more government regulation. Now they are beginning to see the advantages of it."

"On this island we still lack an institutional framework for proper environmental management," said Gregor Williams, acting director of the St. Lucia National Trust. "We have droves of technical people who seldom meet each other, let alone the supposed beneficiaries of the services. While some of the highfalutin people don't want to admit it, the CANARI program has been highly successful. Its problems have come not from within, but from outside." Indeed, accomplishing anything on the island involves overcoming huge obstacles—whether getting people to attend meetings or surmounting the formidable legal barriers to the formation of associations and the use of idle government land. Nevertheless, Williams added, the Southeast Coast Project "demonstrates that nothing can really work if it does not involve the user of the resource."

Renard places St. Lucia's prospects in a wider context. "Other Caribbean islands like St. Maarten and Antigua have already made their decision—development at any cost," he said. "In St. Lucia the issue is still open, and it is still open in Vieux Fort. Whether we like it or not, it appears that the future of this region lies in the service sector. Either Vieux Fort can be a nice service station or it can be a mess. Whatever happens, my hope is that the community will handle it well. And I'm more confident about that than I used to be." Currently, Renard is confident enough of the Southeast Coast model to be selecting other eastern Caribbean regions where it might be replicated.

During a 1988 visit to the remote canton of Talamanca, on Costa Rica's Caribbean coast, I encountered a similar situation. A local conservation and development organization called Asociación ANAI[1] dates

1. The acronym initially stood for "Asociación de los Nuevos Alquimistas," in honor of a now defunct affiliation with the U.S.-based New Alchemy Institute. Despite the separation, the Costa Rican organization continues to use the initials as its name.

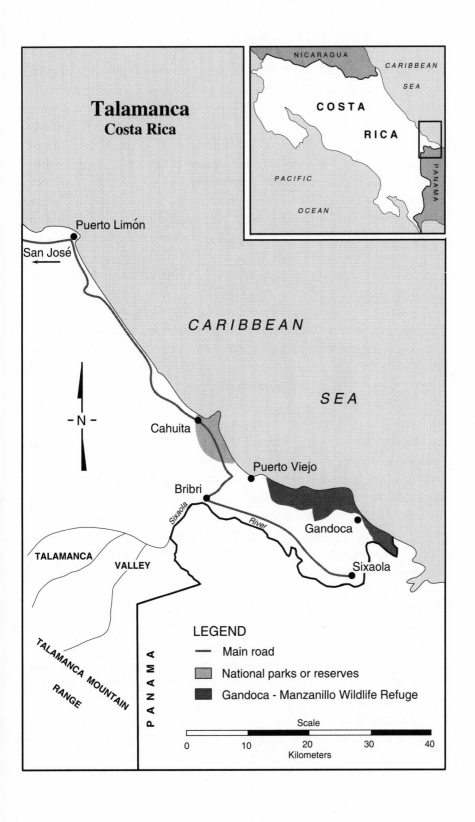

Talamanca
Costa Rica

NICARAGUA

CARIBBEAN
SEA

COSTA

RICA

PACIFIC

OCEAN

PANAMA

Puerto Limón

San José

CARIBBEAN

SEA

Cahuita

- N -

Puerto Viejo

Bribri

Gandoca

Sixaola

TALAMANCA

VALLEY

River

Sixaola

TALAMANCA MOUNTAIN

RANGE

PANAMA

LEGEND

Main road

National parks or reserves

Gandoca - Manzanillo Wildlife Refuge

Scale

0   10   20   30   40
          Kilometers

from the early 1970s, when the American fisheries biologist and community organizer Bill McLarney developed an itch to help bring about ecologically sound development somewhere in the "icky-sticky tropics." On foot he searched the Caribbean coast of species-rich Costa Rica for a place to put his ambition into practice. Before long he found lightly populated Talamanca, then a place of scattered villages, towering tropical forests, and clear waters where jaguars, tapirs, monkeys, and manatees thrived. Motorways, telephones, and electric power were absent from most of the region. A good plot of shorefront property could be had for $500. McLarney bought some and settled in. Soon he gathered a band of Costa Rican and American colleagues, and the fledgling ANAI, which came to depend less and less on its founder, set about its task.

A striking characteristic of Talamanca is its polyglot assortment of citizens and settlers. Indians had long lived close to nature in the region's forests, hunting and gathering, speaking their own languages. Since early in the nineteenth century, black families speaking a rich English-based Creole, many of them descended from Antillean contract construction workers in Panama and Costa Rica, had also settled on land along Talamanca's reef-lined coast. Their traditional livelihood came from fishing, farming, and light agroforestry. Starting in the 1920s, Indians displaced to the mountains of Alta Talamanca began to filter back toward the shore; some found work on black-owned farms. Most recently a new mestizo population arrived. These new settlers brought with them the Spanish language and a clear-cutting form of agriculture that contrasted sharply with the blacks' and Indians' softer techniques. The mestizo value system, which would come as no surprise to many North American real estate developers, placed a premium on cleared or "clean" land as opposed to uncleared land designated as "dirty." Never prosperous on their small plots, the Talamanca farmers faced worsening conditions soon after ANAI appeared. The cacao seeds that make chocolate, which grow on short trees, had long been their principal cash crop. Since cacao requires shade, orchards in the region looked less like farms than like bucolic shrub-dappled glens, the ground covered with low green plants, parrots and toucans screeching and roosting in tall trees overhead. But now the cacao was being attacked by a fungal disease called monilia pod rot that almost completely destroyed the crop and moved the growers to the edge of despair. Some turned back to subsistence farming. Others abandoned their farms and became fishermen or peon laborers. All but a few slid deeper into poverty.

With growing human suffering came also the threat of grave ecological damage from people whose range of choice was narrowing. At the time the monilia struck, wildlife populations were already dwindling and biological diversity declining, in part because of relentless hunting. Deer, wild pigs, and tapir were going fast; the jaguar had all but vanished. "There was plenty bad thinking around here," Florentino Hansel, a native of the region who had a job as a wildlife refuge guard, told me. "Them went into the forest and took what them could find. Have some guys what even eat the red monkey. I was a bad guy too." Along the coast shrimp and lobster were being overharvested. Because of logging and the accelerating influx of new settlers, or *precaristas*—who occupied and deforested "idle" land in hopes of eventually achieving legal status—the forests were suffering from the relentless onslaught of chain saw and bulldozer. The dire consequences included erosion, siltation of rivers, and loss of habitat for many wildlife species.

It was obvious that if the fragile beauty and abundant resources of the Talamanca region were to be preserved, people seeking a better life would have to abandon the heedless practices that damaged the environment without helping them. Far-off government specialists offered little help. "No one knew what to do about it," said Levy Bryant, a veteran farmer and innkeeper in the coastal village of Puerto Viejo. The local farmers themselves had little experience beyond cacao and subsistence crops for their own households. Injecting something new and ecologically positive into the equation was the urgent challenge that ANAI faced.

Saving the local cacao industry might tide many farmers over, but it would also entrap them within a risky monoculture. In the longer term, this dependence could be reduced if efforts were made to have some diversification of crops. An early ANAI step was, therefore, the purchase of farmland for experimental plantings. Still, new tree varieties or agroforestry techniques did not solve an equally fundamental problem: practically no one owned a legal land title even though many families had been living in the area for several generations. According to a 1949 law, occupants without title could best demonstrate "possession" by showing that they had "improved" their land for farming by clearing it. Entitlement would not stop farmers from cutting and selling trees to supplement their income, but would relieve them of the pressure to deforest for legal reasons only. Land titles would also give them new access to bank credit to enable them to turn away from logging and concentrate on more sustainable, less destructive activities.

As ANAI, together with local citizens, addressed the twin objectives of agricultural diversification for development and land titling for conservation and economic benefit, new factors were quickening the pace of local change. Sediments from reinvigorated banana plantations, on rich alluvial soil along the swift-flowing Rio Sixaola and the nearby Rio Estrella, began to pollute mangrove and coral-reef sites within the project area. An expanding road network provided ever greater access to the region's ample timber supplies. Tourism accelerated with the creation of a shorefront national park at Cahuita, just inside the coastal boundary of ANAI's territory. Growing numbers of banana workers and *precaristas* swelled the once sparse Talamancan population.

Two government actions raised the region's political temperature even higher. One was a well-intentioned declaration, in 1976, of reserve areas to protect the Indian population. Few found reason to contest the portion of the reserve land in the high mountains (encompassing much of the ANAI program area) to which the Indians had clear ancestral rights. But blacks could and did assert a claim on part of a coastal section called the Cocles Indian Reserve. Once occupied by Indians, this area behind Puerto Viejo had been empty when the blacks arrived and, on portions of it, founded the cacao plantations where returning Indians later found work. The mistake, the blacks asserted, was the government's inability to distinguish, on aerial photographs used to demarcate the reserve, between untouched forest and cacao farmland. Initially, the Indians advocated reducing the size of the reserve and restoring to the blacks the land they claimed. In the pro-Indian national climate, however, this just solution ironically proved, for legal reasons, to be impossible to implement. The Indians then

ANAI representative Alberto Salas (pointing at map) meets with residents of San Miguel to discuss a land titling program.

began to talk of a swap that would give the blacks the land they wanted but also keep the reserve about the same overall size.

Polarization in other quarters came in 1985, when the government—at the urging of ANAI—created the 9,449-hectare Gandoca-Manzanillo Wildlife Refuge to protect at least a portion of the forest and a biologically important coastal stretch encompassing coral reefs and mangroves. Hunters and prospective land developers or speculators objected to the loss of free access to this land. Conservation's cause was hardly helped by the fact that the government failed to compensate owners of land expropriated to create the nearby Cahuita Park. Many Talamancans instinctively concluded that changes imposed by outsiders could only be for the bad; some were quick to label the ANAI group as meddlers responsible for the imposition of the refuge.

What had started as a challenging agricultural conservation and development project had thus turned into an even more absorbing three-dimensional chess game. Beyond the region's basic economic and ecological woes, sensitive cultural and political conflicts had come to the fore. After 1983, bolstered by support from several new funders, ANAI responded by diversifying its program. It continued to plug away toward the achievement of its original goals, but it also, almost always , jointly with clever and increasingly sophisticated community leaders, pieced together an intricate mosaic of new projects and subprojects. One way or another, they now affect many of the 17,000 people living within Talamanca's 300,000 hectares.

Land titling alone was no easy matter. The government's cumbersome procedures call for dozens of individual steps in a process that, at its speediest, takes years to accomplish. And border, coastal, and wildlife refuge lands are each subject to special rules. Some properties that straddle two of these categories present exquisite difficulties. Yet ANAI, in cooperation with several state institutions, had after six years of patient involvement moved the government close to being able to award titles to 597 landholders occupying 11,000 hectares of land within and near the wildlife refuge. The cost to individual farmers, which would have been prohibitive if they had worked with the government only, was far lower because of ANAI's involvement.

In anticipation of the breakthrough, some farmers in the titling area long ago planned to expand and change their activities without placing greater pressure on forest lands that they would at last own. In the village of San Miguel, whose forty-three farmers were scheduled to be the first in the region to receive their titles, Remigio López looked forward to credit that would enable him to buy a milk cow and a motor vehicle. Another farmer's bank loan would decrease his dependence on cacao, which had recovered somewhat from the monilia but was, in 1988, selling for less than half its 1983 price. Marcos García, an ardent believer in ANAI's philosophy and a keen student of new agroforestry techniques, was impatient to get on with improvements to his nearby five-hectare finca and the addition of black pepper as a cash crop.

José Luis Zuñiga, the articulate head of the citizens' association in San Miguel, took a broader view: "The titling program, though important, is only one of many aspects of what we are trying to do," he said, as a community meeting began to break up. "In the old days, when everyone was doing all right with cacao, we did not need an association. Now that the cacao price is down and our forests are

Community residents work at one of twenty-four ANAI
tree nurseries in Talamanca.

disappearing, we have to think harder and work more together. Of
course, we need credit, and the titling will help with that. But we must
also work hard to get better technical training. And we will have to
plan together to save our forest lands."

ANAI stands quietly behind the creation of Zuñiga's association and
many other community groups in the program area. Tree nurseries lie
at the heart of it. "Our approach is very straightforward," said Jim
("Diego") Lynch, an outgoing, Yale-educated forester and agronomist
who joined the ANAI team in 1979. "We convene a meeting in a village
and explain what it takes to run a nursery—land and commitment—
and what the results could be. We say that we'll be back on such and
such a date, and if you're interested show up then and we'll get to
work." Results were impressive, with twenty-four separate nurseries
functioning within the region. Six hundred farmers—men, women, and
teenage boys—donated half a day a week to work in them. They
planted, weeded, and watered. They also learned grafting, pruning,

and special techniques for raising individual crops. The nurseries were classrooms too.

Hours worked by each member of a nursery team were being carefully recorded, and seedlings apportioned to individual growers in strict accordance with these numbers. During the life of the nursery program, millions of trees have been raised, distributed, and replanted; hundreds of farmers no longer work in the nurseries because they have already taken home as many plants as they can use. More than half the nurseries' output has been cacao hybrids—productive specimens that bear fruit within eighteen months and are far more compact, thus easier to manage from the ground, than the region's leggier traditional varieties. Many other plants—particularly black pepper and the popular fruit called soursop—have gone out as well. In all, about seventy species, including exotics from as far away as Asia, have been raised at the nurseries. At the time of my visit, crops still at the experimental or household-use level included cinnamon, nutmeg, mangosteen, several delicious fruits that are little known beyond their native Amazonia, the tree called *achiote* whose seeds produce a red dye for food coloring, and a local vanilla species that had previously only grown wild in the forest. More than 100,000 seedlings had been distributed purely for reforestation, which is now as urgent a need for the region as farm diversification.

Thinking ahead to the marketplace and the need for high yields and reliability, ANAI was trying hard to supply germ plasm of the highest quality. Under no circumstances, though, would dramatic results come quickly from the nurseries. Some species are very slow-growing, some require years before bearing fruit, some may never do so for lack of local pollinators. For want of local support mechanisms that were created too late to be helpful, one pilot effort to market Talamancan turmeric in the United States did not yield sufficient income to justify a full-scale venture. Yet the basis for farm production at a commercial scale was clearly being laid. The future held promise.

From the nurseries have sprung many other agroforestry development activities that are guided from the capital city of San José by Robert Mack, of the ANAI staff, who along with Lynch has served from the outset. Training of local *técnicos* is far enough advanced so that ANAI is less and less involved directly in nursery management;

*Biologist Julio Barquero
and green iguana*

many different technical materials have been prepared. Women's groups were working on spin-off environmental education and farming projects. Development associations had been legally constituted in several Talamanca villages, and more were being formed. In 1990, two community farms were functioning as experimental extensions of the local nursery.

In the wildlife refuge and also in the "buffer zone" on its margins, the spreading practice of agroforestry protects the refuge itself. Within its boundaries, ANAI's energetic Alberto Salas, a ten-year veteran of Costa Rica's National Park Service and former director of several of its key parks, directs three locally based employees. The refuge staff, led by administrator Herman ("Benson") Venegas, who although young was already a community leader, was watching over sea turtles that use local beaches as nesting grounds. Biological studies were in progress on nearby reef deterioration and on the tarpon, a valuable sport fish for which the refuge's lagoon is a nursery area. While tourism is envisioned for the palm-fringed shorefront of the refuge, and because of recent road improvements has already established a beachhead at its northern edge, ANAI is trying to make sure it will be along environmentally sound lines and will benefit the local people, rather than outside speculators. Small-scale facilities and eco-tourism projects are being promoted.

The inventive roster of ANAI projects ranges far beyond this central core. On the edge of the Kékoldi (Cocles Indian Reserve) and in the town of San Miguel, biologist Julio Barquero was assisting a group of Indians who were incubating green iguana eggs and raising hatchlings in cages. When old enough, batches of the animals would be distributed to nearby Indian families to be used, like chickens or rabbits, for food and profit. An enthusiastic young teacher named Marilín Villalobos was giving farm-management courses to rapt students. Two Indian women, Juanita Sánchez and Gloria Mayorga, with assistance from ANAI and from the American sociologist and oral historian Paula Palmer, had assembled a booklet describing Cocles Indian life and values. This work, published by the University of Costa Rica, was being used with slides in meetings where the Indians lobbied to gain support from black and mestizo neighbors for their conservation practices.

What makes the variety and sheer volume of ANAI's work all the more impressive is that, in the core of a program area that still lacks a single reliable telephone, each step of each activity requires face-to-face contact. Simply keeping the pieces of the program together, let alone moving things forward, demands considerable skill and energy. From dawn to dark and often well after, Lynch, Salas, and other ANAI staffers patrol the region. Afoot (the only means of locomotion in half the territory) or in aging four-wheel-drive vehicles, they hear complaints, announce meetings, deliver messages or seeds or equipment, pass out advice. Because of poor communications between Talamanca and the outside world, both Salas and Lynch need to spend substantial portions of most working weeks in San José, keeping up the requisite contacts with government officials and funding sources. Almost invariably, each tackles the drive between the capital and the project area at night to avoid taking time out of the working day. "This truck knows its own way home," laughed Salas as he once again began the long haul.

ANAI has won many skirmishes over Talamanca's future, but the

*Logging trucks passing through the town of Bribri,
in the heart of Talamanca*

war goes on. Fresh dangers emerge. Each day, large trucks overloaded with immense newly cut logs trundle out of the region's narrow dirt roads onto the highway toward San José. Pollution problems are on the rise. Swarms of *precaristas* (including even a naïve gringo who once tried without permission to build a house on the beach near Manzanillo) arrive and cause defoliation. A proposed oil pipeline remains a possible blight, and ill-considered highway plans forever threaten.

The longer the agricultural crisis persists and the easier overland travel becomes, the more tempting it is for farmers to sell out to eager weekend-home buyers from San José. Ominously, many young Talamancans express less interest in farming than their parents did. For all ANAI's efforts to neutralize it, local opposition continues. Twice in recent years, appeals to get the wildlife refuge annulled and leave a freer hand for land speculation were presented at the national legislature.

What, then, *has* ANAI accomplished? A rangy black farmer named

Emmett Roy ("Jimmy") Walker held an unqualified opinion. "If it hadn't been for what ANAI did after the monilia hit," he said flatly, "I don't know what would have become of us." In the absence of firm figures, ANAI staff members were more guarded in their assessments. "The refuge, the land titling, the nurseries—all the things we've done are nothing more than techniques," said Salas. "People don't eat better just because of them, and our work here will not be finished until we can really say with numbers that we have achieved conservation through development." Said Lynch: "A farmer with the old cacao might be making five hundred dollars a year now. The prospects through our renovation of the cacao industry have increased substantially. A farmer who has been in the nursery program since the beginning also might have five hundred well-established fruit trees. Many will soon start producing, and this in the future could mean a *dramatic* increase in income. But we still have to prove it."

At least ANAI has helped to bring about a burst of hope and a sense of orderly progress. In the canton there is, today, a bustling atmosphere, and sound development is a very real possibility. Despite the other occasional efforts to discredit ANAI its work is winning ever more supporters even in the coastal village of Manzanillo, from which the loudest negative voices emanated. "I'd guess that about half the people around here have become believers in conservation, and that number is growing all the time," said "Benson" Venegas, a black who lives in Manzanillo. "Now," said Lynch, "we can really talk to the people about conservation. Of course we care deeply about it. But our caring by itself is not enough. As a development group with a lot of experience in the area, working with local priorities, we have the credibility. We're seen as more than just flakes wanting the people to starve to death for the sake of the wildlife."

"We think that it's right-on," said Jeffrey A. McNeely, the experienced deputy director-general of the Switzerland-based World Conservation Union. "Here's something new being tried in an area where the old things didn't seem to be working very well. New approaches were needed. The ANAI people treat the area as it deserves to be treated." Said sociologist Paula Palmer: "If people can stay with agriculture and make a living, it will make a real difference. Otherwise the changes in the economic and social structure of the region will be tremendous. The nursery program may prove to be a decisive factor."

ANAI's ultimate objective is to work itself out of a job in Talamanca, but its program is far from finished. Marketing expertise is urgently needed as new crops reached the commercial stage. Land entitlement makes the banks more responsive, and a push from ANAI helps to get credit into needy hands. But local government structures remain weak, and the need for sound planning sharpens as the canton and the world come together and as tourism and resort development pressures mount along the vulnerable coast.

Indeed, the day may never come when ANAI's task in Talamanca will really be complete. Some staff members, and some community leaders as well, interpret even partial withdrawal as desertion. Surely the deepest lesson to be derived from the organization's efforts is the importance of tenacity. For all that, the time has come when ANAI, having handed over more and more responsibility to skilled Talamancans, can consider applying what it has learned to the broader task of ecodevelopment throughout conservation-conscious Costa Rica.

In this small country, 11.3 percent of all land is protected in parks (3 percent is the world average), and another 13 percent is in forest or Indian reserves. Dedicated to the idea that ecologically sound development will win tangible returns in the tourism sector and elsewhere in the economy, the Costa Rican government is engaged in a spirited $70 million effort to assemble, manage, and endow a system of "megaparks" around the nation. USAID and the Inter-American Development Bank, as well as several European governments and many private funders, are involved. Much of Talamanca itself forms part of an International Biosphere Reserve stretching from Panama across to the heart of Costa Rica.

Though the Costa Rican Park Service has been criticized in the past for not paying attention to the needs of local people living on the borders of the already extensive park system, this attitude is changing. National Parks Foundation director Mario Boza said that it is the government's "clear" and "very natural" policy to organize ecodevelopment efforts on behalf of such people. He further suggests that nongovernmental organizations are usually in the best position to take on those sorts of responsibilities. He and others agreed that ANAI has precisely the right kind of experience for the job.

ANAI staff members, who have already been accused of running a series of small projects rather than a tightly integrated program with clear objectives and priorities, resist the temptation to go national. "How far can you stretch a cucumber?" asked Lynch. Along with most others at ANAI, he expressed determination to keep the organization small. McLarney, still a participant in the program though he spends only four months a year in Talamanca, expressed the dilemma frankly: "I don't want to sit at the big table just as a means of earning a full-time living even though we are rottenly paid. Nor do I feel comfortable about being removed for long periods of time from the grass-roots level. There are dangers in being a generalist. Yet we have been immersed in the development of an effective methodology, and if the kinds of stewardship models we've developed don't affect the broader picture, we're just a drop in the bucket. I'd like to think that it is possible to keep my boots muddy and also make a broader contribution by sharing our experiences."

Whatever the future holds, these plucky people will keep on breaking new ground in the absorbing task of promoting sustainable development. Costa Rica, indeed all of Latin America, needs far more such efforts.

CHAPTER 7

❧

Africa:
Tendrils of Hope

Dressed in a cloak of chicken feathers and a frightening wooden mask, Mabu once protected the lush forests of Kilum Mountain in northwest Cameroon. Often this fierce deity of the Oku tribe drove women away if they were caught trying to plant beans or maize within the forest's boundaries. A more serious offender would, thanks also to Mabu, find a sprig of a plant called the *boboi* on the ground of his compound. This was a summons for the culprit to visit the Fon, or regional chieftain, and be sentenced to a stiff fine of perhaps several goats.

Kilum clearly merits such careful attention. Almost ten thousand feet high, it is the second-highest mountain anywhere in West Africa, dominating an upland farming region of great beauty called the Bamenda Highlands. From the 6,885-hectare forest on the mountain's slopes, Kilum offers broad views across deep valleys to grassy, rock-strewn ridges. Puffy clouds swirl around Kilum, sometimes darkening to produce sudden brisk showers, and clear streams and waterfalls descend to thickly settled villages below.

What interests naturalists about Kilum is its concentration of rare or unusual species. Though not so diverse in its wildlife as a lowland tropical forest, this montane area contains one of West Africa's few

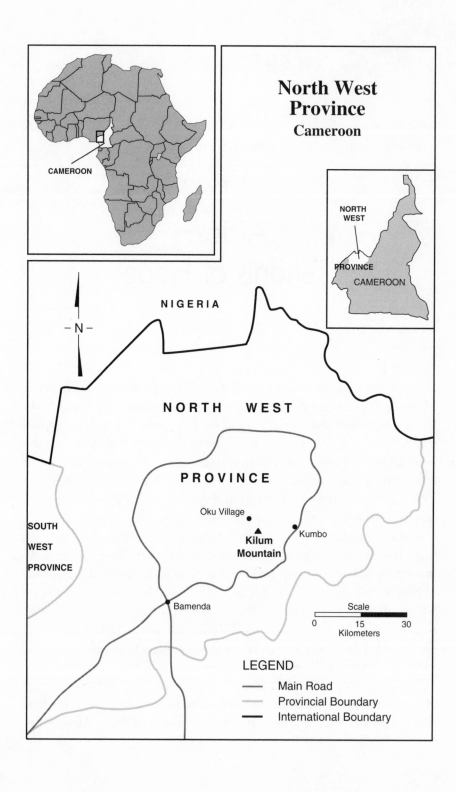

NORTH WEST
WEST

PROVINCE

CAMEROON

CAMEROON

North West Province

Cameroon

NIGERIA

-N-

NORTH   WEST

PROVINCE

Oku Village

Kumbo

Kilum
Mountain

SOUTH

WEST

PROVINCE

Bamenda

Scale

0   15   30
Kilometers

LEGEND

Main Road
Provincial Boundary
International Boundary

People and farmland near Kilum Mountain

remaining stands of a tree called *Podocarpus*. The handsome black-and-white Preuss's monkey is endemic to the region. So are twenty bird species. Most notable of these is the red-crested Bannerman's touraco—a bird so bright that it makes you wince when you see it in the sun-dappled forest. Along with that of seven other threatened bird species, the survival of Bannerman's touraco probably depends on the fate of Kilum Mountain.

The more than 100,000 people who live in the villages on Kilum's lower slopes still have no telephones or electric power, and are severely limited in their mobility by rough and tooth-jarring dirt roads. On rolling land, steeper as it rises to the forest edge, farmers plant annual crops—maize, Irish potatoes, yams, beans—as well as a little coffee. Traditionally the Oku people, and some members of three other ethnic groups with whom they share this land, have also depended heavily on the resources of the forest itself. They are linked more to the mountain than to the outside world.

From a tree called *Pygaeum* they have, for good wages, harvested the bark. The product derived from it is used internationally as an effective medicine for men with prostate problems. Many other forest trees and plants contain substances used in the region's sophisticated practice of folk medicine. Hives in the forest have been reliable suppliers of good honey and marketable beeswax. Tree trunks and branches made fences, fuel, and raw material for wood carving. The forest's softening "sponge" effect guaranteed a reliable flow of clean fresh water even during the pronounced November-to-February dry season.

When independence came to northwest Cameroon in 1961, tribal authority began to yield to the central power radiating outward from the faraway capital city of Yaoundé. Four-wheel-drive vehicles and motorbikes penetrated the challenging Oku roads with increasing frequency. The passengers they carried brought new styles and new values; many of the newcomers swelling the local population, particularly those who farmed on Kilum's western slopes, had little traditional affinity with the forest. Handsome, nomadic Fulani tribespeople from the north brought more and more cattle into the region. The Western seven-day week, with a day-and-a-half weekend, began to overtake the traditional Oku calendar based on a market holiday each eight days.

Oku people continued to scream when Mabu came out. But for all his fearsome ways, the power of this especially important "juju" in their traditional cosmology faded as well. Farmers now could more safely take quick, easy steps that would have profoundly negative consequences over the long term. With growing abandon, they cut and burned forest to make farmland on ever more precipitous slopes, thus hastening the erosion of the thin but rich volcanic crust that overlay the subsoil in some places. Landslides became more frequent. In 1987 an Oku woman was killed in one.

At the same time, herdsmen released goats, up to one hundred of them per owner, to graze freely in the forest's understory. Eating tree seedlings as well as other plants, the animals greatly impeded forest regeneration—and compacted the fragile earth as well. Trees used by honeybees or valued for carving or medicines disappeared along with less useful species; the walk to obtain fuel wood grew ever longer. Most ominously, people began to observe a lessening of the freshwater flow during the dry season. Erosion clouded and dirtied what remained of the fresh water available to many villagers. The loss of the forest's protective cover was affecting the Oku just as it had the people of San Lorenzo in Ecuador.

By the mid-1980s the Kilum forest was reduced to less than half its size twenty years before; a third of what remained was severely degraded. Still far and away the region's most important montane forest, Kilum faced complete obliteration by 2000 or soon after. Its unwanted disappearance, which no one seemed able to prevent, would leave the Oku people and their neighbor farmers with but one sad option: an ongoing struggle for survival, against lengthening odds, as subsistence farmers on ever more exhausted soil. Gone with the trees would be the choices that had long given the people of the region good health and relative prosperity.

Periodically since the 1930s, local authorities have recognized the Kilum forest's significance, and tried to protect it with boundary markers and restrictions on grazing and farming. But no program has ever worked for more than a short time. Nor, until the late 1980s, was any effort made to change the destructive behavior that was precipitating the crisis. Fresh eyes were needed at Kilum. John Parrott, a Londoner with a degree in zoology and a yen to get away from big cities, first arrived in Cameroon as a biology teacher in the late 1970s. Later he honed his knowledge of the country over two years of work at the Korup National Park, a beautiful tract of lowland tropical forest near the southern coast. In 1979 Parrott, a keen birder, first visited Kilum and glimpsed its great beauty and resources as well as its colorful touracos, sunbirds, and bulbuls. In 1983 the ecologist Heather Macleod, then a recent University of Edinburgh graduate, joined an expedition organized by the International Council for Bird Preservation (ICBP) to study the birds and bats of the Cameroon Highlands. Macleod too became a Kilum addict.

Later, when both had returned to the United Kingdom, Macleod and Parrott met, married, and resolved to carry out conservation work in the Third World. In 1985 Macleod returned to Kilum and prepared a forceful report on its condition that won warm endorsements from several levels of Cameroon's government. Subsequent proposals for a three-year project gained financial backing from the World Wildlife Fund and from Britain's Overseas Development Administration, administrative supervision from ICBP in Britain, and a pledge of assistance from several Cameroon government agencies. On Christmas Eve 1987, Macleod and Parrott, having navigated the Sahara by compass in their heavily laden new Land-Rover, lumbered into Oku village.

By December 26 they had already found a place to live, moved in, and begun to assemble a staff, led by a seasoned Oku medicine man with intimate knowledge of the forest flora, who arrived at the doorstep that very day. It took Macleod and Parrott not much longer to adjust the project's original goals to the realities they found. "We knew all along that a purely conservationist approach would never work," said Macleod. "The people are so dependent on the forest, for so many reasons, that we had to address their needs in a number of ways that we had not anticipated. So we started to change. We also became aware that we would need more time if any results were to show, and so we added a fourth year to the project. The government welcomed this idea."

At the outset, their intentions were to mark the forest boundaries clearly, develop a management plan, and by means of audiovisual aids "promote" sustainable practices in farming, honey collecting, and animal husbandry. But soon they instinctively moved the project far beyond the limits of traditional conservation practice. By 1991, they were hip deep into a series of uncontemplated actions to bring about, not just encourage, changes on the human side: goats would have to be removed from the forest and new grazing regimes instituted; soil conservation and agricultural diversification programs were a must; new perennial crops had to replace the relentless pattern of shifting agriculture that was dooming the forest.

Late in 1988, I went to Kilum Mountain. My trip began in Cameroon's humid commercial capital of Douala, which lies beside moist lowland forest along a meandering brown river. At the gloomy airport, as I emerged from Customs and Immigration, I was confronted by a large sign reading MR STONE borne by a small and intense Frenchwoman. She led me to a basement garage and we checked out the four-wheel-drive Suzuki Samurai that I had reserved but not fully expected to find awaiting my arrival. It was in excellent shape. After a comfortable night at the Hotel Ibis on Avenue Charles de Gaulle, I drove, early on a Sunday morning, through Douala's quiet broad streets. It seemed a shabby port town, on the order of Palembang or Guayaquil, with a faint whiff of France about it.

Once across the river and clear of the coast, I moved into lush green plantation land (oil palms, rubber) that was also full of people—heading for open markets along the highway, dressed in brightly colored robes and dresses. Farther along, the road began to climb into a belt of rich farmland: many fruits and vegetables, herds of long-horned Brahman cattle. Eventually the French language gave way to English as I entered the northwestern sector of Cameroon, once a British protectorate, which at the time of independence opted to affiliate with the rest of Cameroon rather than throw in its lot with the powerful neighboring nation of Nigeria. Late afternoon found the Suzuki poised on the top of the cliff that dominates the eastern edge of Bamenda, the bustling capital of this province. I plunged down into the sprawling town and soon found the Tabong family, for whom, at the request of a man named Simon, a relative working in the United States, I had brought a child's bicycle. "This is great," Simon's wife, Julia, kept saying. We assembled the bike in the dim light of her house in the family compound. Soon the boy for whom it was destined, the oldest of her three sons, wobbled off into the cool dark evening. Various relatives greeted me. Simon's brother Daniel, the family's big man, gave me a tour. "Would you like someone to stay in the hotel with you?" he asked. He shrugged when I declined his offer. "Some do, some don't," he said.

Over dinner the burly Daniel, wrapped in a blanket to ward off the evening chill, gave me a glimpse of African family life. He was too busy at home, he explained, to accept Simon's invitation to visit him in the States. Though his only income was a civil-service salary, he cared for his aged mother, a sickly brother, and several other families with a total of twenty children. "I'm alone," he said. "Everyone expects me to produce. You saw me handing out money earlier today. This is expected here, just as it is expected that if there is a death in the family you will have a celebration that lasts a week and might cost a million CFA francs. If you don't do it, evil spirits will know. I wish Simon would come home. Then there would be two of us to do all this." (Late in 1989 Simon did come home.)

Rain pounded all night against the windows of my room at the hotel on the cliff above Bamenda. In the morning it was clearing when I began the hard part of the trip. The well-paved highway gave way to dirt a few kilometers outside of Bamenda and the fastest possible pace slowed to 50 kilometers per hour. Now again I was in rich black-soil farmland: rice, coffee, fruits, and vegetables being grown in small plots by many farmers. After a pause for lunch (peanuts, bananas, Guinness stout), I passed through the town of Kumbo and left the wide dirt road for an even rougher and narrower one that would carry me the final stretch to Oku village. Deep wallows, hairpin turns, and mounds that were more rock pile than road characterized this route.

By three-thirty in the afternoon, I was at last in Oku village in bright sunlight, looking with admiration at the mountain looming to the south. Many people were gathered at the dusty market square even though it was not market day. I asked for Parrott and Macleod. "Oh, you mean the conservation," said a young man who hopped into my vehicle and guided me to a compound a short distance from the Kumbo road. Two houses, one a single-story dwelling, the other a workshop, flanked the parking area. Macleod and Parrott materialized soon after my arrival, expressing relief that I had managed to horse the Suzuki up the rugged road. They showed me quickly around the compound, which featured unanticipated luxuries: a portable generator that powered a full electrical system, running water and flush toilets, a computer rig, a gas-fueled refrigerator and freezer alongside the gas stove. Our group included Stan Kozak and Leanne Johns, a visiting Canadian schoolteacher couple, and Angela, the Valley Girl–speaking Peace Corps volunteer then assigned to the honey cooperative. We ate chicken cacciatore and talked about farming.

The next morning I walked uphill through fields of old maize and freshly planted beans and potatoes to the clearly marked edge of the forest. Within it I continued upward along an open path. Hearing a soft coo, I looked up and glimpsed a bright flash of crimson. Was this Bannerman's touraco? (From my description Parrott later confirmed the sighting.) I saw many other birds, including a wood hoopoe that Parrott himself had not seen. Reluctantly turning back toward the village as the day began to wane, I treasured the long view across the green valley. I also felt grudging respect for the ability of the farm women to plant crops on the precipitous hillsides, unwise as the prac-

tice is. Goats scampered along the roads. Children giggled and said
hello.

On market day we walked down to the town's main square and
wandered among the stalls. Food was plentiful, with many varieties of
fruits and vegetables (some trucked in from far away) on display. One
of the butchers had killed a cow and its carcass hung from a hook.
Little at the market was handmade: no handwoven goods, only one
stall offering carved wood (though later I found a dealer with an in-
different collection, mostly imported from Cameroon's Muslim north),
an abundance of plastic ware. Tall, graceful Fulani women, their eyes
glowing under the hoods of their cloaks, inspected the goods. I bought
chili peppers for hot sauce and beer and soft drinks for the project
larder.

One sunny morning we drove an hour in the Land-Rover, whose
ride seemed as smooth as a magic carpet after my many hours aboard
the bucking little Suzuki, to a small village on the mountain's south-
western slopes. We disembarked. Parrott led about twenty assorted
people up a slippery path to the highlands above. Along were village
leaders, including (at Macleod's insistence) a woman; a representative
of the Forest Department; and several project staff members carrying
freshly stenciled signs, brushes, and small pots of whitewash. Upon
reaching an open pasture above a residual forest patch, the villagers
unhesitatingly climbed to the top of it. Pius, the department representative, lingered below. Parrott and his crew remained in the middle.

It was a pattern often to be repeated throughout the day. Local men,
wanting to save the forest but also hoping for a little insurance, would
claim to have been planting beans for years in a given area. Pius would
swear that the very same place had been thickly wooded just a year
before and should therefore be allocated to the reserve, within whose
boundaries farming would be prohibited. Then Parrott and Macleod,
with a government mandate to settle the forest's boundaries even before its official declaration as a reserve, would negotiate a compromise.
Here they might nip off a small planted patch. There they would leave
a little woodland for farm expansion. Upon agreement with the villagers, who had been softened up to the procedure by means of a carefully
orchestrated advance meeting to stress the importance of the forest,
the project crew would whitewash a tree or plant a sign to establish

Villagers mark boundary of Kilum Mountain Forest Reserve

the edge. "Kilum Mountain Forest Reserve," the sign read. "No farming. No fires. No goats." Then the party would move to the next marking point along the one-hundred-kilometer periphery of the forest, and the negotiating would begin anew.

On through the day the party trudged up and down the rough country. Occasionally Macleod stopped in the corn fields to chat with women working there (in this male-dominated society, women do most of the hard farm labor). By early afternoon even the wiry and compact Parrott, in fine condition from many long marches in the forest, professed fatigue. But the group pushed on for several more hours before returning to the village for cool fizzy wine made from the raffia palm, chicken stew, *foufou* (cornmeal mush), and congratulatory speeches.

As an expression of his satisfaction with the way the day had gone, the village headman presented Parrott with two live chickens. Squeezed into a small flat basket, they squawked feebly as we jounced homeward in the Land-Rover. The next morning, early, I heard their louder voices abruptly trail off. Peter, a deaf man with an extraordinary football-shaped head who worked as a project assistant, had dis-

John Parrott and villagers discuss results of
boundary marking expedition

patched them. Later he washed them at the sink with great care, his
long delicate fingers caressing the pieces as he scrubbed them. Peter
explained to me in rapid-fire pidgin English—spoken by most men and
some women of Kilum as a common alternative to their tribal languages—about his work and his problems. I needed subtitles. But I
needed no such crutches to understand the importance of involving the
villagers in the boundary-marking process. Their participation made
the effort's longer-term success far more likely than the subsequent
official gazetting of the reserve. "As far as I'm concerned," Parrott had
said, "it's a forest reserve when we put up the signs."

Adjacent to the project compound was a small plot of well-watered
land that was not in use when the project began. It lay just downstream from a small "law forest" where Oku spirits dwell. Working
with the owner of the vacant plot and with the Fon, Parrott and Macleod got permission both to establish an experimental nursery there
and to irrigate it by means of a small gravity-flow channel from the
stream that passes through the sacred little forest. I walked often among

the neat rows and pots of nursery seedlings, and talked much with Parrott about his plans for them and with the headman Alfred and the other nursery workers about their operations.

Since *Pygaeum* bark cannot be harvested for ten or more years after the tree is planted, cultivation of this crop is a long-term investment. Villagers had expressed so much enthusiasm for it, however, that it was being emphasized at the nursery. Propagation experiments were also being conducted on fourteen other tree species, including soft-woods for carving, several that are suitable for reforestation, and three nitrogen-fixing legumes for soil enrichment. Composting tests were also under way to see what might be done to improve the acid, nutrient-shy soil. A eucalyptus tree on the premises, one of many planted in the region, was felled because it hogged too many nutrients, needed too much water, and shed toxic leaves. Though the Kilum region is too high and too cool to grow many vegetables, such possible new staples as cabbage, kale, onions, cauliflower, and broccoli were being attempted. By 1990, total nursery production reached an annual level of twenty thousand plants of fifty species, many of them indigenous. Since demand for seedlings soon exceeded supply, Macleod and Parrott established more than forty satellite nurseries, managed by women and children, involving three hundred farmers.

One afternoon Macleod and Parrott were to make an appearance at a meeting of the women's cooperative. Outside the building that housed the 2,053-member organization, people started gathering a full four hours ahead of time. Arrayed on the grass, apart from the others, were ten of the Fon's fifty-five wives. Each wore a cowrie shell band across her head, shaven to honor a recent death. The meeting had been called to honor Madame Celine Chin, one of the local district's four delegates to the national legislature, and a Canadian visitor representing a cultural exchange program. When the speeches began the room was full, with perhaps three hundred women and a handful of men in attendance. Madame Chin drew more than perfunctory applause only when she unveiled an old wheeze of a pledge to improve the minimal road to the nearest town, Kumbo, to facilitate crop marketing.

Macleod and Parrott had requested and been granted permission to show the group their slide show, entitled "Trees for Life," after the formalities had been completed. In advance, the project's portable gen-

Heather Macleod and Kilum women

erator and slide-tape equipment had been carried up from the compound and set up in the hall. Parrott stood up and gave a brief introduction. Macleod reiterated her interest in working with women, saying that she would gladly bring the slides to women's groups anywhere in the region. Then they darkened the room and ran the show, which, thanks to a local volunteer, was narrated in the Oku language. It emphasized the importance of saving the forest and the grim consequences of its loss; the room collectively caught its breath when the image of starving Ethiopian children came onto the screen. At the end of the presentation, Parrott, speaking easily in pidgin, urged the women to sign up for forest preservation. He promised that he and Macleod would be around to help. "We dey here for at least three years," he said. "We no de hurry for finish." As the women filed out, some facing a two-hour walk home, Macleod and Parrott moved among them making new contacts and dates for future meetings.

The slide shows are one of the two principal dimensions of the project's strong educational thrust. The other is a newsletter, called *Fen* in honor of the Oku name for Bannerman's touraco. Printed in two col-

An early issue of FEN

ors on the sole photocopier in Oku (the color red was being added by hand to highlight the crest and wing feathers of the bird), *Fen* reaches leaders throughout the Kilum area. It simply and persuasively states the case for forest conservation and defines new rules governing behavior in the forest reserve. The newsletter's no-nonsense tone and the lack of much else to read that is free had made *Fen* an immediate hit. The first edition underwent four printings on the balky photocopier, and the second, just out at the time of my visit, was being eagerly sought by streams of visitors to the Parrott/Macleod compound. Some were farm extension workers commissioned to carry bundles of copies to outlying villages where they work; others were passersby not on the official list but simply hoping to scrounge an extra copy. And the project files bulge with solemn, carefully written letters to the editor, almost all of them congratulatory.

With additional staff and a second vehicle added in 1989, the educational effort has expanded to encompass teacher workshops, school visits, nature walks, and T-shirt production. In 1990, a conservation-oriented juju dance group became an instant hit in performances at special celebrations and public events. "The Fon loves it," Parrott told me.

While taking the initial steps that they had long planned, Macleod and Parrott discovered unexpected ways to assist Kilum. One of their principal achievements was helping to improve the honey cooperative. When they arrived, its operations were primitive despite a decade of experience. Beekeepers, who often needlessly destroyed hives when they collected honey, carried it to the cooperative building in rusty tin cans. Their mixture of wax, bees, and solidified honey remained there, often for months, before further processing—cooking the honey over an open wood fire until the mush turned to liquid and could be strained, boiling, into a plastic bucket; skimming off the wax after its rise to the top (which after further refining would be sold to nearby craftsmen who employ the lost-wax process to make brass castings); and then packaging the honey, now dark in color and smoky-tasting from its fiery catharsis. Not competitive in the world market, whose wholesale prices were far lower than those paid to the 1,000 honeybee workers in the Kilum region, it was sold within Cameroon. Such was the co-op's sluggish style and poor cash flow that in an economic environment where payment on the barrelhead in cash or goods is standard practice, the beekeepers were not getting paid for at least six months after first collecting their honey.

Parrott persuaded the beekeepers to transport their honey in clean plastic buckets, he introduced a water-bath cooking technique to replace the wood fire, and he encouraged prompter payment. Though major packaging and marketing problems remain, cooperative membership and sales have grown. If the trend continues, the community's enthusiasm for beekeeping will lead to heightened pressure to preserve the forest, which contains the nectar and pollen that the bees require.

Unlike bees, the free-ranging goats of the mountainside are a problem. By recycling nutrients in the forest, they encourage the growth of nitrogen-loving weedy plant species to the detriment of trees, and they trample down very young tree seedlings. The destruction they cause makes their removal a top priority, but their owners resist this, since they have nowhere else to put them. An order from the regional government banning goats from the forest has reduced but hardly eliminated the problem, since enforcement is lax.

Though neither pastoralists nor agronomists nor soil conservation experts, Parrott and Macleod were also trying to find ways to improve soil quality, diversify away from annual crops, and reduce the pressure on the forest. Controls on burning, which tends to destroy the soil's structure, needed tightening. To avoid erosion and landslides, Parrott sensed from the outset, permanent trees such as *Pygaeum* would have to replace annual crops on the steeper slopes. Shifting the Kilum people from slash-and-burn farming to reforestation of this sort and to agroforestry systems where trees complement ground crops, and giving the Oku people reasons to want to pursue these goals, are the project's most important challenges. By 1990, a strong four-person team had been assembled to pursue them.

At the outset, Parrott and Macleod enjoyed remarkably smooth sailing. The constant stream of visitors to their compound and the lively conversations, in pidgin and in the Oku language, which both continue to study, gave evidence of their warm reception. Their cheerful energy was contagious, and their son, born in 1990, was a popular addition to the community. But difficulties loomed as well: staff problems, enforcing the goat rules, stormy interactions with people from tribes with no traditional concern for the forest. Radical change in an established rural agricultural system never comes easy, particularly if there is no promise of a quick return.

As they began the fourth year of their Kilum residency in 1991, Parrott and Macleod showed firmer resolve than ever. Before going home, they hoped to have set off no less than a revolution in the habits of the people living around Kilum Mountain. They planned to have the reserve gazetted and the goats out, and even to have institutionalized a new set of values. "Incomes around here have improved anyway," Parrott told me. "More cash crops, like the new Java variety of arabica coffee, are being produced. But the people are borrowing from the future by overworking the land. We're hoping to reestablish among them a genuine wish to protect the forest, and thereby enable the people here to enjoy at least a reasonable standard of living for a longer time. If we can accomplish these things, the project will have succeeded."

"Go softly," the people of this bewitching region say in bidding each other farewell. The morning of my departure, Parrott and I drove up to the sparkling clear Lake Oku for a picnic lunch. Little grebes and black ducks populate the water of this sacred place that holds the spirits of its dead, and the rare Preuss's monkey is one of several primate species living on its shores. In the shallows swam swarms of nimble toads, of a species that may exist only in this lake, frequently gulping insects from the surface. Brilliantly colored sunbirds, Africa's answer to hummingbirds, fluttered in nearby thickets.

Before we left the project compound Emmanuel Ngamgon, an elder from a faraway village, had stopped by to pick up his copy of *Fen*. We talked about the project, about the forest, about the need for people to change their ways. Mr. Ngamgon peered up at the mountain, now sharply etched in shimmering sunshine, and glanced in the direction of the sacred crater lake. "These things will happen," he said. "It has to be gradual. But it will come. We have no other choice."

From Kilum Mountain, I jounced back to Bamenda in the little Suzuki, admiring once again the beauty of the high valley farmland and of the Fulani women at the roadside. In Bamenda, Daniel Tabong was again wrapped in a blanket and shivering, possibly from malaria. His niece Evangeline gave me a letter to carry to Simon in the States, and Julia followed with a whole packet of mail for her husband. She also handed me a small blue backpack of special local foods to take to him (these, alas, I had to abandon since some were powders that a customs officer could easily take for drugs). From Bamenda, I retraced my tracks back to Douala to catch an Air Gabon flight to Libreville. There I lay over a day, writing and strolling along the quiet waterfront past assorted ministries, airline offices, and the inevitable palace, awaiting the weekly east-west flight that would carry me into a vastly different Africa: its heart.

* * *

It was blue and crisp and dry at Lilongwe, the capital of Malawi, when the well-managed UTA plane set down on schedule at midafternoon. At the pleasantly rambling Hotel Lilongwe, I dined with Martin Lewis, a leathery Brit who had first come to what was then Nyasaland in the 1940s and never left, and a young African woman named Diane. She, Lewis said, had been with him for a few months. "Drink and women— these were always the most available things out here," he explained. "I always have an African woman. I have two middle-aged children and then succeeded in producing my own grandchildren. The last one is just finishing school." Lewis lives "in the bush," he said, in an unchanged area close to Blantyre, Malawi's other major city. He represented a British company, was enjoying the slower pace of old age, and was harboring deep apprehensions about the fate of Malawi after the eventual demise of its longtime ruler, Hastings Banda.

With Lewis's undiluted colonialism embedded in my brain, I drove the following morning toward the close-by Zambian frontier. The road, paved in Malawi, turned to washboard dirt soon after I had crossed the border at Chipata. But it was good enough to keep the little Daihatsu saloon shuddering along past flat farmland at 60 to 80 kilometers per hour, fast enough to reach the town of Mfuwe by lunchtime. Now I was in the land of national parks for game-viewing tourists. Tame vervet monkeys roamed the premises of Norman Carr's Kapani Lodge, just across the Lupande River from the South Luangwa National Park, and a fish eagle (Zambia's national bird) soared overhead. Baboons, geese, and one large white stork guarded the watering hole below the comfortable camp with its genial young British tour guides. Here, later in the afternoon, I met the earnest American scientist Dale Lewis, an employee of Zambia's National Parks and Wildlife Service (NPWS), and his Japanese-American wife, Julia.

An hour before sundown we set forth along the narrow, deeply rutted dirt road toward the village of Nyamaluma two hours away. Frequently we pitched sharply down into dry riverbeds, lurched across them, then clawed back skyward to level terrain. Along the route, in a region where wildlife had all but vanished a few years before, we saw remarkable concentrations of giraffes and impalas as well as many waterbucks, bushbucks, warthogs, and several magnificent elephants. After a pause to repair a flat tire—the local product is so poor in

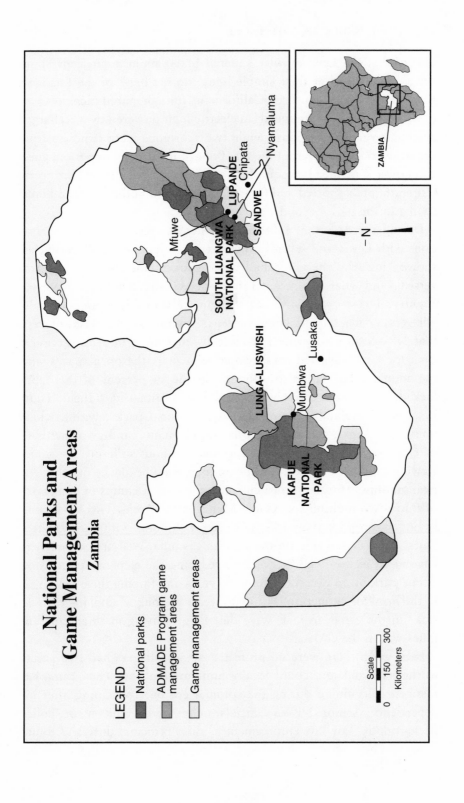

National Parks and Game Management Areas
Zambia

LEGEND

- Natrional parks
- ADMADE Program game management areas
- Game management areas

Mfuwe

SOUTH LUANGWA NATIONAL PARK

LUPANDE

Chipata

SANDWE

Nyamaluma

LUNGA-LUSWISHI

Mumbwa

Lusaka

KAFUE NATIONAL PARK

ZAMBIA

-N-

Scale

0   150   300

Kilometers

quality that the Lewises once suffered four flats in a single five-hour drive—we arrived at their simple house on the bank of the Luangwa River. Incorrigibly southern Californian, Julia prepared tacos over an open wood fire. We ate under an electric light powered by a recharged auto battery. After a pause while two scorpions were removed from the straw matting covering the dirt floor of my nearby one-room guest cottage (a staff member squashed one under a bare foot), I gingerly retired. Hippos snorted and fought and splashed in the river, and lions roared in the park beyond.

During the days that followed, further travels and long conversations with Lewis and several other keenly enthusiastic NPWS officials showed me why the game had come back to the area we had traversed—and what this meant for village economics in a hard-pressed country. The story involves the changing relationship among animals, villagers, poachers, and game wardens. Central to it is a series of steps that NPWS took to protect wildlife by turning it into an economic asset for long-neglected rural people who share the open spaces with the animals. The latter still abound in the 30 percent of this land-locked, Texas-sized country that is allocated primarily to them. Tourists who visit Zambia's nineteen large national parks, within which hunting is illegal, can see leopards and elephants, and great herds of antelopes as arcane as the black lechwe, without suffering the game-viewing gridlock that has become an increasing headache in other African nations. Hunting safari customers, based at camps in a network of thirty-two multiple-use Game Management Areas (GMAs) serving as buffer zones for the parks, have returned home with excellent trophies. But as elsewhere on the African savanna, well-armed poachers have fared all too well in Zambia, reducing the elephant population in one park by 70 percent in only ten years and forcing the black rhino to the brink of extinction. For many years the only Zambians with no stake in the game, in fact, were the villagers living in small communities within the GMAs.

Back when there were no protected areas, villagers had free access to the parkland and could legally hunt for the pot. Then came harassment. Beginning during the colonial era but continuing after independence, senior NPWS officials, many with military or police backgrounds, saw law enforcement as their principal duty and found the local people to be their most convenient target. The guards they hired, civil servants brought in from other places, seemed to pursue poor, ill-equipped local poachers far more vigorously than they did the well-armed professionals who did most of the damage. "The department would track a suspect to his house and inspect his fire, even if he was only cooking a rat," said Willard Ntalasha, the spirited governor of the Mumbwa district adjacent to the Kafue National Park in western Zambia. "To say there was friction between the park officials and the local communities would be a vast understatement." So widespread was the antagonism toward the game department that big-time poachers had no need to bribe local citizens not to inform on them.

Villagers were equally estranged from the professional safari hunters, who had virtually cost-free rights to utilize the very game areas that were forbidden to the locals. The hunters, usually white expatriates with permits to work in Zambia, staffed their camps not with community residents but with outsiders. No wonder, I heard from Ackim Mwenya, then deputy director of NPWS, that the villagers thought of the safari hunters as "legalized poachers." Often, in fact, the villagers' best friends were the true poachers themselves, who hired local men, most of whom had no other source of cash income, as porters or assistants.

Opposed or ignored by the very people who might have been their principal allies, NPWS could not control rampant poaching in the strictly protected parks, even with such luxuries as a helicopter and a fleet of airplanes. The sound of gunfire was almost continuous in and around the parks. In one GMA, the crisis was so serious that villagers, fearing that they might get hit by gunfire or hounded even more severely by park rangers, moved to take over game-management responsibility from NPWS. Pressure for change mounted within the department as well. "I was working my tail off, but I was failing," said Lewis, an outspoken wildlife biologist and conservationist who first came to South Luangwa National Park in the mid-1970s as a researcher supported by the New York Zoological Society. "The people who lived with the wildlife were angry over our failure to recognize that they were part of the equation. In not addressing their needs, we were making a big mistake. It was not the way to save our elephants."

The frustration that Lewis and others felt led to two important shifts in bureaucratic procedure in the early 1980s. One was that NPWS was allowed to go beyond the civil service in hiring employees to help conserve wildlife and enforce the law. This meant, for example, that Lewis, a North Carolinian with a University of Texas doctorate in zoology, who is the department's only non-Zambian employee, could now begin working experimentally with community assistants. The results were dramatic. "The villagers walked all over the bush with great zeal and determination," he said. "They'd go out with a couple of shotgun shells and bring back ten poachers. So we began to look for ways to recognize and respect what they were doing." The decision to allow the wildlife department to establish its own revolving fund was the second, equally important innovation. For many years, NPWS was required to hand over all of its earnings to the Finance Ministry, and it often complained that central authorities did not reinvest these revenues in wildlife protection programs. Now it could channel some of the money back into local communities.

These were the first building blocks in NPWS's revolutionary new game-management design. At a workshop held in 1983 in the village of Nyamaluma—a meeting attended by national and regional political figures, NPWS officials, and village dignitaries (including the local chief, Malama, whose eloquent complaints had done much to provoke action)—the major components of the new program were pieced together. The experimental Lupande Development Project, conducted between 1985 and 1987, led to a more comprehensive Administrative Management Design for Game Management Areas, or ADMADE.

A new corps of paid village scouts, young men who had seldom earned money before, would play a leading role in the task of wildlife management and law enforcement in the GMAs. The distinction of being a village scout was to be conferred by panels of local political leaders, chiefs, and headmen. "We wanted these men to stand ten feet taller than anyone else," said Lewis. Wildlife management and anti-poaching efforts in each GMA were to be led by a new NPWS manager called a unit leader, who would supervise the village scouts, work hand in glove with local communities and with the NPWS, and to the extent possible lend a hand within the parks as well. Intensive training programs for unit leaders and village scouts, emphasizing elements as diverse as military drill and animal identification, were to be established at Nyamaluma, a remote location that would provide opportunities for practical experience as well as work in the classroom.

Changes in money handling were also key in ADMADE's design. Sources of revenue for the newly established revolving fund included concession fees that safari companies would be asked to pay for the exclusive use of hunting blocks in the GMAs; sales of meat, hides, and other products from culled game; and the legal purchase and resale of government stocks of poached ivory that had been apprehended. Funds generated within each unit would be divided between national and local entities. Thirty-five percent would be allocated to community development projects—schools, clinics, wells, and similar grass-roots improvements—40 percent to managing the resource within the GMA, and the remaining 25 percent divided between national tourism promotion (NPWS is a division of the Ministry of Tourism) and the costs of managing the wildlife in the national park adjacent to the GMA. Activities in the buffer zones would thus help to support the strictly protected national parks, the backbone of Zambia's conservation system. Decisions about many aspects of the program, including how to spend the community share of the proceeds, would rest in the hands of local wildlife management authorities and subauthorities; the commanding voices would belong to chiefs and other local or regional officials.

From the outset, ADMADE faced daunting problems—virtually nonexistent communications capabilities; chronic shortages of weapons, ammunition, transport, clothing, and even food during the wet season, when dirt roads become impassable and supply lines are severed; and malaria, widespread in Zambia. Bilharzia and AIDS are growing threats. Hampered by a heavy external debt, insufficient foreign exchange to purchase imports, and growing political instability, Zambia's national government has not provided the equipment and logistical support that it originally promised. Road maintenance and other services pledged by the Lupande Integrated Rural Development Project (LIRDP), a sprawling entity created in large measure by international aid donors to expedite development around Nyamaluma, have not met expectations.

Still, the spunky staff has scored some remarkable accomplishments. In the pilot area, the lower Lupande hunting block adjacent to the

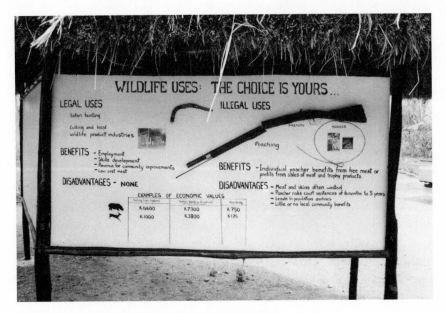

Training billboard at Nyamaluma camp

South Luangwa National Park, once relentless poaching has all but vanished. Wildlife populations in the region are up more than twofold. "That area is under control," said Mwenya with dramatic simplicity. In early 1988, with the lower Lupande success well documented, NPWS stretched ADMADE even further. "At Lupande we demonstrated that wildlife is an important renewable form of land use and that it can bring in more revenue than other ways of using that same land," Mwenya continued. "It then became logical to apply the concept more broadly." By 1990 the program was reaching every GMA in Zambia with sufficient wildlife to warrant inclusion, and the numbers of trained village scouts and unit leaders had grown dramatically. Added Gilson Kaweche, the articulate head of research at NPWS: "The program is mushrooming at such a rate that we're having a hard time keeping up with ourselves."

My purpose in coming to Zambia was to study ADMADE at a critical moment in its evolution and at the beginning of the rainy season, when an annual drama was once again commencing. Safari hunting and game-viewing camps were shutting down for the season, and trucks were hastening to carry out the operators' gear while the roads were still passable. NPWS officials were busy as well, ferrying sacks of corn-meal, the staple food of the region, out to remote camps where scout units would ride out the wet season in isolation. This was also the time when bands of poachers began to slip into the game areas under the cover of rain and to mount their most intensive attacks.

The morning after my arrival at Nyamaluma, Lewis conducted me on a brief tour of the camp, which since the outset has been ADMADE's nerve center. Here were classrooms for the village scout and unit leader training programs; a housing compound where trainees live, often with wives and children; a tannery, slaughterhouse, and other facilities for the game-culling program that is a critical element of the project and a source of local employment; a small shop for repairing vehicles and other machines; an office.

Lewis expressed special enthusiasm for wildlife utilization or game culling, as successfully practiced in several African countries. Trimming fast-multiplying herds of antelopes and other species, and selling the meat locally, is not a universally popular technique in conservation circles. It is, however, essential to ADMADE's economics. "We're using the entire product," he said. "We can earn far more money than a poacher can. Our meat is cheaper, and there's more of it per animal than there is of illegally hunted black-market meat. The hides we tan here go to a modern shoe factory, and we make glue as well. From each hippo we cull we earn five thousand kwacha—more than six hundred dollars at the official exchange rate." In many parts of Africa, the tsetse fly (which kills cattle and people by carrying a parasitic infection called trypanosomiasis, or sleeping sickness) prevents people from keeping cattle. While international agencies seek to exterminate the fly, conservationists regard it as a means of preserving wilderness. Lewis sees the fly's presence as a way of using hippos, which are not affected by it, as an ecologically sounder alternative to cattle: "In dense numbers, placidly grazing the riverbanks, hippos have the potential to be the cattle for this area," he said. Antelope harvesting has also been a success, he added. "Each impala we cull brings us about a thousand kwacha. We're selling the whole animal, wet weight, to the lodges and to the market down in Chipata. And it's all sustainable. In one test area, we're taking seventy-five impalas per year from a population of twelve hundred that is continuing to grow."

Back at the Lewis house, Patson Mwimanzi, unit leader for the lower

Village scouts receive new boots at Sandwe camp.

Lupande hunting block, described the progress he and his unit had made. The wiry Mwimanzi is a villager from the region and a seasoned wildlife manager. Tapped in 1985 to instruct the first detachment of village scout trainees, he moved from that to his unit leader job. Community relations, particularly with the originally skeptical Chief Malama, was a high priority. "At first we went very slowly," Mwimanzi said. "Then we started becoming very familiar and open to the chief, reminding him of the profit that his community could get from the wildlife. Now we're in cahoots, and all the chiefs in the area are cooperating. Often instead of apprehending poachers in the bush, we can catch them in the villages before they go out. These villages are very small, and often the sons of people who used to be poachers are now employed in our program. So it's not so hard to keep track of things."

In 1985 Mwimanzi's unit arrested eleven poachers; by 1987 the total had risen to fifty-six, and elephant poaching in the lower Lupande had dropped by 90 percent or more. With the local situation in hand, Mwimanzi was able to send his men on patrols beyond his own region, to an area on the other side of South Luangwa National Park that was under heavy pressure from professional poaching gangs. He could also assign scouts to duty in hunting safari camps, where after an uneasy start they became welcome, and he developed a sophisticated data-collection program that helps science while it trains scouts. "It's amazing," said Lewis. "These guys will come back from a patrol and report there are twenty-seven elands out there, not eighteen as we had thought. Three or four years ago they hardly knew what an eland was." The unit's greatest achievement was to have rediscovered the black rhino in the lower Lupande, where it was thought to have been poached to extinction.

One day Lewis and I drove from Nyamaluma down the river valley to an adjacent GMA called Sandwe, where a small group of village scouts had just established a provisional camp. Lewis wanted to see how things were going and to deliver to each scout a pair of shiny black boots that had been donated by Barclay's Bank. Entering a village near the camp, Lewis stopped the Toyota and was immediately surrounded. A headman wearing an olive-drab cloak pointed to a shy little girl hiding behind a tree. "She is the one who was attacked by a lion a month ago," said the man. "She is lucky to be alive. Last night the same lion came back. It killed a dog and a duck. What can we do?" "We'll have to kill that lion," said Lewis. "We have the authority to do it, and we will get the job done." In an aside, Lewis told me that although it does present difficult choices, this sort of community-relations work was a particularly important aspect of the ADMADE structure.

We walked from the village for half an hour across sunbaked open farmland to the separate village scout camp. Fifteen of the scouts mustered, marched, then stood at attention while we interviewed them. Since their arrival two months before, they had managed to flush only one poacher, who escaped before they could apprehend him. But the scouts had not found any carcasses of freshly poached animals, and had discovered only three snares. They also reported having seen "plenty" of animals in what had once been a bereft region, and they believed that their mere presence had been enough to scare poachers away. With more weapons and ammunition, they said, they could become more active and do a better job.

"You are here to be real men," said Lewis in his formal speech to the scouts. "We have not put you out here to be farmers. You can grow what you need to eat, but no more. This is an area for wildlife. Your job is to take care of the wild animals as if they were your cattle. Take care of them, and they will take care of you." Then the footwear was distributed, along with one aged rifle—the detachment's second weapon—and three rounds of ammunition. "These boots are given to you," said Lewis. "The next pair you will have to get on your own." Driving back to Nyamaluma under darkening clouds, Lewis confessed that two years before he could not have entered Sandwe without armed men at his side, so intense was the local hostility. Now he looked forward to promoting the provisional village scout unit to permanent status.

It was difficult to leave the Nyamaluma region without being impressed by the program's accomplishments there. Local employment in wildlife-related activities had risen tenfold. Substantial sums for a virtually cashless rural society ($35,000 U.S. at the time of my visit) have been returned to the communities for development projects. Whereas poaching once was the only possible source of cash income for villagers, most people had come to feel that protection and utilization of the animals was their principal economic opportunity. "It's sometimes dangerous and there are many problems," said village scout Weston Mwembela. "But we love this work and we are committed to it."

From Nyamaluma I went via Lilongwe to Zambia's capital city of Lusaka. From here, with help from Mwenya and others at NPWS headquarters, I arranged to survey the GMAs bordering the large Kafue National Park in west-central Zambia. The sandy soil of the region would provide better driving conditions than the clay and mud of the Luangwa Valley; around Kafue I would find newly installed village scout detachments and see the deployment of the program at its very earliest stage. I traveled now in the excellent company of Flywell Munyenyembe, a senior NPWS official with an Australian master's degree in resource management. Once clear of Lusaka we passed rich, flat farmland. The cotton was in and the maize harvest being completed.

Our first stop was at the village of Nalusanga, bordering the park, and headquarters for the unit patrolling the Mumbwa GMA. From this base, in just five months, the unit had managed to arrest and

Unit leader Godfrey Mubita

charge more than seventy poachers; all but a handful of those prosecuted had been convicted and fined. The arrests, said unit leader Leonard Lubinda, had been achieved in spite of the usual shortfalls in supplies and sometimes in the face of strong opposition. Once, he said dryly, when a group under his command encountered a band of poachers, "all but one of them ran away. The one who remained opened fire on us with an AK-47. We took cover until he ran out of ammunition. Then we apprehended him."

Already the Mumbwa unit's efforts were resulting in new attitudes in the region. "The idea caught on very fast," said its most important chief, Mulendema, as we sat in small chairs on the dusty ground in front of his house. "Most people view the program as good for them not only because of money and jobs but also because there has been a shift in ownership from the government to the people. Now we view the wildlife as our own." With initial revenues for the community expected from the NPWS revolving fund within a few months, Mulendema's chiefdom was looking forward to making improvements in the local school. Wildlife was already making a comeback. Elephants, which had all but disappeared, had returned to the sparse forests and open grasslands of the region. Populations of buffaloes, zebras, and hartebeests were beginning to recover. For want of sufficient baseline data, it was too early to begin culling operations; the community therefore could not yet enjoy the full benefits of income from the revolving fund. Even so, said Mumbwa district governor Ntalasha, "we have made a good start. Over the past six months, more has been done than in the previous two years. To replace the old hostility and antagonism, there has been a relaxation on both sides. And the poacher is aware that his village will excommunicate him if he continues."

During unit leader Godfrey Mubita's first year at the remote Lunga-Luswishi GMA, which I also visited, he was plagued with almost every imaginable problem. His house literally fell in upon him and his ailing family. His aged vehicle, on which he relied to feed and pay his scouts, gave him frequent trouble. "I lack spare parts," he said at his riverside camp. "I have to use initiative to make it run." Though the Lunga River is the best highway in the region during the wet season, Mubita had no boat. His radio had been out of action for almost two months; it is a two-hour drive, during the dry season, to the nearest telephone. His men were so short of weapons and ammunition that only with help from the safari hunting companies could they go on long patrols. Medical assistance is far away. At Mubita's camp we found one scout who had been suffering from a long bout of diarrhea, which in Zambia is a common cause of death among children and can be fatal even to adults. I gave him Bactrim tablets from my medicine kit and crossed my fingers. About $50,000 U.S. is usually needed each year to make a GMA fully self-sufficient, but Mubita's entire budget, to cover every aspect of his thirty-scout, four-camp operation except for his own salary, came to little more than $20,000.

Despite his severe handicaps, the tall and determined unit leader was able to point to accomplishments and express optimism. Twenty poachers had been caught and many others deterred. The Wildlife Management Authority had convened and community development projects had been decided upon. New camps along the GMA's northeast frontier, a particularly heavy poaching area, were being established. Neighborhood reaction, Mubita told Lewis in a long letter, had been "very whelming and pleasing." GMA residents had "seen a good result comes to them through their own wild animals . . . proper explanations have been said loud and clear . . . the way I look at the coming sphere on wildlife conservation will be very good . . ."

Munyenyembe and I spent a night at a brand-new Circuit Safaris hunting camp at a beautiful site on the Lunga River, enjoying such comforts as a hot shower, a flush toilet, and cold drinks from a gas-fueled refrigerator. Ben Labouschagne, the Zambian assistant professional hunter in residence, was only dimly aware of the ADMADE concept, but he expressed great enthusiasm, and pledged full cooperation, after Munyenyembe's succinct and articulate explanation. From the camp we drove back toward Lusaka by way of the flat, grassy Kafue National Park. Within its boundaries we saw many species of antelopes, a splendid young male lion as well as a pride of females, an orange-and-blue bateleur eagle, a safari lodge closed for the season—and, ominously, a newly built lean-to for use by poachers during the rains. The problems had not disappeared by any means. Night fell as we left the park and continued toward Lusaka on the highway. From the tall grass at the road's edge a leopard, the first I had ever seen outside of a zoo, suddenly materialized. Its eyes glowed yellow in the beam of our headlights. Then it vanished.

Back in Lusaka, I attended the annual professional hunters' dinner at the Inter-Continental Hotel. "So sad, isn't it?" sighed a British lady. "The 'game department' just can't seem to cope." A farmer told me he had heard a report that a Norwegian development assistance agency, which has run a major program in Zambia, had become so frustrated that they were plotting simply to take over the management of all Zambia's wildlife and wildlands. "It would be a good thing too," the man added. The suggestion is not new. In the name of wildlife protection, donors have periodically proposed to dismember the department and employ international forces to control poaching.

But as I wandered among the several hundred people in attendance, I learned that the better acquainted the safari hunters were with ADMADE, the more they liked it. "It's excellent," said Peter Swanepoel, a Zambian professional hunter who has cooperated with the program from the start. "No one cares more about conservation than we do, and they've clearly hit on the right way to go about it. We've been getting better trophies each year for the past five years." Several other hunters voiced similar sentiments. Even David Frost, a prominent businessman who chaired the hunters' association, professed guarded respect. "Of course there are problems," he said. "But I honestly believe that some progress has been made."

Hunters complained that confusion and disorganization had occurred over the issuance of licenses, and that NPWS had sometimes embarrassed them and disappointed their clients by double-booking the hunting blocks. For their part, wildlife officials said that the safari companies fudged the required reports about how many animals they killed, and manipulated clients' hard-currency payments in ways that prevent a rightful share from entering Zambia—and the revolving fund. But for all the inevitable tensions between hunter and gamekeeper, the relationship seemed generally comfortable. Annual kills from professional hunting remained minimal in number, and the mere presence of the safari camps in the GMAs deters poachers, at least during the dry season. While the indirect assistance that safari hunters give village scouts and unit leaders could be corrupting, there was no talk of this; more important were the four million kwacha (about $500,000 at the 1990 official rate) in concession fees collectively contributed to the revolving fund each year. Unity between NPWS, villagers, and professional hunters seemed fairly well established even in the newly patrolled areas. Where once NPWS stood alone and ineffective against the poachers, now it is the poachers who have few allies.

In search of clues about the program's future, I visited NPWS headquarters in the town of Chilanga at the edge of Lusaka. There, Mwenya and Kaweche with great enthusiasm described a cluster of new plans. The Japanese had been asked to help improve the department's lamentably poor communications capabilities, and Barclay's Bank was supporting the restocking of a GMA that had been depleted of wildlife. Dutch aid had been sought to develop a land-use policy for the GMAs to prevent the spread of agriculture into wildlife habitat. ADMADE principles of community involvement were being applied to a project to manage the nation's extensive system of wetlands. Using a new grant of five million kwacha from the USAID mission, NPWS would soon greatly improve its supply system by adding new vehicles and warehouses. Cornmeal-grinding mills and wells would be installed in villages in the GMAs, and new professional analysts added to the department. "We think what's been done is great," said Alan van Egmond, a USAID official in Lusaka. "We'd like to make it a model."

Still, the usual threats and obstacles remain. At Lupande the rural development officials, who have a lot of power but limited achievement to date, inhibit and frustrate ADMADE's no-nonsense efforts. With Zambia's national economic woes causing continuing shortfalls in government assistance, political rivalries in Lusaka and global market fluctuations might at any time undercut progress. Zambia is not overpopulated and it is the most urbanized country in Central Africa; but its 3.1 percent annual population growth imperils wildlands, and the international ban imposed on all ivory sales in 1989, supported by Zambia's then president, Kenneth Kaunda, cut deeply into the NPWS revolving fund.

For all the difficulties, Zambia may soon become one of the very few African nations to have effectively combated poaching. The situation in Kenya before the ivory ban was, in contrast, "completely out of control," according to one wildlife manager. At the heart of Zambia's success is a pragmatic perception of wildlife as a resource for its rural citizens and as an important element in the national economy. "We had a big problem," said Dr. Harry Chabwela, a former NPWS director and tourism official. "And we found a solution—to treat our animals as a serious component of economics. We are using professional hunters as a method to conserve the resource available. We have put the industry on the right course. We look forward with some confidence to the future."

Sub-Saharan Africa, long viewed by romantics as "Eden," is modern economic development's most conspicuous disaster. During the past decade, the burst of hope that accompanied independence in the 1960s gave way to gloom and even despair. Economies that had enjoyed growth began to level off, then decline, while those of other developing regions continued to expand. According to the World Bank, Africa's share in world markets dropped by almost half during the 1970s and 1980s, and the continent remains "simply not competitive" internationally. Poor and hungry Africans relentlessly continue to do grave harm to their natural surroundings: overgrazing leads to widening bands of desert, deforestation disrupts water supplies, resources are overexploited. People and nature are the joint losers, with two of every three Africans without safe water and 50 million of them facing acute fuelwood shortages. The human population continues to grow inexorably: from fewer than 100 million inhabitants at the beginning of the current century to a projected level of one billion by 2010.[1]

In listing the reasons for Africa's nondevelopment, many analysts have highlighted the hostility of its natural environment. From prehistoric times Africa has suffered from the poor quality of its soils, which never received the benefits of the glaciation or volcanic activity that enriched those of other continents, and from extremes of weather, including soil-leaching torrential downpours and severe drought. Wideranging disease epidemics have felled scores of millions of Africans over the centuries. Ill health is a major cause of one of Africa's principal economic problems: the irony of its chronic labor shortage. "Environmental crisis and demographic collapse," wrote the British scholar John Lonsdale, are "as old as the continent's ascertainable history."[2]

While nature has done much to obstruct progress, making Africa far less amenable to human activity than either Asia or Latin America, *Homo sapiens* has also been at fault. The slave trade ranks almost as high as disease as a cause of human decimation in Africa. Colonial governors tended to respect neither the continent's complex tribal mosaic nor its challenging ecology. Those who managed the artificially contrived new nations emphasized industry and urban development. Their efforts in the countryside often abruptly substituted new techniques and crops intended to satisfy European needs in place of farming traditions based on the local people's experience with difficult conditions. Half of sub-Saharan Africa's gross domestic product in 1990 (*up* from 40 percent a decade before), farming still receives only about 10 percent of government spending. Throughout the postcolonial

1. Figure is from the 1989 World Bank report, *Sub-Saharan Africa: From Crisis to Sustainable Growth*.
2. In David Anderson and Richard Grove, eds., *Conservation in Africa* (Cambridge, Eng.: Cambridge University Press, 1987).

era, authoritarian centralism, corruption, administrative disarray, capital flight, and neglect have been powerful obstacles to the sound management of rural development.

Nor did the aid agencies help much. The voluminous literature on the subject is replete with examples of failed dam projects and irrigation schemes, of integrated rural development programs that produced neither integration nor development, of disease and environmental degradation arriving along with aid-donor largesse. The World Bank has forthrightly admitted that its failure rate in Africa has been about double what it experiences elsewhere; the solution it advocates rests on the shaky assumption that the key to a reversal of Africa's "backsliding" is to pour in ever greater amounts of money, proposing to quadruple its support to $22 billion by 2000. Meanwhile, traditional conservation efforts throughout the region focused far more intently on nonhuman than on human needs and on ways to sequester wildlife within parks and protected areas.

Yet Africa's farmers and villagers have shown remarkable skill in coping with their severe environmental shortcomings. And few commentators on the African crisis fail to advocate greater and more pluralistic attention to the rural sector. The kinds of interaction that I saw in Cameroon and in Zambia, with newly empowered local people working with outsiders toward self-reliance, neatly exemplify what can be done. And they demonstrate that for all Africa's ecological shortcomings, the African people can overcome these tremendous obstacles by applying sound development strategies from the bottom up.

PART III

MAKING
A DIFFERENCE

CHAPTER 8

ᚵ

The Perils of Percolation

Sian Ka'an, the Maya term for "birth of the sky," is also the name of a gorgeous, little-touched 110-kilometer stretch of Mexico's Caribbean coast in the Yucatán state of Quintana Roo. Clean, clear waters, empty beaches, a profusion of coral reefs and wetlands provide excellent habitat for many important marine species, including sea turtles and manatees. Until Hurricane Gilbert tore up the region in September 1988, the spiny lobster (crawfish) bred abundantly in Sian Ka'an. Fetching an international price of eighteen dollars a kilo, a reduced population still provides a good living for the region's few fishermen. The dense forest that cloaks the land close to shore contains jaguars and four other cat species, tapirs, and a great diversity of birds.

So near (150 kilometers), and yet still so far away, is the burgeoning resort community of Cancún, which in 1990 boasted 16,000 hotel rooms and a population of more than 250,000. The island of Cozumel, another tourist destination, lies even closer to Sian Ka'an. Although unfavorable economic conditions made rapid development unlikely, the shoreline between Cozumel and Sian Ka'an, along which lies the ancient Maya settlement called Tulum, was in 1990 zoned to permit an additional 36,000 hotel rooms. An international airport at Tulum, proposed to relieve congestion at the Cancún and Cozumel airports, would, if built, accelerate the pace of nearby development. If environmental degradation does not yet seriously affect the Sian Ka'an region and its 25,000 people, most of them indigenous Maya, it looms as a mounting threat.

Early on, when Cancún was still small and uncrowded, conservationists began taking steps to safeguard Sian Ka'an. In 1982 the state government was persuaded to declare as a protected area a 528,000-hectare section of the region, within which fewer than 1,000 people were living. The 1986 inclusion of the reserve in UNESCO's Man and the Biosphere program gave the effort great prominence. That year, with the enthusiastic support of international funders, a local private organization called Amigos de Sian Ka'an was also established to work with state and federal agencies on managing the reserve and bordering communities. With little pressure on the reserve, lobster and other renewable forest and marine resources to harvest, and good early cooperation from the local communities, a quick victory for ecodevelopment in the region seemed imminent.

The Amigos' initial objectives were to help fishermen in the village of Punta Allen organize a cooperative to achieve proper management of the lobster resource. To forestall the likelihood that a gradual, ten-year lobster decline would continue if they did not set and enforce new rules, the Punta Allen fishermen (whose group is called the Pescadores de Vigía Chico, or Little Lighthouse Fishermen) agreed to stop harvesting during the late-winter egg-laying season. Studies of the lobster's reproductive cycle were also launched, as well as a program to protect the several marine turtle species that deposit eggs on Sian Ka'an beaches. Later, the Amigos as well as state and federal authorities sought both conservation and development goals for the far larger population in the Zone of Cooperation by encouraging and helping to maintain ecologically sound standards of farming and of harvesting forest resources. The Council of Sian Ka'an Representatives, whose members came from public and private organizations sharing responsibility for managing Sian Ka'an and adjacent areas, was formed. Between them, they launched several projects having to do with ecologically sound farming and controlled use of forest resources. A management plan was drawn up.

In mid-1990 Juan E. Bezaury Creel, a former official in Mexico's National Park Service who served as the Amigos' executive director, could cite a variety of accomplishments after eight years of work. For one thing, the reserve was intact, he noted when we talked in Washington. The 104-member fishermen's cooperative, though financially beset because it purchased a million-dollar freezing plant and was then hit by Hurricane Gilbert, was nevertheless functioning. Much research had been conducted, and more was in progress. Techniques for the sustainable harvest of forest resources, including chicle and vines used to make baskets, had been introduced. Planning for new activities ranging from eco-tourism to organic corn farming was under way.

But between 1986 and 1990, with no appreciable change in pollution levels or in the composition or behavior of the region's light population, the program also suffered from grievous growing pains. International funding for turtle protection was phased out, and poaching of the animals and their eggs increased. In 1988 the initial head of the Amigos, Arturo López, walked away from the assignment, having, in the possibly skewed opinion of one observer, "managed to alienate everybody." Early in 1990, extension workers on village-level projects were buffeted by problems ranging from broken-down vehicles to what the writer Jerry Emory called "rather intense personality conflicts."[1] Several withdrew from their posts. The Council of Representatives stopped meeting. Disputes raged among the agencies involved in the project: the federal government's Secretariat of Urban Development and Ecology (SEDUE), several departments of the Quintana Roo state government, and the Cancún-based Amigos. The management plan was never approved.

During our conversation Bezaury conceded the irony that it had been difficult for the program to make the transition from thought to action not because of intrinsic pressures on the ecosystem but because of human factors. "Conservation is a social development science," he said. "We're working on the development technologies that are right for the region, and on the kinds of social organization that will be required to use them. But we don't want to open the Pandora's box of these

1. "Where the Sky Was Born," *Wilderness*, Summer 1989, pp. 55–57.

technologies without knowing how to control their use. It'll take us another five years to get the first of them into *some* communities." Then Bezaury added the kicker. "I cannot say that this schedule pleases our funders," he said. "They want faster action."

Bezaury did not want to talk much about the personal rivalries. "We try to be very careful," he said. "Sometimes we play one side, sometimes the other. It's complicated." If his comments seemed very Mexican, the situation that he was describing differs only in detail from what rural ecodevelopment schemes anywhere frequently encounter as they move from planning to implementation. In Irian Jaya in 1990, WWF manager Stephen Nash was grappling with unforeseen adversities ranging from ill-advised sexual adventurism on the part of one employee to misunderstandings and "often ridiculous" arguments between community leaders and project staff members; Nash later left the province for another WWF assignment. At Kilum Mountain, an in-house squabble of intricate complexity became the project's most severe setback. For all his energy and chutzpah, Nikhom Putta, the TEAM fieldworker in Thailand, had great difficulty in adjusting to the more measured style of Wildlife Fund Thailand and was almost let go. Differences crop up between community views and those of faraway agencies. Corruption, or the threat of it, hovers around as funding and temptation increase.

The excruciating difficulty of accomplishing *anything* in rural work of this sort underscores the critical importance of giving success the best possible chance. This means that one must observe a number of dos and don'ts that have been learned during the grass-roots experience of several previous decades, and confirmed as ecodevelopment's boots have muddied. These are consistent with attitudes that have long prevailed within such institutions as the International Fund for Agricultural Development (an innovative branch of the United Nations), the Peace Corps, the Inter-American Foundation, and the sensible Oklahoma-based NGO called World Neighbors. Heifer Project International, a church-supported organization based in Little Rock, Arkansas, has fine-tuned its techniques of advising villagers in developing countries in ecologically sound livestock management. The book *Two Ears of Corn*, by Roland Bunch of World Neighbors, contributes much to the summary. So do the more academic but no less important observations of the British rural development analyst Robert Chambers,[2] which are also based on many years of fieldwork, and the careful 1988 World Bank analysis of its twenty-five-year record in rural development.[3] Not all points apply to every situation. But no effort that ignores most of them is likely to get very far.

The first point is about help from outside. Dalmiro Cortez of Ecuador is far from the only foresighted community leader who has taken action with no prompting from anyone else. Left to their own devices, however, villagers will often carry on with a rather narrow range of traditional farming or resource-gathering practices—to the bitter end, even if the resource is disappearing. In the absence of encouragement from elsewhere to try something new, St. Lucia's charcoal makers would have stripped the locally accessible mangrove down to the last stalk before stopping their harvesting of it. The same is true of the *Pygaeum* bark on Kilum Mountain or Khao Yai's sandalwood. Among such groups of local people, self-policing programs to conserve resources that enable them to survive will seldom arise from within the community when it is harvesting them.

A formidable obstacle to change is the absence of effective community institutions in places, such as Khao Yai, where migrants from many different areas have recently converged to take advantage of the available natural resources. Where tribal societies had been stable for generations, as was the case until recently among Cameroon's Oku people, or among the blacks who occupied the San Lorenzo region of Ecuador for four centuries, self-restraint is more likely, but as the Hatam example in Irian Jaya illustrates, the mere fact that a people have been in place for decades or centuries is no guarantee that old techniques of self-governance will continue to work. Even the Oku could manage only to reduce the intensity of their traditional behavior. They lacked another principal ingredient of successful sustainable development: the technical know-how to innovate. When monilia pod rot struck the cocoa plantations of Costa Rica's Talamanca canton,

2. As particularly recorded in his book *Rural Development: Putting the Last First* (Harlow, Eng.: Longman Scientific and Technical, 1983).
3. "Rural Development—World Bank Experience 1965–86," published by the Bank's Department of Operations Evaluation.

the growers did not try other crops, but instead simply abandoned their farms and shifted to other occupations. Although sea moss had been gathered around St. Lucia's Vieux Fort for generations, no one had invented the technology of planting the algae on a raft, anchoring it in shallow water, and letting nature then produce an easily harvestable commodity. Nor had any local person done the research to establish which of the many sea-moss species grow best in Savannes Bay. It took a Canadian marine biologist to do this.

So a nudge from outside is often needed to encourage or even precipitate a shift. The best way to deliver it is by means of a trained person who is of the same nationality or closely resembles those being given assistance. Much of the initial success of Wildlife Fund Thailand's Khao Yai program may be attributed to the presence, in the keystone village of Khlong Sai, of Nikhom Putta. He was born, as were many of the villagers he served, in Thailand's drought-ridden northeast. He himself had lived through periods of extreme poverty. A veteran of service as a Khao Yai National Park warden, he knew the region's plants and animals. He found it fairly easy to communicate his values to his peers in the villages. This sort of symmetry is ideal, but emissaries from the capital, with sharply divergent backgrounds, may also be highly effective agents for rural change if they have the people's interests at heart. The chemistry can work even if the agent comes from another country: to Ecuador's Awá, the capable Ecuadoran diplomat who until 1992 ran UTEPA in Quito, Carlos Villarreal, was every bit as "foreign," or as welcome, as the gringo fieldworker James Levy, who for years has worked and lived among them.

Recognition and rapport will usually follow the realization of financial reward flowing directly and visibly from the outsider's work in the village. The more quickly a tangible result can be achieved, the more popular the program will be. The butterfly scheme in Irian Jaya is particularly promising for this reason. But even when quick financial reward is not in the cards, conservationists tend to be well received when they state it as their purpose. Said Dale Lewis, the sole American in Zambia's National Parks and Wildlife Service: "Things were much easier for us because we could say that our business was to bring about development for the people living in the GMAs. If we had presented ourselves as conservationists, the people would have seen us as just another agency trying to keep them down." "Diego" Lynch, the hardworking ANAI fieldworker in Costa Rica's Talamanca canton, expressed almost identical sentiments about a project in which conservation only belatedly became an instrument for development. On the slopes of Cameroon's Kilum Mountain, Heather Macleod and John Parrott achieved a remarkable rapport with the community even though it will be well into the 1990s before financial returns become visible.

Whatever the nationality of the chief field honcho in the program, decades of grass-roots experience have demonstrated and early returns from the ecodevelopment sector have confirmed, progress is most likely if local citizens are full partners. Top-down planning seldom flourishes in the field. Even with the asset of an immediate economic incentive, it is doubtful whether WWF's Ian Craven would have generated much interest in butterfly ranching among the Hatam of Irian Jaya if he had not worked long and hard to achieve mutual respect between himself and them. In all five of the other projects I visited, community participation is an article of faith. The Vieux Fort waste-management example shows how involvement can grow into positive leadership.

Over and above local participation, progress seems to come most readily when local committees or associations have decision-making power. Although the World Wildlife Fund supplied the building materials for the shorefront storage and marketing facility that improved conditions for the fishermen in St. Lucia, it was the fishermen who did the construction work and laid down the rules for the building's use. In Irian Jaya's Arfak Mountains, Craven learned that if the Hatam people helped to decide upon and mark the exact border of the Strict Nature Reserve, within which no farming or hunting would be allowed, they would never violate that boundary. "They will even come and tell me if a boundary stake is missing," said Craven. John Parrott's Kilum Mountain boundary-marking expeditions illustrate the same principle. Even better results occur when, as in the instance of Zambia's ADMADE structure or the Khao Yai credit scheme, one puts financial responsibility and accountability in the hands of villagers.

Education, too, works best as a participatory experience. The schoolchildren of Khlong Sai were learning more about farming by actually growing crops than by viewing slide shows or looking at books or even watching videos. The tree nurseries of Talamanca and Kilum

Mountain are as important for learning as they are for reforestation and agroforestry. One of the principal and most appealing features of Heather Macleod's *Fen* newsletter is the fervor of its "Letters to the Editor" section. In the eastern Caribbean, the British-born conservationist Paul Butler gets his best results through gleeful leaps into the popular culture: he persuades local breweries to sponsor calypso or reggae videos with titles like "Leave de National Bird in de Wild," and builds environmental protection motifs into children's carnival costumes; his wife dons a parrot costume to accompany him to lectures at schools. Similarly, Kilum Mountain's juju dance group, which wears wooden masks depicting forest birds and animals and performs to drum and xylophone music, has, according to the program's managers, been highly popular. The T-shirt, whose use in grass-roots conservation education was pioneered by primatologist Russell Mittermeier of Conservation International, has become the leading cliché in the field.

Conservation is also facilitated when the program is aligned with the communities' traditional allegiances and values. By enlisting as leaders the very men who were already serving as *gembala,* or "shepherds," for the missionaries, Ian Craven in Irian Jaya activated an existing community hierarchy to generate enthusiasm for his program. Hatam people generally welcomed the new program not only because it held the promise of income but also because it helped them defend their territory. The essence of the Zambia model was the shift from an authoritarian relationship between gamekeeper and villager to one of more or less equal partnership against a common enemy. Ethnic Thais were sympathetic to the WWF low-interest credit program at Khao Yai in part because it freed them from the domination of Chinese village moneylenders. In Costa Rica, there is a direct relationship between the ANAI program's overall success and its ability to dampen antagonisms among the three distinct ethnic groups occupying the Talamanca region.

In their efforts to line up symmetrically with traditional community values, ecodevelopers often encounter one fundamental dilemma. According to the World Bank, women do 60 to 80 percent of the agricultural work on small farms in Africa and Asia, and 40 percent of it even in "macho" Latin America. Particularly in Africa, where women are responsible for virtually all food production as well as half of the animal husbandry, incorporating them into development activities is profoundly important. Their lack of access to credit and their inability to join cooperatives or to benefit from training programs have set back many large-scale rural development efforts, prompting the World Bank to establish a special Women in Development office.[4] Yet to favor women in rural African micro-projects is to flout long-standing traditions and to risk losing the community's support by abruptly undermining its value system. At Kilum Mountain, no sector of activity is trickier or more significant than Heather Macleod's involvement of women (and sometimes children) in tasks, such as boundary marking, that might otherwise have been left to the men.

Odd as it may seem for conservationists to reach this conclusion, WWF's planners have been recommending an *increase* in the kinds of human activity permitted within some protected areas. It is not always desirable to relax the rules. Thai government officials and Wildlife Fund Thailand fieldworkers agree, for example, that if Khao Yai's doors were set ajar for local villagers, the consequences for the park would be sudden and dire, despite the presence of guardian personnel and the park's well-equipped rangers. Anyway, overutilizing the park's resources would only be a temporary solution. Still, the search for longer-run sustainability becomes all the harder when economic gains must be wrested entirely from already degraded lands beyond the park's borders. Similar constraints affect programs in Costa Rica as well as in St. Lucia, where local divers could not harvest the plentiful white sea urchins near the Maria Islands Nature Reserve. (By 1990, they were illegally gathering the "sea eggs" in the knowledge that they would soon die if not taken; members of the Southeast Coast Project staff were working both with them and with the Fisheries Management Unit to see if rules to establish sustainability could be set and observed.) Following rigid models established by Dutch colonials, Indonesian parks administrators long ago favored the classification called Cagar Alam, or Strict Nature Reserve—lands within which no hunting, farming, or resource harvesting is permitted. Since the Arfak Mountains Nature Reserve in Indonesia's Irian Jaya falls into this category, economic opportunities are reduced for the Hatam people who live in

4. See ibid., p. 58.

villages adjacent to the reserve but can legally make no use of it. With proper discipline the Hatam could ranch butterflies and conduct other income-generating projects within the reserve without harming it. In general, then, the prospects for villagers living adjacent to reserves will improve if conditions permit them the maximum tolerable access to the resources within them.

Very little improvement will occur unless the outsiders entering the world's remote corners are willing to make long-term commitments to them. One of the first decisions that Parrott and Macleod made in Cameroon was that it would take longer than the three years originally scheduled to give their project's goals a chance of being achieved. Otherwise, they figured, the Oku people would quickly abandon the recent innovations and revert to their previous practices. In Talamanca and on St. Lucia, progress began to come clear only after about a decade of concentrated effort. At Sian Ka'an, the question is whether the program will ever produce the forecast results.

One difficult aspect of the marriage between conservation and development agencies, as in all marriages, concerns differing levels of patience. Conservation organizations have become increasingly businesslike and are much more interested in demonstrable results than they were in earlier, more relaxed times. WWF, for example, has ended its support for ANAI in Costa Rica, in the belief that Lynch, Salas, and Mack have failed to transform a series of projects into an integrated program. But their tolerance still is generally greater than that of government aid dispensers, who need to report dramatic strides forward at regular quarterly intervals—and whose home offices are all too likely to put a premature end to their support unless there is rapid and measurable accomplishment. Executives of the big private foundations also became restless in the information-cluttered spirit of the late twentieth century. No longer content merely to receive grant proposals, they began to patrol the periphery themselves. Greater conviction, if not always more profound understanding, made them more demanding as a result of their often hurried research trips.

All these obstacles notwithstanding, a careful study of projects such as those I visited evokes a sense of modest but significant achievement. For the rank and file in places where the development-for-conservation methodology arrived very recently, it was too early to forecast results. Some, like the Maya living near Sian Ka'an, will not benefit from ecodevelopment's messianic arrival for many years. They may never see any. But measures introduced to achieve sustainability have demonstrably improved the lives of the fishermen on St. Lucia's southeast coast, the long-ignored villagers near Zambia's national parks, farmers in Costa Rica who were in desperate straits before ANAI came along, the abandoned Awá. In these places progress could be seen and even measured.

What has happened out there suggests some even broader thoughts about the relationship between environmentalism and everything else. Back in the Stockholm era, it was generally assumed that cleaning up the environment was important—and expensive. Economics stood at one pole, the environment at the other, and future actions would involve "trade-offs" between the two. Still, today, such choices are often required. Fortunately, however, synergies have also emerged. In Japan and Germany, energy efficiency leads to competitive advantages. In the tropical villages I visited, the cluster of ideological forces deployed on behalf of a sustainable environment include democracy and market economics. Pluralism is an essential element of the micro-projects, and the economic incentive is what motivates people to participate. If either is removed, the project collapses. Properly conducted, then, the struggle against extreme poverty in the rural tropics unites several positive forces.

The question that many development professionals now ask is not whether the micro-programs can work; it is whether their principles and methodologies can be effectively applied to *nations*. It is all very well, they argue, for a tiny staff working in a far corner to do a good job meeting a limited objective for a small number of community beneficiaries. A solitary Peace Corps volunteer might work wonders within a single village, but who ever heard of the Peace Corps collectively influencing the course of an entire country? Sensitive to such criticisms, grass-roots agencies constantly search for ways to "scale up" the models and become more respectable among the bureaucracies by achieving broader "impact." An entire recent issue of *Grassroots Development,* the Inter-American Foundation's pioneering publication, was devoted to examining how "a conscious effort to expand operations, impact, or both"[5] might be implemented. Seminars and conferences about "rep-

5. From lead article by Mary Morgan, *Grassroots Development,* Vol. 14, No. 1, 1990.

licating the models" are frequent. In fact, modest efforts sometimes do resonate at the national level or beyond. One example is the influence that La Planada, a small ranch in a remote corner of Colombia, has quickly exerted on countrywide public opinion and on the attitudes and practices of the nation's leaders.

This property, only 3,200 hectares in size, covers one of the most biologically diverse places on earth. With 4,500 millimeters (180 inches) per year of rainfall, it is also one of the rainiest. It is classified not as moist, but as *wet* tropical forest. Until the biologist Jorge Orejuela surveyed it in 1981, science had only a dim understanding of what it contained. Hardly any Colombians could appreciate what its resources meant for them or the world. Early in the 1980s Orejuela, born in Colombia and equipped with a U.S. doctorate in ornithology, managed to convince a straitlaced Colombian institution called the Fundación para la Educación Superior (FES) of the region's virtues and of the need to save La Planada from a furniture manufacturer who wanted to buy the ranch and harvest its trees. Though FES was far more accustomed to working in the traditional fields of health, education, and social welfare, it agreed with Orejuela's idea.

The result has been a remarkable flowering of conservation and development activity. The ranch, which might have been stripped of its trees to become only another cattle pasture, came to serve a rarer function. Science entered to discover and study many previously unknown species of flora and fauna. More than eight hundred species of orchids, scores of them endemic to the region and new to science, have been documented. Ecodevelopment programs involving both the mestizo people of the lowlands below La Planada and its neighboring Awá, some 12,000 of whom live on the Colombian side of the border with Ecuador, have flourished. Beyond the striking local success of La Planada, which merits far more space than it is being given here, is what it has accomplished at the national level.

Thanks to a boost from a popular television show, viewed by two-thirds of Colombia's 33 million people, the little ranch late in the 1980s became something of a national shrine—a place whose colorful birds and trackless forest offered citizens a vision of their nation contrasting with the poverty, drug warfare, and guerrilla violence to which many had become accustomed. In growing numbers vacationing Colombians began making the long trek by auto (a four-hour drive from a town called Pasto, which itself is far off the beaten track) to visit La Planada and experience its wonders. But La Planada's national success is far more than a matter of mere imagery. FES, an important private institution that cleverly combines the features of a commercially successful finance company and a grant-making social-welfare foundation, has been transformed through what its senior managers originally saw as the gamble it took at La Planada.

From that small beginning has sprung an energetic Environment and Natural Resources Division under whose auspices, in 1990, a dozen projects were functioning throughout Colombia. New conservation organizations tend to regard La Planada as the quintessential example of what they seek to accomplish. Guillermo Hurtado, an alumnus of FES who was deeply involved in developing the La Planada idea, now heads one of these newer groups. In partnership with some thirty schools in the region, La Planada's environmental education unit was in 1990 testing materials and techniques that were destined to go national as part of a Ministry of Education program called Escuela Nueva. In few countries, in short, can the rapid growth of a new conservation ethic be so largely ascribed to the success and immense popularity of a single project. Biologically, moreover, few countries anywhere are as important—in endemism and species diversity—as Colombia.

Another "model" with a long reach is the attempt, in the Palcazú Valley, low on the eastern slopes of the Peruvian Andes, to carry out sustainable forestry activities in the humid tropics. Integrated planning for this remote area originated in the 1960s when Peru's president, the visionary architect Fernando Belaúnde Terry, proposed the so-called Marginal Road (Carretera Marginal) to run eastward from the Andes and link his country with Brazil and Argentina. Initial planning, interrupted when Belaúnde's regime was swept away in a military coup in 1968, called for the road to set off a burst of agricultural development along the "eyebrow of the mountains" (*ceja de la montaña*), of which the Palcazú Valley forms a part. Back in power in 1979, Belaúnde once again rolled out the Marginal Road idea even though science had done much during the interim to reveal its environmental shortcomings. USAID's research made it evident that the Palcazú region's poor soil was inadequate for the types of agriculture proposed, and accordingly "reoriented the project in favor of natural forest management as the principal activity."[6] Under a contract to the nonprofit Tropical Science Center in Costa Rica, a sustainable forest management system was designed, principally by Gary Hartshorn, now vice president for science at the World Wildlife Fund.

According to the conventional wisdom about humid lowland tropical forests, this is a contradiction in terms. For many reasons—including the tropical forest's high species diversity, lack of scientific knowledge, and institutional policies and practices—there had arisen "a pervasive attitude among forestry professionals, development agencies and the public in general that it is economically unjustifiable and ecologically impossible to manage tropical forests,"[7] as several planners of the Palcazú Development Project put it. Only mahogany, ebony, and a few other species had commercial value. As is characteristic of tropical-forest ecology, individuals of these prized species are to be found not in groves but widely scattered throughout the forest. To extract them foresters had employed notably heavy-handed methods, causing severe attrition. In recent years, however, the increasing scarcity of these top-grade species has caused a trend toward market acceptance of a far larger variety of native trees. In turn, say the planners of Palcazú, this change "opens the door to intensive management of tropical forests as an alternative to the selective exploitation of a few species." Now foresters could make economic use of the most prevalent form of succession in the tropical forest, which occurs when a large tree falls and is replaced by fast-growing, light-seeking "gap" species. Artificially emulating these "gap-phase dynamics" at Palcazú, project managers found that they could commercially exploit a number of these species, and sustain their population on a regeneration cycle of thirty to forty years. Selling lumber, charcoal, and other by-products would earn a handsome income for about one hundred Amuesha In-

6. From "Conserving Tropical Forests and Biological Diversity," the 1988–89 report to Congress on the USAID program.

7. Gary S. Hartshorn, Robert Simeone, and Joseph A. Tosi, Jr., "Sustained Yield Management of Tropical Forests: A Synopsis of the Palcazú Development Project in the Central Selva of the Peruvian Amazon," English version of a paper published in Spanish in 1987 (San José, Costa Rica: Tropical Science Center).

dians, from five communities, in a cooperative that harvests, processes, and markets the resources. Palcazú is the first forestry cooperative to be founded by indigenous people anywhere in Amazonia.

In 1988 USAID suspended its support for the experiment due to the nearby presence of guerrillas from the Maoist Shining Path movement, which has been active in many parts of Peru since the 1970s. Weakened for want of adequate funds, Palcazú's overall importance remains conjectural for other reasons. As in the instance of the extractive reserves for which the Brazilian rubber-tapper Chico Mendes fought and died, the number of people for whom Palcazú can provide a living is sharply limited relative to the swelling numbers of rudderless Amazonians about whom something must be done and for whom there is little hope. "Every time I go to Palcazú, I see more forestry professionals than Indians," observed Marc Dourojeanni, director of the Inter-American Development Bank's Environmental Protection Division. Some scientists worry that, despite the extreme care taken there, nutrient losses will eventually inhibit the trees' regeneration. For all the question marks, the project represents a refreshing wisp of hope, and it has attracted wide attention within the development community. In an article noting many failures elsewhere, the tropical-forest ecologist Robert Buschbacher calls Palcazú "one of the most exciting and promising experiments in natural forest management ever carried out in Latin America," and a project that "will be closely watched in both the conservation and development communities as a possible model for environmentally sound rural development."[8]

Careful programming and good public relations will extend the influence of a well-located small endeavor, as La Planada shows. And Palcazú indicates that technologies that may be applicable in many environments will emerge from applied ecology. Zambia's national ADMADE program, now being adapted to the needs of several other African nations, started out as a "demonstration project." In its issue on the subject of "scaling up," *Grassroots Development* offers several Latin American examples of this: the financial practices of a Uru-

8. "Ecological Analysis of Natural Forest Management in the Humid Tropics," in Robert J. A. Goodland, ed., *Race to Save the Tropics* (Washington, D.C., and Covelo, Calif.: Island Press, 1990), p. 66.

guayan wool growers' cooperative worked so well that the Central Bank adopted the same system for all growers; a cultural center in northeast Brazil succeeded in getting no less than a constitutional guarantee for alternative education programs for slum dwellers.

The people who brought about these accomplishments merit hearty congratulations, and many involved want more of the same to happen. "It's time we took aggressiveness training," said Charles Reilly, vice president for learning and dissemination at the Inter-American Foundation. Yet it is unlikely that success will strike with dozens and dozens of small rural efforts scattered around the world, and it is not necessarily desirable for their managers to want to expand as a principal objective. The larger the project, the less likely it is that a bona fide grass-roots manager will possess the right kind of skills to run it properly. The difficulties that Sian Ka'an and other projects encountered during their adolescence hardly suggest that expansion should become a goal. To put it the other way, the people who can make the switch are often not those who function best at the micro-level. "We're not affecting the big picture," said Deborah Szekely, then head of the Inter-American Foundation and Reilly's boss. "We're doing demos. We're a laboratory for learning and teaching, and what we do cannot be scaled up."

Here was a California businesswoman talking, the successful operator of a spa for women called the Golden Door, who at the outset of the Reagan era requested—of all things—the Inter-American Foundation as the prize she wanted in return for devoted political service. Professionals in the field were appalled, particularly since Reagan loyalists, hastily appointed to the IAF board, had unceremoniously dumped Szekely's respected predecessor, Peter Bell, a Harvard-educated alumnus of the Ford Foundation, to make way for this less "liberal" successor. But Szekely turned out to be a doughty, if unconventional, believer in the grass-roots philosophy. She thrived in the field. She survived on Capitol Hill, where she had to defend the congressional appropriation for a small, countercultural institution whose ideas were hardly in the spirit of the times, and the agency remained intact. Szekely surprised almost everybody by enduring into the Bush era, until 1990, when she finally withdrew. Along the way, this determined antipoverty crusader came also to believe that "scaling down" the programs of the bigger agencies is more important, and maybe even more feasible, than trying to stretch the cucumbers. "The banks need to become more responsive and involve more people," she said as we sat in her office in Rosslyn, Virginia, just across the Potomac from Washington. Popular art mementos from her travels lined the room. An Andean singing group clad in handwoven cloth, en route to the Smithsonian Institution's annual Folklife Festival, patrolled the corridors after having given a fund-raising concert for the IAF staff. "I think it's really happening," Szekely continued between interruptions. "Five years ago it would not have been possible to imagine the things that Barber Conable is saying at the World Bank, what Enrique Iglesias is doing at the Inter-American Development Bank. Their point of view has really changed."

Is it feasible, then, for the big lenders and donors—the foundations and large government or semipublic agencies—to slice up their programs into little segments to accentuate these values? As Szekely suggested, the banks have made sincere efforts to move in these directions. Their voluminous policy papers, environmental guidelines, and proclamations express concern that goes far deeper than mere protective interest in stifling criticism. In recognition of their own limitations as ecodevelopers, they now work far more closely than ever before with smaller nongovernmental groups. But can they scale themselves down? Can they themselves achieve flexibility any more readily than the little programs can achieve sustainable growth? Their own defensive answer is negative. To maintain the kinds of controls and discipline their bureaucracies require, said John Spears of the World Bank, could never be cost-effective, since it would involve enormous staff increases. The game is not worth the candle, the development economist Sheldon Annis, then of the Overseas Development Council in Washington, told *Grassroots Development*. Rather than attempt such massive adjustments, he recommends that they strive "to create propitious conditions—legal frameworks, social structures, economic systems—conducive to smallness thriving."[9]

Annis is surely correct. Rural development will function best if the large agencies, for the most part, relinquish field activities to the new clusters of smaller national and international nongovernmental orga-

9. Mary Morgan, op. cit.

nizations. The strategy is not without dangers, for no rule prevents these organizations from atrophying as they "mature," taking on the very rigidities their designers founded them to correct. "I'd be very careful about putting all my eggs in the NGO basket," says one seasoned international environmentalist, Jacob Scherr of the Natural Resources Defense Council. When in 1990 Bush announced his Enterprise for the Americas Initiative, a new effort to give economic and environmental assistance to Latin America, some critics faulted its small but significant environmental component for favoring NGOs over government agencies. But in general, the NGOs have been more sensitive and less wasteful than all but the very best of the public sector, and their presence will be invaluable. As the economist Albert Hirschman noted in his book *Getting Ahead Collectively,* in Latin America as in so many other regions the gulf between the state and the poor is usually too great for effective interaction to occur. As one NGO representative, Roque Adames Rodríguez of the Dominican Republic, put it at a recent Inter-American Development Bank conference: "The low level of motivation of government officials and their lack of contact with reality meant that efforts to resolve problems at the source almost invariably ended up a total failure." The solution, he continued, is for small and flexible NGOs to act "as a bridge between the needs of people and the resources of the national and international communities." Hence, in Latin America, Hirschman found growing interest among educated young men and women in *"promoción social"* as a new sort of career. According to Maria Helena Allegretti of the Institute of Amazonian Studies in Brazil, a fervent advocate of the principles that Chico Mendes espoused, the very growth of NGOs in Latin America shows the "deep-seated crisis between civil society and the state," and how the NGO community needs to "develop two relationships, one with local communities and the other with public authorities."

In his often-quoted essay "The Tragedy of the Commons,"[10] the biologist Garrett Hardin reflected gloomily on "the solemnity of the remorseless working of things." Since each individual gains incrementally by adding to the planet's overcrowding or further pollution but

10. First published in *Science,* Vol. 162 (December 1968), pp. 1243–48.

shares with others the negative consequences, he argued, "ruin is the destination toward which all men rush, each pursuing his own best interest in a society that believes in the freedom of the commons. Freedom of a commons brings ruin to all." In his own search for "corrective feedbacks," Hardin concluded that the abandonment of the commons concept was required, and that the only acceptable way to achieve it would be by means of "mutual coercion, mutually agreed upon by the majority of the people affected."

Where smallness does thrive, I would counter-argue, the commons can still flourish as a principle. The lobstermen of Sian Ka'an, the sea-urchin gatherers of Savannes Bay in St. Lucia, the *Pygaeum* harvesters of Kilum Mountain have all gained by applying their own standards to the use of their resources. They have employed Hardin's concept of "mutual coercion, mutually agreed upon" *without* relinquishing their freedom of access to the resource. Community control of fragile environmental assets may not fully merit the accolade of a "long and successful history" that the environmental economist Robert Repetto has ascribed to it.[11] But my experience suggests that, like all others, the very poor people at the margins of the rural Third World are usually the best judges of where their self-interest lies. With direct but gentle assistance from small-scale development agents, and the backing of the large agencies, they have demonstrated their ability to exercise restraint—and, concurrently, to achieve both economic and environmental progress.

The question is not whether the villagers can adjust to the world. More likely, it is whether the world can adjust to them.

11. Repetto, ed., *The Global Possible* (New Haven: Yale University Press, 1985).

CHAPTER 9

ॐ

New and Old Voices
from the South

To this day, there are political and social leaders who argue that poverty can be alleviated only if environmental goals are set aside. The
dialogue about the global environment is itself, they continue, complicated by the major differences between industrial and developing
nations regarding priorities and techniques. An eloquent spokesman
for these attitudes is the Pakistani economist Mahbub ul-Haq, currently a senior official at the United Nations Development Program.
During a brief but pungent meeting in his New York office, he crisply
outlined to me the principal "difficulties" he sees in discussions between
the powerful North (the community of industrial nations) and the developing South about environmental matters.

In poor countries, he said, it is not the environment but people's
"compulsion for survival" that must be addressed. While water pollution is the most pressing problem, the man-made disturbance of the
atmosphere remains no more than a distant threat: "The Third World
will blow up before the globe warms up." With regard to money, ul-
Haq feels that not only should industrial nations clean up the environment as part of their debt to the planet, but paying back the "debt of
human neglect" is an urgent and separate obligation. He and many

Food riot in Third World

other Third World leaders were alarmed, he said, that participants in the 1989 Group of Seven meeting in Paris talked "only about global warming and so forth, not about who will pay for global poverty." Ul-Haq, moreover, regards the creation of the United Nations Environment Program as "a terrible mistake because you should not treat the environment alone, but address it while dealing with poverty issues." He is, of course, right to suggest this sort of integration. But in stating his case he relegates the environment to such a minor role that one must question how "sustainable" his model of development really is. His demands on the North are, moreover, so strident that they make one gloomy about the prospects for North-South cooperation in integrating environmental and economic strategies. Little can be expected of agencies, or countries, as hesitant as he to let the environment onto the playing field.

Nor will progress come easily in poor countries where grotesque styles of political leadership persist. Though it is easy to make too much of this, one force working against environmental stability is surely insatiable acquisitiveness at the top. The application of its lead-

In Abidjan, a $200 million cathedral

ers' Swiss bank holdings, it has been suggested, could shrink all of sub-Saharan Africa's debt to zero and relieve its citizens of most of the hardship and deprivation that they are compelled to endure. Money that might be allocated to social progress in the provinces goes instead to the excessively expensive monuments, such as the Ivory Coast's infamous $200 million cathedral, that adorn some capitals. As one disheartened World Bank economist with Latin American and African experience stated, "It's hard to be optimistic when you're working in countries with governments that don't care what happens to the people they are governing."

As a means of maintaining political control, moreover, national leaders favor military over social expenditures. The United Nations Development Program specified the problem in its *Human Development Report 1990:* "The rapid rise of military spending in the Third World during the last three decades is one of the most alarming, and least talked about, issues. It continued even in the 1980s despite faltering economic growth in many developing countries and despite ma-

Militarism ranks high in many poor countries.

jor cutbacks for education and health." In 1987, it continued, arms imports by developing countries reached nearly $35 billion, or three-quarters of the global arms trade. While more than twenty-five developing countries spend more for military purposes than for health and education combined, in some of them almost three-quarters of the total for the three categories goes to the military.

The traditional forms of inclusive grass-roots participation we find in many societies of the Third World demonstrably encourage environmental health. Yet, in order to consolidate their power, the insecure leaders of poor new nations tend both to suppress decentralization, depriving and squeezing the countryside, and to pamper the urban sector, where dangerous opposition is likelier to crop up. How health and education services are allocated reflects the urban bias. Many hospitals in Third World capitals have sophisticated equipment and well-trained doctors, yet medical aid for the rural poor hardly exists. Many parts of the rural tropics have no schools. In most developing countries, city folk receive four or five times the per capita volume of direct antipoverty assistance that is extended to the country-side. Government technical assistance programs seldom reach the rural poor. All too often, competent governmental functionaries are unwilling to undertake field assignments. Sometimes xenophobic Brazil makes life difficult for foreign scientists conducting basic research in Amazonia, and meanwhile the Brazilians who might be doing the same work are sitting, feet to the fire, in the paper-shuffling Brasília bureaucracies where the better-paid jobs and promotion opportunities are to be found.

In countries where regional politicians are somewhat influential, the opposite problem may occur when the hope of larger allocations from the federal pork barrel tempts them to lay out welcome mats in ecologically inhospitable regions. So it was in Brazil's Rondônia, whose governor of the early 1980s energetically recruited immigrants, and so it now is in the relatively undisturbed Brazilian state of Amazonas in the central Amazon. There, the governor elected in 1990, a seasoned politician named Gilberto Mestrinho, who had previously occupied the same office, adopted a strongly pro-development stance in spite of all the ecological warning signals. "I wasn't elected by the trees," said Mestrinho, who won handily on a platform that, in part, consisted of accusations that "foreign ecologists" conspire with international business interests to keep Amazonian mineral riches out of Brazilian hands. As his campaign symbol Mestrinho used the *boto,* or river dolphin, a species widely believed in Amazonia to have magical powers. "The center of ecology should be man," the *boto* told James Brooke of *The New York Times.* "Ten million people can't be condemned to hunger so the animals and trees can grow." Displaying remarkable ignorance of how his state's ecosystem works, he accused its trees of being riddled with termites and fungi, and recommended that they be cut down and replaced with more wholesome species.

A similar example comes from Thailand. For some years USAID has been experimenting with coastal-zone management programs, and has had notable success in balancing the needs of wild shrimp harvesters and shrimp farmers in Ecuador. Now, on the fast-industrializing Thai coast, it again tried to strike bargains between watermen, operators of tourist facilities in the town of Phuket, and people wanting to put up factories. At the outset, the provincial governor showed great enthu-

THE PITONS

The Pitons, gateway to the Caribbean, present fascinating opportunities for recreation in the form of nature appreciation, hiking, wind surfing, sailing, snorkeling and scuba diving.

The Pitons, referred to as Plug Domes, seem to defy gravity, and are considered by many to be the "most spectacular piece of scenery in the Caribbean." They owe their magnificence to their proximity to the sea, from which they rise in towering twin peaks. The Petit Piton, which rises a veritable Matterhorn, was long considered unscalable. It was first climbed by Abdome Deligny in 1878.

The geological formation of the Pitons is obscure. Four separate accountings exist in the literature. You may well disagree with all of them, and formulate your own opinion.

One theory states that the Pitons are the remains of a crater ruin, which has since fallen away, leaving only the Pitons. Another states that the Pitons are viscous extrusions which grew within a sheath which surrounded the "Plug Domes", and has since eroded away. Whichever theory you choose, intense vulcanism, erosion and earthquakes have certainly played their part.

The interior of St.Lucia is dominated by mountain peaks, steep ridges, and deep narrow valleys. The highest mountains are, Mt.Gimie (3117 ft.), Piton Canaries (3012 ft.), Mt.Tabac (2270 ft.) and the Gros and Petit Piton (2619 and 2469 ft.) respectively. Fast flowing streams with high gradients occur in the valley bottoms emanating in a radial arc from the central volcanic ridge. Relief tends to be very high, with a 3000 ft. drop over a four mile horizontal distance in some areas. The volcanic geology of the interior is the dominant factor that produced this landscape. Shifting volcanic vents created a somewhat jumbled topography with several major peaks, each having numerous ridges radiating from them. The Qualibou Caldera, which takes in the entire region around Belfond and the Sulphur Springs in an immense crater with numerous faults, is an excellent

St. Lucia's Pitons

siasm, and local communities joined in with excessive vigor. In one well-publicized, if perhaps overdramatized, 1986 incident, a group of them set fire to a newly completed plant just before it was to begin operating, in order to prevent the pollution it would cause in local waters. But after several years of promising activity, a local political change brought into office a new governor more interested than his predecessor in real estate development. The USAID program's effectiveness abruptly diminished.

Bad planning, influenced by the wrong people, blunts the effectiveness of many Third World economic development efforts. A telling example is to be found in the Lesser Antilles. The Caribbean's most spectacular stretch of scenery, its Yosemite Park, is the stretch of St. Lucia's southeast coast that is dominated by twin peaks called the Pitons. Geologically, the Pitons are defined as plug domes, remaining from intense volcanic activity during ancient times. A mile apart, they explode out of the cobalt sea and rise steeply to heights of 2,438 and 2,611 feet. Between them lies a well-watered saddle of green vegetation—the remains of an old plantation near the shore, tropical forest at higher elevations. In the bay, corals attached to the Piton walls plunge downward to depths of three hundred feet or more, housing an abundance of species. They are the preferred destination for scuba divers visiting the island. The Pitons, which decorate the national flag and postage stamps and tourist brochures, are as much the symbol of St. Lucia as is the Eiffel Tower of Paris or the Statue of Liberty of New York. On one of my flights to St. Lucia from New York, the young man in the next seat could not suppress his excitement as the plane descended toward the airport. "There are the Pitons," he said. "There is my home." The spires have a regional importance as well, for their natural beauty surpasses that of any other site in the eastern Caribbean.

Although the peaks themselves are public property, the land in the saddle between them has, since the eighteenth century, been divided into plantation estates belonging originally to the Devaux family and later in the island's tormented history[1] to a succession of owners. Sugar was cultivated on these plantations until slavery ended. During later times of declining use, various crops, including cocoa, coconuts, bananas, and other fruits and vegetables, were grown there. No one prospered on the farms, or in the pretty nearby fishing village of Soufrière, where Napoleon's empress, Josephine, spent much of her childhood. The region remains subject to natural violence: heavy rainfall, earthquakes, landslides, flooding during the hurricane season. "Five times during my lifetime," said Robert Devaux, a descendant of the original owners and president of the St. Lucia National Trust, "the region has been hit by fifteen-foot waves that resulted in flooding as much as three hundred and fifty feet in from the beach."

---

1. It changed from French to British ownership, and back, fourteen times before 1814, when it became firmly British, remaining so until independence in 1979.

Such dangers notwithstanding, it has long been the ambition of many St. Lucians to make the Pitons and their environs into a national park. The designation would make them eminently eligible for inclusion as a site in UNESCO's World Heritage program. As such, they would become a magnet for hikers, divers, and eco-tourists of all sorts. According to a plan prepared by consultants to the Organization of American States, who worked closely with the Soufrière Development Commission, the park would become the keystone of a badly needed regional development program. Residents of the shabby Soufrière region, which has long suffered from heavy unemployment, would, it was stated by park proponents, benefit from 1,200 new jobs as park managers and rangers, tour guides, and employees of appropriately scaled hotels that would be carefully sited at suitable locations on the park's periphery. "Magnificent Soufrière" itself would undergo a renaissance, with the addition of a shorefront esplanade, marina facilities for passing yachtsmen, and new restaurants and shops. The overall scheme, put together with the heavy involvement of community leaders in Soufrière, seemed the very model of enlightened eco-tourism and wise national development.

For almost all of the 1980s, as these plans were being assembled, they seemed to have the blessing of the national government in Castries. Repeatedly, top officials asserted the designation of the Pitons as an area for "active conservation." On several occasions a committee called the Development Control Authority (DCA) rejected proposals from private landholders for permission to develop parts of the critical plantation area lying between the two peaks. One such came from the elegant Briton Colin Tennant, a tall, well-groomed socialite who with a boost from Princess Margaret had transformed the nearby island of Mustique from a scruffy fishing settlement into a coveted jet-set destination. In 1981, on the lookout for new challenges, Tennant bought the 123-hectare Jalousie Estate that dominates the saddle between the two peaks. Although the history of what happened during the next seven years remains murky, a burst of activity began in 1988, when the estate was sold to M Group Resort SA, a Swiss-based company of Iranian origin. In 1989 the Jalousie Plantation Development Company, with Tennant as its head, won the government's "approval in principle" to proceed with the farm's development as a resort containing a minimum 150 residential units, a Great House, and associated recreational and agricultural facilities.

No public statement was made, either by the government or by the developers. In 1989, however, construction began on the site—a jetty to off-load materials from lighters on the water, earthmoving and road-building operations by the giant Brazilian Andrade Gutierrez company, which had worked on such Amazonian mega-projects as the Carajás iron mine and the Tucuruí dam. Tennant's architects, the Miami-based firm of Lane Pettigrew Jones, set up shop in the old courthouse of Soufrière, one of the village's most striking buildings. There, by September 1990, could be seen the working drawings forming the basis of the entire project. As this work progressed, rumors began to swirl that it was but the beginning of a larger assault by private developers upon what was to have been the park's centerpiece. Tennant still owned an adjacent section of land that he would, as he had at Mustique, sell in small parcels to individual buyers. Proposals were pending for other developments on adjacent estates called Palm Beach and Beauséjour, and some said that these too had already been approved "in principle" by the government.

All along, many people in St. Lucia—Robert Devaux, former forest supervisor Gabriel Charles, a blunt American named Kenneth Green who served as OAS representative on the island and supervised the elaboration of the park plan—did their best to dissuade the government from making such an unannounced and unexamined policy shift. Private development of the Jalousie Estate and adjoining areas, they argued, would emasculate the park plan and cut the heart from the entire Soufrière region development program. Tampering with the natural contours of a disaster-prone area would cause sediment-laden runoff into Jalousie Bay. These sediments would lead to the early death of the sensitive reef systems, which are one of the region's principal tourist attractions. The hotel jobs created by the project would then be threatened. Local citizens' access to Jalousie Beach, though guaranteed by national law, was in jeopardy as a practical matter.

Though the government never officially acknowledged receipt of the OAS proposal, it mutely reacted to the criticism by requesting, from the Antigua firm of Ivor Jackson & Associates, an ex post facto Environmental Impact Assessment (EIA) of the Jalousie project. Work on the EIA was begun well after the initiation of construction activities. The resulting report, which reiterates the desirability of the park proposal and the awkwardness of implementing it with private development at its core, also questions the suitability of the rainy site for development as an "up-market resort." In early 1990, with this document as added ammunition, a new group, called the St. Lucia Environment and Development Awareness Council (SLEDAC), was formed in opposition to Tennant's plans. The prominent poet and writer Derek Walcott was recruited as a member, an aggressive press campaign was launched with the support of one local newspaper, the *Star,* and expressions of concern came from such international groups as Friends of the Earth and Greenpeace. At the 1990 annual general meeting of the Caribbean Conservation Association, a SLEDAC representative, the Barbados-based St. Lucian Dr. Len Ishmael, gave a passionate and moving speech protesting the recent "radical, unexplained, complete shifts of government policy" toward the Pitons region. She particularly decried the "lack of information" about the government's new position. "Don't we have the right to ask questions deemed to be political?" she rhetorically asked an aroused audience. "The arguments advanced about jobs can no longer be justified as an excuse to desecrate a national treasure. Development is about people. Citizens should have the right to enter into debate about this matter, free from fear of professional or personal reprisal. In conclusion, I should like to quote to you one of the phrases listed on a placard placed by the St. Lucia National Trust upon one of our monuments. 'This is all we have,' says that sign. 'Let us protect it.' "

Natty even in a cotton shirt and a pair of torn white trousers, the pale-eyed Tennant reacted blandly to such remarks when I saw him in Soufrière a few days after Ishmael's speech. "The environmentalists don't have the right information," he said. "They're just in this to get attention for themselves. This is a farm, not a forest. What are we supposed to save? The pigs?" He confirmed that the Jalousie development would be completed and open by late 1991, at which time he would begin the conversion of the remaining land he owns into private villas. He took care to point out the low profile of the resort, claiming that very little of it would be offensively visible from the water. The plantation style of his plan, which calls for the restoration of farming activities on a large portion of the property as well as the maintenance of a small forest reserve on its upper slopes, would have environmental safeguards. Tennant added that he had tried to work with the community, had even raised money to support the activities of the Soufrière Development Commission. One way or another, he continued, these initiatives had been rebuffed. We browsed among the antique furniture, destined for the Jalousie Plantation Resort's Great House, that he had temporarily stored in his Soufrière courthouse. "So much for dialogue," murmured this polished man.

What is dismaying about this story is not that hotels are being built near the Pitons. There is little disagreement with the idea that Soufrière needs hotels. The problem is their location in what was to have been the very heart of the park. It is still possible that a deal could be made in which the Jalousie resort would fall within the borders of a national park, in the same way that Yosemite, St. John, and Royal Chitwan parks accommodate private hotels. More probably, Jalousie will become mostly a self-contained enclave for the rich, with entry by common folk discouraged though not prohibited and jobs consisting mostly of bed making and toilet cleaning for hotel guests and private villa occupants. More a socioeconomic than an environmental tragedy, this affair illustrates the sharp cleavage between the elitist and populist views of tourism development. The very poor people of Soufrière, though well represented by their local development commission, will have had no influence whatever on the outcome. It provides what one observer, an aroused Floridian named Jay Randal, calls "the clearest example I've ever seen of a government betraying its own people." At one hearing with government officials, Tennant was asked why it was that he wanted to develop the Pitons. He flushed slightly, then said: "Because they're unique."

Just so.

Skewed national priorities mean terrible economic hardship for the Third World's small farmers. One major problem for them is the artificially low prices that governments set for such basic foodstuffs as milk and bread. Pricing issues had a negative effect on 68 percent of the rural projects the World Bank included in a recent study of its own rural development experience; positive implications were noted in only 10 percent of the cases. Though some governments give farmers subsidies (for fertilizers and other inputs that themselves can do environmental damage), the "beneficiaries" are usually large landholders rather than the small farmers for whom they were mostly intended. The pressure to repay debt makes governments push farmers to produce export crops that bring in foreign exchange but often do major environmental damage. As in the instance of Myanmar, which overharvests its forests to finance warfare against border insurgents, Third World regimes still often ravage their own *campesinos* to further national economic or political objectives.

The basic question of land tenure lies at the heart of the matter. In his Latin American travels, the often counterintuitive economist Albert Hirschman ran across one situation where he felt that land titling would result in environmental degradation. Squatters in an urban slum told him that improving their dwellings offered some protection from the bulldozer; the granting of land titles would remove both the threat and the incentive. In the countryside, however, ownership of small holdings and wise use are far more likely to coincide. Talamanca precisely illustrates the point. In Costa Rica, and many other countries as well, laws making it easier for squatters to gain title to cleared or "clean" land than to become owners of "dirty" forested areas need to be repealed. Better still would be their reversal, in order to encourage limited cutting and agroforestry. If more Brazilian peasants had access to land used inefficiently by the "colonels" who still dominate rural life in much of the country, the rate of their migration to hard-pressed Amazonia would slow down. Globally, the magnitude of the problem is substantial: from late 1970s data, the World Resources Institute in 1990 concluded that, by 1981, 167 million households, or almost one billion people, were "landless or near landless," and expected the number to rise to 220 million households by 2000. In some countries, notably the Dominican Republic and Guatemala, virtually all rural households fall into this dismal category.

An international event much heralded at the time was the adoption in 1985 of a global Tropical Forest Action Plan elaborated by the World Bank, UNDP, FAO, and the private-sector World Resources Institute. Coordination, it was hoped, would improve national and international actions to slow down tropical-forest destruction, raise more funds for forest conservation and management, and in other ways stabilize the deteriorating situation. In the five years after the program's initiation, funding did indeed double—to a 1990 level of about $1 billion a year. Over the same period, seventy-nine developing countries began their own efforts to help implement the global plan. Nevertheless, tropical deforestation also doubled during the 1980s, interagency friction mounted, and so did conflicts between developing countries' national objectives and those of the donors. By 1991 the sponsoring agencies were trying desperately to revamp the sputtering program or possibly even abandon it in favor of a new one.

North-South differences on tropical forestry also surfaced at meetings of the International Tropical Timber Organization (ITTO). Dating from 1983, this organization professes a belief in the sustainable management and conservation of tropical forests: forty-four countries that either produce or consume tropical-forest products are members, and one of these is Malaysia. In Sarawak, the Malaysian portion of the island of Borneo, there is a formidable stand of important dipterocarp forest that will be totally logged out by soon after 2000 unless the intensity of production is reduced. After visiting Sarawak an ITTO-sponsored mission accordingly recommended that the cutting rate be modestly reduced from 43 to 30 million cubic feet a year over five years, that the size of the Permanent Forest Estate be increased, and that other protected areas be created.

At an ITTO meeting held in Yokohama in November 1990, representatives of Sarawak's native peoples gave further reason for the state and national governments to cut back. The logging concessions they had awarded to private companies were in violation of "our native customary land rights," and had severely damaged their water and food resources, their moving statement continued, and "appeals and discussions" with loggers and local authorities had been "useless." When the tribespeople, frustrated in their conventional efforts, moved to blockade the logging roads intruding on land they consider theirs, the consequences included many detentions and a new law declaring such obstruction a criminal offense. Since 1987, reported a group of nongovernmental organizations represented in Yokohama, 340 natives had been arrested for defending their lands.

In its rebuttal the Sarawak government noted that its principal economic policy is to "eradicate poverty" and that so many "well-paid jobs in the timber industry" are at stake that native opposition is, in fact, limited to a disgruntled few; that a slowdown in logging would not reduce the deforestation problem because newly unemployed natives would turn to shifting cultivation. Still, despite this defense of its old practices, Sarawak said it would accept the ITTO mission's recommendations. The Malaysian government, emphasizing that it had invited ITTO to Sarawak, and suavely suggesting that national forest resources need to be "managed for the full range of benefits that they provide," also pledged its intent to implement the mission's recommendations. Japan, a leading consumer of Malaysian hardwoods, pledged $6 million in support of the work. But Malaysia, acting in the spirit of ul-Haq, strongly resisted proposals that a firm timetable be set for its actions and waffled on suggestions for external monitoring of progress. The ITTO Council's resolution on Sarawak likewise failed to specify an agenda for action, causing one NGO observer to comment: "We should abandon any illusion that this political forum will ever be capable of compelling compliance with strong measures contrary to any government's perceived self-interest."

Malaysia's ambivalence is one of countless examples of how national economic policies, often made with the laudable intentions of creating jobs and earning export revenues, have led to economic dead ends and environmental degradation. In the 1950s, persuaded that "import substitution" would be the key to rapid development, many countries stressed industrialization. The steel plant, no matter how uneconomic, represented prestige and advancement. Pressure on the rural sector, then light, increased when these import substitution programs failed to achieve the desired results and export promotion became the new vogue. But developing countries need foreign exchange to purchase manufactured products and oil, so they often made expedient but environmentally negative choices about what crops to produce for the export market.

Indiscriminate use of hazardous chemicals frequently results. According to the Latin American and Caribbean Commission on Environment and Development, "approximately 75 percent of the pesticides used in Central America are either prohibited or restricted in the U.S." The commission's report goes on to state that, despite the general unavailability of credit to poor farmers, Central America nevertheless ranks number one in per capita use of pesticides. The "excessive and careless use" of these and other agrochemicals has caused many thousands of cases of chemical poisoning and dangerous residue levels in water supplies and food chains.

The developing countries' efforts to escape from these environmental traps are constrained by the habit of doggedly depending on a single agricultural product—a habit that tends to lessen soil quality and prolongs dependency on fickle world tastes and volatile market prices. The Central American beef industry is a good example. Expansion of the fast-food trade, beginning in the 1960s in the United States, created growing demand for lean Central American beef. The governments of many of the region's countries, such as Costa Rica—wanting foreign exchange for imports, debt servicing, and funds for development— were eager to offer incentives to those wishing to invest in cattle. Through land-ownership laws that encouraged the "improving" of land by clearing, often to be sold directly into pasture, through low-interest loans, and through government investment in the necessary infrastructure, the beef industry grew; Costa Rica's beef exports to the United States eventually surpassed those of any other nation.

From a short-term economic perspective these decisions seemed to make sense. But the overemphasis on cattle led to record levels of deforestation, water shortages, siltation because of the erosive effects of overgrazing, and depletion of the soil. Simultaneously, more benign forms of agriculture that would have helped to feed Costa Ricans were neglected. *Campesinos* who had practiced swidden farming on what became pasture were forced onto even more unstable land, often found on steep hillsides subject to erosion and landslides.

Because of changing U.S. food preferences, Costa Rica no longer enjoys the same high levels of U.S. demand for its beef. Nonetheless, it is left with the aftermath: denuded land and depleted soil. By as early as 1983, according to a World Resources Institute report, only 17 percent of Costa Rica's original forest cover remained. Pastures ("the worst and least sustainable use of tropical forest," according to the ecologist Robert J. A. Goodland of the World Bank) covered half the nation's arable land. Although the need to diversify is understood, introducing new crops on the degraded land is not an easy task.

In Botswana, the colonial government established a beef industry, first in response to the growing South African market, later to fulfill demand for lean grass-fed beef in the European Community, which provided preferential trade arrangements and ended up consuming two-thirds of what Botswana could produce. Since cattle were not well suited to the environment, however, large landholdings were almost essential to recoup losses due to water shortages. As a result, more and more land was put into pasture while people and other animals suffered: Botswana's once vast wildebeest population has been reduced to some 10 percent of its original size.

In Thailand, cassava, or manioc, of the sort grown around Khao Yai National Park, offers a classic example of how an export crop can constitute a mixed blessing. Cassava is a dietary staple in many poor countries, but it is not important to the citizens of Thailand, which enjoys a surplus of other, more nutritious foodstuffs. So the cassava flour is converted into pellets and chips and sold, almost entirely in Western Europe, as feed for livestock. Overall cassava production has grown fivefold since 1973. Between 1983 and 1989, exports of this commodity more than tripled. Many poor small farmers have been the beneficiaries of this boom. The plant grows on poor soil, is well adapted to low or erratic rainfall, and in Asia resists all but a few pests even if pesticides are not applied to it.

Yet at least 60 percent of the land used to grow cassava in Thailand was once tropical forest, which now occupies only a small fraction of the nation's land surface, and profitable cassava cultivation has forced subsistence farmers to move deeper into the forest in order to survive. Cassava is therefore a principal contributor in Thailand to the usual consequences of tropical deforestation: soil erosion, watershed disruption, microclimatic change. Grown as it usually is in Thailand—as a monoculture, without fertilizer, by small farmers—the crop may also deplete the soil's nutrient supplies and bring about deterioration of its structure. In short, cassava is not here a sustainable crop without major changes in how it is cultivated.

By diversifying, some countries have begun to work their way out of the export monoculture trap. The small African nation of The Gambia, which once relied almost entirely on peanuts to generate foreign exchange, has greatly reduced its dependence on that monoculture for export earnings. Judicious diversification can also help to regenerate soil: the peanut plant is itself a legume, fixing nitrogen in the earth where it grows. Industrialization is another way of taking pressure off the land, creating job opportunities for people who might otherwise invade forests for subsistence farming, and supplying capital for fortified social services. The example of Thailand, however, raises a question about the longer-term consequences of the strategy. In this prospering country, land values have risen dramatically—as much as fiftyfold in some areas over the last several years. As in the United States, the amount of land allocated to any form of agriculture is diminishing as manufacturing, services, and other nonfarm activities become ever stronger in the national economy. If industrialization is to represent an environmental gain, however, the factories themselves must not be allowed to be heavy polluters, as they still are in many parts of the world. Whether this can be accomplished, whether developing countries will manage not to repeat the environmental follies that industrial nations have already committed, remains an open question and a dangerous gamble. But it must not be forgotten that clean industry and a rural agriculture built around villages is the optimum way for the South to confront the reality of fast-rising populations.

Fortunately, fresh ideas gaining currency in some quarters of the South tilt more toward this sort of integration than back to ul-Haq's pre-Founex disregard of the environment. *Our Own Agenda,* the thoughtful report that the Latin American and Caribbean Commission on Development and Environment issued in 1990, underscores the point. It contains frank and clear environmental recommendations that will be in the region's interest in the decades to come. In a report issued in mid-1990, the South Commission, a group of leaders from developing countries, suggests similar approaches. This sober and balanced document, entitled *The Challenge of the South,* encourages Third World nations to decentralize and to pay far greater attention to the principles of sustainability:

> The North is responsible for the bulk of the damage to the environment because of its wasteful life-style. However, poverty is also a great degrader of the environment, and an effective strategy for the removal of poverty is, in the final analysis, a strategy for protecting the environment. . . . Ecologically viable patterns of

development will in many cases need more resources in the short run than conventional development strategies. But this cannot be an argument for not taking a serious view of environmental degradation. To do so would amount to condemning the South to an insecure future in the twenty-first century.

Brazil, of all countries, seems at last to be heeding these messages. At the time of the 1972 Stockholm conference, says José Goldemberg, the fervent environmentalist serving in 1991 as his government's cabinet-level Secretary for Science and Technology, the need for jobs was so critical that " 'development first, then worry about the environment' was the only position Brazil could take, and it did." At Stockholm the Brazilian delegation shocked others with their anti-environmentalism. Their warm welcome for imported pollution permitted an overconcentration of chemical plants in the small coastal town of Cubatão that made its "Valley of Death" one of the world's most dangerously contaminated places. Pressure from Brasília as well as from Washington led to the debacle of the Amazonian development effort during the 1980s. Just a few years ago, the caretaker regime of President José Sarney, reacting nationalistically to misinterpreted comments by visiting U.S. politicians, defiantly told the world that only Brazil would set policy for the deteriorating basin.

Still, even this weak government managed to remove some of the incentives that had encouraged unwise migrations to Amazonia. Functioning in a region not known for observing legal niceties, Sarney's justice officials also started the unusual process that brought the rubber-tapper Chico Mendes's killer to trial and, ultimately, conviction. At Cubatão, 90 percent of the pollution was removed in a vigorous campaign. The new spirit got another boost when in 1990, reflecting a dramatic swing in public opinion, incoming President Fernando Collor de Mello announced further improvements in Amazon policy and unexpectedly appointed Goldemberg and another dedicated environmentalist, José Lutzenberger, to key government positions. In the United States the equivalent of Lutzenberger's appointment as Environment Secretary would be to name the head of Greenpeace as Environmental Protection Agency administrator. The conversion, many would argue, is still only skin deep—*p'ra inglês ver* (for British eyes), as a local cynic would suggest. For every Lutzenberger there is a *boto*. But the start that Brazil has made is nonetheless encouraging.

For all the reasons outlined in this chapter, the challenge of finding sustainable ways to help the poor in the rural tropics is vastly complicated by how their societies are organized. As the World Bank's Rural Development report puts it: "Indifference to the plight of the rural poor could be as destructive as outright exploitation of them." But while Southern attitudes and policies have begun to change, this shift alone is far from enough to carry the day. As the South Commission forcibly states, industrial nations as well will need to make major adjustments in their economic policies and practices, which affect all countries, and which touch the lives and economies of poor farmers in remote corners of the rural tropics. The next chapter reviews a series of these connections.

CHAPTER 10

২✦

Distant Thunder

Early in this century, colonial planters in Antigua grew sugar to grace English tea tables. Though the plant was originally from Asia, it thrived in Antigua despite the island's poor soil and fluctuating climate. It produced good yields and, for slaves as well as masters, fringe benefits ranging from bagasse (sugarcane residue used as fuel for cooking) to rum. Today in Antigua, where expanses of forest once rippled in the easterly trade winds, goats and chickens now scrabble on bare brown hardpan. Except in landscaped tourist areas, the island is largely a desert. The reason is not only the Antiguan public's distaste for work in the sugar fields, a practice that evokes images of servitude, but also that the world market for cane sugar has withered.

Because of tightening U.S. quotas imposed to protect domestic producers, U.S. sugar imports from the Caribbean Basin dropped 73 percent from a 1975–81 average of 1.66 million tons a year to 442,200 tons in 1989. Despite high U.S. prices, the net loss to the region was $312 million in 1989, according to the Overseas Development Council. While the U.S.-sponsored Caribbean Basin Initiative is said to have added up to 136,000 jobs between 1983 and 1988, the decline in quotas cost the region 400,000 jobs over the same period. European Community sugar

Cutting cane in the Caribbean:
a dwindling trade

policy compounds the problem; through it Western Europe has become a subsidized net exporter (of beet sugar, not cane) and has flooded the global market; developing-country producers suffer except for the ex-colonies of France and the United Kingdom, whose output has long-term protection under the Lomé Convention. In part also because soft-drink producers have switched to high-fructose corn syrup, a product that is economically competitive in the United States only because of the artificially high United States prices for cane sugar, global demand for cane sugar has dropped 25 percent from its peak despite the world's rising population.

On some Caribbean islands, one result of the inability to sell sugar has been diversification into export crops that do greater environmental damage. Banana trees, which require substantial chemical inputs, now climb high up the steep hillsides of Dominca, St. Lucia, and St. Vincent and cause erosion and watershed problems. More commonly, nothing has replaced sugar's dominance, and on islands where growth in tourism has failed to make up for lagging agriculture the result has been spreading poverty and mass out-migration. Late in the 1980s, as a direct consequence of sugar policies controlled elsewhere, the hard-pressed Dominican Republic's efficient sugar industry reduced production by 40 percent. Its U.S. quota had been drastically lowered and producers could not compete internationally, where prices during the 1980s remained no more than half those that prevail in the protected U.S. market. Efforts to generate equivalent returns from non-traditional crops proved unsuccessful and, in some instances, environmentally harmful. In current dollars, per capita GNP sank to two-thirds its 1980 level. Many farm workers left the country: late in the 1980s the Dominican Republic became the world's top supplier of emigrants to the New York City area.

Sugar is but one example of how the economies and the environments of poor countries are deeply affected by the policies and practices of people and institutions in advanced nations. Rich countries control the mechanisms that govern world trade in farm and other commodities, decide how and where public and private investment capital shall be allocated, and own the problem of developing-country debts. During the 1980s all these forces worked against the developing world. Between 1980 and 1987, the prices of thirty-three commodities monitored by the World Bank fell by 40 percent to the lowest levels since the Great Depression; the cost to developing countries was scores of billions of dollars per year in lost sales and depressed earnings.[1] Total developing-country debt reached the staggering level of $1.3 trillion in 1991; the Philippines owed $30 billion, a figure representing 87 percent of the nation's entire GNP. Capital flows turned sharply negative, with the poor paying the rich about $50 billion a year by 1989. Former West German Chancellor Willy Brandt called this trend "a blood transfusion from the sick to the healthy." No quest for sustain-

---

1. According to calculations made from World Bank figures by Maria de Lourdes Davies de Freitas, who served on the Latin American and Caribbean Commission on Development and Environment, the total may reach $100 billion a year.

able economic growth in the rural tropics can fully succeed without Northern cooperation in reversing these patterns.

In January 1991, just before the hostilities broke out in the Persian Gulf, a group of concerned individuals reviewed the relationship between global economics and sustainable development in the rural Third World. During a three-day colloquium in New York co-sponsored by the Council on Foreign Relations and the World Resources Institute, the forty-one participants—environmentalists, foreign affairs scholars, businesspeople, and representatives of international organizations— explored the ways the North might respond to the economic and environmental needs of the rural tropics. Much of what follows reflects the colloquium's mood and content.

The developed world's high domestic farm prices and protectionism contribute massively to what the agricultural economist G. Edward Schuh, dean of the Hubert H. Humphrey Institute of Public Affairs at the University of Minnesota, terms "a grossly inefficient global agriculture" in which rich countries produce too much food, poor countries too little, and the environment suffers everywhere. The generous subsidies that rich nations often give to their own farmers (which in the twenty-four wealthiest of them amount to some $300 billion a year, or six times what they provide in official aid to developing countries) lie at the heart of the problem. Feedlot cattle-raising programs in the European Community helped to create a vast artificial market for Thai cassava. The same pull-factor caused much fertile farmland in southern Brazil to be converted from foodstuffs for domestic consumption to soybeans for export. Environmental and economic difficulties arise not only from what developed countries choose to buy from the South but also from what they choose to sell. In Togo, a carefully designed program to encourage the raising of small ruminants was destroyed when the EC decided to supply the nation with subsidized meat. The dumping—selling excess production at a very low price—of rice and other basic commodities undermines local balanced rural development.

Developing countries, Schuh adds, compound the problem by overvaluing the foreign-exchange rates for their currencies, levying export taxes on farm products, and shifting the domestic terms of trade against the agricultural sector. The distortions affect large-scale farmers less severely than less competitive small farmers, who are squeezed off fertile lands and into marginal areas, where they cannot help inflicting environmental damage. Land values drop, and landowners' incentives to husband their resources are reduced. Protectionism by developed countries against imports of labor-intensive manufactured products also intensifies the stress on the rural South. "The dumping from the European Community and the United States makes global prices even lower than they would otherwise be," says Schuh. "Developing countries become net importers of what they could be producing for themselves, and because of the cheap imports they do not need to make more rational policy at home. And the fact that they continue to import means that it remains easier for developed countries to continue to practice their predatory or dumping policies. They've developed a nice little symbiotic relationship that is very difficult to change."

So the South is playing the game, but the North still sets the rules. World trade of most sorts is regulated through the General Agreement on Trade and Tariffs (GATT), a club of trading nations whose policies have until recently been established with no regard to environmental considerations. Within the GATT structure, in ponderous multi-year "rounds" of negotiation, basic decisions have been made about matters affecting some 85 percent of the total volume of some $4 trillion in annual international trade. While the GATT served its purpose well during the early years after it was founded in 1947, many have more recently found fault with its structure—and in particular with regard to farm trade. Said Roger B. Porter, assistant to President Bush for economic and domestic policy, in a recent speech:

> The GATT rules on agriculture, for which the U.S. shares blame as a principal author, have been widely discredited and are in need of drastic revision. They have permitted a huge expansion of farm subsidies, encouraged massive overproduction of certain agricultural commodities, and fostered trade barriers that permit inefficient producers to exclude competitive imports.

Developing countries have seldom had much of a voice at GATT discussions, which long centered not on how these countries' producers could gain greater access to the international economy, but on how rich nations could sell more to them. Over the course of the latest of these sessions, the Uruguay Round that began in Punta del Este in 1986, the South grew stronger as a result of its increasing role in world trade. As strapped as they are, developing countries currently manage to buy about 40 percent of all U.S. exports, and the figure could climb to 50 percent if their economic health were to improve. For the United States economy, conversely, these markets are of critical importance if U.S. exports ("our most important product," the analyst Paula Stern said) are to grow as rapidly as is hoped. As the Uruguay Round progressed, it became evident that advanced trading nations would gain even greater access to the South's rapidly expanding high-technology and service-sector markets only if, in return, they offered better terms of trade in food and textiles, over the objections of strongly protectionist domestic lobbies. Complaints from the North that their "intellectual property rights" were being violated by cut-rate pirate producers—of products ranging from pills to audio cassettes—were met with well-reasoned counter-arguments that such genetic resources as fresh germ plasm for new hybrid plants, which are the intellectual property of native peoples in poor countries, are in jeopardy on the same grounds.

The United States pressed hard for liberalization of agricultural trade during the Uruguay Round's early stages. Backed by a consortium of fourteen agriculture exporting countries called the Cairns group, it originally called for the removal of all forms of farm support within ten years. Later, unyielding Western European opposition moved the United States to modify this proposal to a 90 percent reduction in export subsidies and a 75 percent cut in domestic price supports. Home to ten million farmers (compared with two million in the United States), the European Community stalled for months, then countered with a suggestion that overall support be cut 30 percent; it made no mention of reducing in export subsidies or easing import restrictions. Other liberalization measures that have been proposed during the Uruguay Round include: less protection for processing industries in the North, particularly in agribusiness, minerals, and timbers; less dumping of farm surpluses in the developing world; more market access for manufactures from developing countries, in order to lessen the degree of their dependence on export crops.

As of mid-1991, the Uruguay Round faced an uncertain future. Its extension, for perhaps two years, would give negotiators a further chance to work out these differences. But without the fast-track procedure that would require the United States Congress to vote "up or down" on trade packages without amending them, domestic lobbyists for special interests (e.g., textiles, farm goods) were likely to prevent the passage of a new program that would be acceptable to other members of the GATT. The congressional votes in May 1991, which sanctioned the use of the fast track, instantly prolonged the Uruguay Round and greatly increased the likelihood of freer trade. Outside the GATT, opportunities to pursue the goal of trade liberalization by means of regional trade agreements will always exist.

For growers of export crops in developing countries, the movement toward freer trade within the GATT system could bring major economic benefits in the form of higher world market prices. Opinions vary, however, as to the environmental consequences of such a shift. Optimists believe that the combined factors—improved returns from the best lands, more international market access for manufactured and farm goods, technical assistance—could spare steep hillsides and tropical forests *and* create jobs. Others doubt that such fortuitous synergy will be the result. The agricultural economist Ernst Lutz, of the World Bank, argues that high unemployment and high population growth will nullify the "offsetting effect," as Schuh has termed it, and that the net environmental result will be negative.

On other grounds, environmentalists harbor apprehensions about liberalized trade under the GATT. A "harmonization" of environmental rules that would facilitate trade might also compel many nations to accept international standards on food safety and pesticides or insecticides that are far less stringent than their own established standards. The United Nations–administered Codex Alimentarius, for example, accepts far higher concentrations of DDT and other dangerous chemicals than U.S. regulations do. The international ban on trade in ivory and other products derived from endangered wildlife, enthusiastically supported by most environmental groups, is subject to challenge under GATT rules. New rules might make it easier for unilateral import bans imposed for environmental reasons to be interpreted within the GATT as protection for domestic industries.

Global agricultural trade: reforms required

Trade in tropical timber products, a principal reason the global rate of tropical deforestation doubled during the 1980s from already un- sustainable levels, gives us a clear example of how the GATT's rules can work against environmental stability. One of the goals of the In- ternational Tropical Timber Organization (ITTO), which loosely reg- ulates this trade, is the achievement of sustainable tropical-forest management. Most of the forty-seven nations that are ITTO members, and have signed an agreement pledging to develop domestic policies toward this end, are also members of the GATT. Yet in making this commitment, acccording to a WWF paper presented at the 1990 ITTO meeting in Yokohama, they risk provoking challenges that are valid under the GATT:

An established principle of the GATT is that trade restrictions cannot be used to discriminate between "like products" on the basis of the method of production. This means that signatories to the GATT cannot use trade tariffs, quotas or bans to favour trade in sustainably rather than unsustainably produced tropical timber.

Yet the ITTO objective . . . will not be achieved unless trade measures which do precisely this are implemented.

At the Yokohama meeting, the WFF proposed that the ITTO request from the GATT a waiver from regulations interfering with the organization's quest for tropical forestry sustainability, and remind member countries of their sovereignty with regard to their own forest resources. To avoid conflict between environmental goals and trade liberalization objectives under the GATT, it will often be necessary to seek this sort of exception.

The very existence of the GATT, as the essential vehicle for trade reform, complicates the task. It would be difficult to work through the GATT toward separate improvements in the way any single commodity, sugar for instance, is traded. "To negotiate anything within the GATT," says Edward Schuh, "you have to negotiate everything." Like it or lump it, though, the GATT is there, and environmentalists cannot wish it away. The GATT would be the logical administrator if a new code of conduct to govern perilous sectors of North-South trade were put in place. "Hazardous substances and wastes represent a trade issue," says Schuh. "There's lots of attention to it, but not much interest in moving it along. What we really need is an environmental code, parallel to the disciplines and codes that we have in the GATT trading system, to prescribe what countries can and cannot do in relation to this form of dumping." *Faute de mieux,* the GATT is where to lodge the code.

Beyond the GATT, some hope for more comprehensive change. In a recent article, the attorney Eric Christensen of the Natural Resources Defense Council argued that "the laws of international trade should be fundamentally restructured to incorporate environmental protection, as well as economic growth, as a goal," and also called for amendments in international trade agreements that would "recognize the legitimacy of national laws aimed at environmental protection."[2] Jim MacNeill, a Canadian environmentalist who served as secretary-general of the Brundtland Commission, advocates intensifying the industrial nations' commitment to recycling efforts as a means of re-

2. Pesticide Regulation and International Trade," *Environment*, Vol 32, No. 9, (November 1990).

ducing their dependence on fresh supplies of raw materials. Structural adjustments within OECD nations, particularly in agriculture, would be helpful—aiming for an overall decrease in agricultural protectionism and in subsidized exports of farm surpluses. Paying off small numbers of domestic workers in obsolete industries is often far more cost-effective, and more helpful to consumers, than doomed efforts to make them competitive.

As to *public* investment in the rural tropics, as I have suggested in previous chapters, there is no development finance or development assistance agency that has not recently taken internal measures to improve the environmental quality of its work. Sector guidelines, new lending commitments, additions to staff, and closer working relations with environmental organizations are all part of the accepted modus operandi. Yet, for all the promise of these innovations, doubts linger about the overall effectiveness of donors' new environmental efforts. Even the moderate wing expresses frustration with the rate of progress. Says Robert O. Blake, a former diplomat and a founder of a private group called the Committee on Agricultural Sustainability for Developing Countries: "The development agencies haven't really tried on sustainable growth even though they have the potential, the resources, and the leadership."

An equally fundamental problem is the *quantity* of overseas development assistance (ODA). Total bilateral and multilateral ODA from the United States in 1989 represented only 0.15 percent of GNP. This level, the lowest ever recorded, placed the United States in seventeenth (last) place among the richest nations in the extent of its total contribution as a share of GNP. The current sentiment, both in the executive and in the legislative branches of government, is to view bilateral assistance programs not as an altruistic vehicle but rather as a means of promoting United States trade.

Other rich nations' generosity is only marginally greater. In 1989 the members of the OECD's Development Assistance Committee (DAC) collectively provided a total of $46.7 billion—only 0.33 percent of GNP, or one-third of the 1 percent mark that, with such passion, Robert McNamara strived to achieve two decades ago. Excluding the United States and Japan, OECD was quick to note in a 1990 report, the DAC group's share rose to 0.51 percent of GNP. This is grievously inadequate in relation to what the developing world faces merely in managing its mammoth debts, let alone allocating resources to the economic growth that its fast-growing populations require. Even if much aid money is poorly used or utterly wasted, more funds are essential for the basic needs of the poorest nations, let alone progress.

Many observers stress the importance of reestablishing a constituency in support of the very concept of foreign aid such as existed, in the United States and other developed countries, in the 1950s and 1960s. "There's little hope today of getting public support in the United States for foreign aid to strengthen Third World economies," says James Gustave Speth of the World Resources Institute. "In fact it's probably a turnoff for many people. It threatens jobs. It means trouble. It is something that people would rather not think about." Many people have lost faith in the development idea, says Speth's colleague, the economist Robert Repetto, since after thirty years it appeared not to have been successful. Yet many people maintain a stubborn belief in the myth of American generosity even though the facts have been otherwise for two decades, and they think they do not have to fight for development. The commitment to foreign aid must be reformulated and reexpressed to incorporate more current public concerns. Says Speth: "If you talk to people in terms of environmental cooperation, alleviating poverty, forty thousand children dying and hundreds of species being lost every day, of land being reduced in terms of its productive capacity—then you can really communicate." Sharon L. Camp of the Population Crisis Committee agrees. "There's a real well of public support for the United States helping to solve world problems like stabilizing the population, saving children, and preserving the environment," she says. "We need to get these things down where the hogs can get at them: set measurable goals and explain them, establish better collaborative relationships, get a narrow focus on the world problems that we want to solve, and *explain* these objectives. The press is very important in all this." Adds Michael Gucovsky of the United Nations Development Program: "We need to demonstrate that a dollar spent on multilateral programs is cost-effective, that the self-interest of the United States is linked to the global environment, to population questions, to a stable political and economic world. I'm convinced that the facts support this."

Of equally basic importance, according to such economists as Repetto, David Pearce in the United Kingdom, and Herman Daly at the World Bank itself, would be aid donors' adoption of new accounting principles in the cost-benefit analyses that are the basis for most of the decisions they make. Under the current system, natural resources are not depreciated, as are capital goods such as buildings or machines, in calculations of national income. Nor is any cost ascribed to the environmental damage that occurs as minerals, trees, or other resources are harvested and brought to the market. Many environmental economists have come to believe that recalculating biological and resource losses to reflect their real costs would make all the difference. Putting true values on biodiversity setbacks, Repetto thinks, is as difficult and as important a task as there is for the environmental community.

Meanwhile it is equally important to get pressure on aid agencies to focus more intently on rural questions. "In the five years that I was at OECD," says Joseph C. Wheeler, then chairman of its Development Assistance Committee (DAC), "there was never a meeting solely concerned with agriculture. There is a need to get a coalition pointing in rather specific ways at the development community, to see if we can't get this priority back again. It's a disaster. When you consider that we're not meeting nutritional needs (on a shrinking base of arable land), it is imperative to refocus on this sector." He particularly urges aid agencies to support specific and neglected aspects of rural development: refining technologies to improve efficiency, emphasizing production on the best lands, strengthening infrastructure and service institutions, including regional agricultural research centers. Blake deplores the drift of USAID away from support for basic farming and toward food processing ("the business side") and suggests that congressional intervention might be the best way to arrest it.

Plentiful enough in earlier decades though not always welcomed, *private* investment in the South dried up in the 1980s as a direct consequence of the debt crisis and the loss of corporate confidence in Third World economies. What had formerly been a net overall inflow of capital to developing countries turned negative in 1982 and has remained so ever since. Given the dismal history of development in the 1980s, a restoration of the private flows is of critical importance. It is the "magic bullet," says the former Mobil attorney William A. Nitze, more recently an environmentalist, that he thinks can hit the bull's-eye of sustainable growth. History also gives us ample evidence that foreign investors will disregard the environmental consequences of their activities, however, and suggests that developing countries' search for sustainability and their desire for private foreign capital do not always go hand in hand.

The end of the colonial era hardly put to rest the saga of environmentally unsound corporate adventurism. An ill-starred effort by the Le Tourneau group to "tame" the Peruvian Amazon during the 1960s left only rusting machinery on the ground. In greatly modified form, the late shipping executive Daniel K. Ludwig's impetuous attempt to establish pulpwood plantations and to grow rice along Brazil's Jarí River carries on in impeccable Brazilian hands. But after two decades of prodigious investments of capital and human talent that few others can afford, this immense project has only begun to break even, although many of its least promising experiments have been abandoned. Although environmental damage along the Jarí has been slight—you can argue, in fact, that what has been learned there has spared other parts of the basin—the outcome also illustrates a temperate-world naïveté about tropical ecology as profound as that of the East African groundnut schemers. Likewise, Japanese investors paid little heed to the health of important coral-reef ecosystems when, in the late 1970s, they planned a major oil transshipment facility for the Western Pacific Palau Islands. The spreading banana monocultures of the Caribbean and Central America cause deforestation, watershed disruption, erosion, and the dispersal of toxic chemicals. Western European and Japanese corporations, whose countries constitute 90 percent of the global market for tropical hardwoods, are intimately implicated in the deforestation of the Philippines, Thailand, Malaysia, and Indonesia.

Still, the greening of corporate behavior has been a remarkable phenomenon of recent years. Large corporations have been ever more beset by environmentalists, government regulators, Wall Street fund managers, consumers with deepening environmental awareness affecting their buying habits, and even their own employees. Having also suffered from the Bhopal catastrophe in India, oil spills, and other well-publicized setbacks, they began to react and even to anticipate their problems. The businessman Maurice Strong, secretary-general for the 1972 Stockholm Conference on the Human Environment and also for the United Nations 1992 "Earth Summit," is impressed. "There's been a tremendous increase in the number of businesspeople who are taking a longer view," he says. "The managers of the big companies have truly internalized the environmental imperative," says Nitze. "Interview the chief executive officers of the principal U.S., European, or Japanese corporations today, and you'll find a level of awareness about the environmental agenda that simply didn't exist even ten years ago. In many areas individual CEOs, like Ed Woolard of Du Pont or the management of 3M, have become environmental leaders in their communities. They are ahead of government, at least the White House, in terms of their willingness to reshape policies in order to protect the environment." No longer do corporate executives so patly assume that environmental progress will require economic sacrifice. More typically, they tell you how energy efficiency has helped the company gain a competitive edge.

Less well understood is how much this generally more circumspect attitude toward the environment applies to corporate operations and investments in poor countries. In the least developed areas of the tropics, where biological diversity is concentrated and where government regulations and procedures are relatively loose, investor interest is intent upon capital-intensive, large-scale ventures to export food and raw materials back to the industrial world. This sort of investment— typically in agribusiness, mining, forestry, or oil—harms the environment even if the best available technologies are applied. The installations are so far off the beaten track, moreover, that local managers can wink at the rules.

Neither host-country governments nor environmental groups have been able to put up much resistance to large projects involving major degradation. Keen to secure the capital investment, host-country governments have looked the other way when environmental issues were raised. And environmental NGOs in developing countries have been small in number, size, and influence, though the situation is now fast changing. Not even the militant United States or multinational conservation groups, successful in campaigning against offending corporations at home, have much influenced the environmental quality of corporate investment in developing countries. "They are very hard to get at," says one Sierra Club activist.

Some corporations have on their own maintained high environmental standards in remote regions of the developing world. Several mining companies working in Amazonia are examples. In Thailand, Uniroyal Chemical walked away from a promising deal when its local partner refused to commit to the U.S. company's environmental standards. In other instances, environmentalist lobbying has helped persuade companies to withdraw from controversial ventures for which they had received governmental approval. Coca-Cola dropped a citrus plantation in Belize that would have caused the loss of some relatively undistinguished tropical forest. As noted in Chapter 5, Scott Paper abandoned plans to develop a big pulp-and-paper complex in Indonesia's Irian Jaya province. In the future, local laws and regulatory mechanisms will stiffen in many countries; in the meantime, there is no guarantee that this kind of voluntary action will be commonplace among investors.

To increase the likelihood that U.S. corporations will adhere to green principles, Robert Repetto has recommended that the World Bank's International Finance Corporation and the U.S. government's Overseas Private Investment Corporation (OPIC) give "special attention to commercially feasible investments that promote sustainable development." OPIC, which issues political-risk and other forms of insurance as well as loans to American companies investing in the developing world, currently claims to follow "World Bank rules" on environmental quality. But such a statement, on the part of this profit-making government corporation, is not wholly reassuring. Even less so is one OPIC official's admission that its two-person environmental staff's monitoring tends to be passive, not active. In order for OPIC to carry out the mandate suggested, in other words, internal adjustments are required.

In the absence of governmental restraints, several private groups have recently composed codes of conduct. In 1989 the U.S.-based Coalition for Environmentally Responsible Economies (CERES)—made up of pension funds, church groups, and other nonprofits—laid down a ten-point set of guidelines. The CERES criteria, known as the Valdez Principles, are currently being advocated at shareholders' meetings in the United States, and are gaining international currency as well. Corporations—which would rather establish their own criteria than be pressured to respond to rules set by others—have swung into action as well. After the Bhopal disaster in 1989, the U.S. Chemical Manufacturers Association drew up a set of "responsible care" principles, to which companies must pledge adherence in order to qualify for membership. The American Petroleum Institute and the International Chamber of Commerce have similar projects under way.

Also involved is the Global Environmental Management Initiative (GEMI), a godchild of twenty-one large U.S.-based corporations whose purpose is to gather and disseminate information on environmental management. While GEMI remains vague about how it will relate to developing countries, it pledges a "worldwide" program to enhance the environmental performance of business, improve environmental management, and encourage sustainable development. It is still small, with a 1990–91 budget of $675,000, but GEMI's very existence manifests a new stirring in large corporate boardrooms. In Europe the multinational Business Committee for Sustainable Development worked closely with Strong's "Earth Summit" secretariat to give the private sector a presence and a voice in Rio. Canada, Germany, and Japan are among other countries that have new environmental business associations.

For those who question whether self-policing mechanisms will "control" the private sector, public-private partnerships are a better solution. One model is the 1987 Montreal Protocol, limiting the use of the man-made chemicals called chlorofluorocarbons (CFCs) that cause ozone depletion when they leak into the atmosphere. In London in 1990, ninety-two nations, including a reluctant United States, took the dramatic step of agreeing on a timetable for the termination of all CFC usage. While governments signed the 1987 agreement and subsequent modifications that tightened it—though not enough to rid the world of the problem, since scientists have reported spreading ozone depletion—their doing so would have been difficult if not impossible if they had not had the support of large corporations like Du Pont that have manufactured the products. "When industry accepted the idea of the Montreal Protocol," says William Nitze, "it actually *did* a lot of the planning for the CFC phaseout, and for the development of substitutes, in conjunction with the U.S. government. I hope the same kind of thing will happen with regard to toxic chemicals—not just their registration, but programs for licensing, storing, and handling them.

And I can see the same principles being applied to the techniques of integrated pest management, though high returns would have to be allowed because the payout would occur only over the long term."

Other forms of partnership between corporations and governments or aid agencies offer similar potential, especially in the important field of technology transfer. Already, several models are at work. In India, USAID supports the Program for the Acceleration of Commercial Energy Research, which tries to encourage energy efficiency by making new technologies available to local enterprise. In a controversial but important move the World Health Organization extended financial support to Roussel Uclaf, a French drug company, to undertake clinical trials of RU-486, the so-called abortion pill, in return for which the manufacturer agreed to market the drug in developing countries at an affordable price. Another interesting model is Fundación Chile (FCh), a mixed-enterprise corporation whose purpose is to facilitate Chilean access to advanced nations' technical know-how. FCh was established in 1976 as a means of resolving a $50 million difference of opinion between the ITT Corporation and the Pinochet regime as to the value of ITT properties that had been expropriated by Pinochet's predecessor, Salvador Allende. To avoid a stalemate, the company and the government eventually agreed to split the difference and invest $25 million each in a mutually beneficial activity. During its lifetime FCh has not only substantially increased its own net worth but also heightened the level of Chile's technology in many fields, from farming to fisheries to light manufacturing. Well-packaged fresh raspberries from Chile that show up year-round in North American markets are a tasty, if expensive, consequence of the Fundación's efforts.

There are many new ways for the public and private sectors to join forces. There is, for example, ample opportunity for private participation in the new Global Environment Facility (GEF). This experimental mechanism for funding sustainable development was established in 1990, under the supervision of the World Bank, with UNDP and the United Nations Environment Program (UNEP) as its partners. Sponsors expect GEF's initial subscription, of over $1 billion in capital from twenty-five countries, to increase substantially. Within GEF there is broad latitude for corporations to seek concessional funding for investment projects in a range of fields from forest management to making the transition from CFCs to other gases that are less harmful to the atmosphere.

Joan Martin-Brown, special representative of UNEP in Washington, suggests that companies as well as nonprofit groups compete for development assistance funds given to reforestation projects and other efforts to restore degraded ecosystems. "We need to throw away a lot of the old assumptions," she says. "One thing that must be stopped is the old isolation of private from public funds." The best way to get the corporate sector involved, says William Nitze, is to apply market forces to create "real public-private partnerships for sustainable development. Get the incentives right and a lot of this falls into place. Put a significant carbon or energy tax on in the United States and boy, you wait and see what happens! Put on an international carbon tax, then have transferable permits and really enforce the program—and you'll see a revolution in five years."

Among specific kinds of private investment in the rural tropics, forestry obviously needs special attention. Here the links between government and business are already so tight that defining responsibility on either side is all but impossible. Since neither ITTO nor the Tropical Forest Action Plan seems able to arrest tropical deforestation, which continues at a runaway pace, new management devices seem to be needed. The aid donors, who until recently perceived forestry in purely commercial terms, can be important enforcers: forestry loans from development finance agencies should follow TFAP guidelines and be linked to debt-reduction efforts, says Repetto. National government policy can also be influential. When Brazil offered tax breaks for reforestation, foreign investors participated enthusiastically.

Investors will still base their decisions on old-fashioned criteria. In older times, many statist Third World nations scared them away by placing restrictions on profit remittances and demanding that subsidiaries of foreign companies share equity with local partners. Now that the free market revolution has prevailed or at least begun in all but a handful of them, they are more lenient toward the private foreign investor. Still, the extent to which they will be willing to adjust "the rules of the game" in favor of investors is an important question. Now as always, investors are free to move on to the next poor country if they dislike financial or environmental curbs in the deal. Changes in

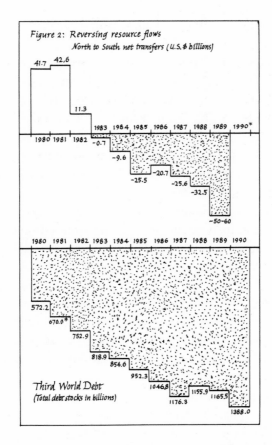

Figure 2: Reversing resource flows
North to South net transfers (U.S. $ billions)

Third World Debt
(Total debt stocks in billions)

industrial nations' economic policies also accelerate the flow of capital. Fiscal balance in the United States, it was stressed in the report of an international conference on the economics of sustainable development held in Washington in 1990, would reduce American demand for international capital and real borrowing costs, whereupon vast resources would, at least in principle, be available for investment in developing countries. Still, not even such broad modifications in both North and South can assure that future private investments in developing countries will be squeaky green.

During the 1970s, when successive "oil crises" beset the global economy and prices soared, the oil-producing nations racked up huge surpluses. These they deposited in Western banks, which then faced the problem of "recycling" the funds and earning their own profits on the differential between interest paid and interest earned. Developing countries snapped up the eagerly offered loans, and for a while the banks were pleased with the outcome. In 1977, fully one-fifth of Citibank's worldwide earnings came from interest payments and other operations, not in the United States, but in Brazil. The bubble burst, though, when developing countries were no longer able to service their growing debt and, in the 1980s, terms of trade continued the previous trend of working against them.

In 1982, Mexico proclaimed that it could no longer service its debt. Since then, at least forty countries have encountered similar difficulties. In 1989, the interest and dividends actually paid by developing countries (let alone what was owed but *not* paid) was just about equal to *all* the financial resources that they took in through bilateral and multilateral development assistance, export credits, and private capital flows. In 1991, the debt's face value surpassed $1.3 trillion. Annual debt service due amounted to $200 billion—quadruple the sum that the OECD nations spend each year on multilateral and bilateral development assistance.

The direct pressures of debt service, as well as a more general crisis of confidence among investors, have resulted in an even larger problem: the reversal in the direction of overall North-South capital flows. In 1981, $42.6 billion net moved from North to South. The following year, when Mexico defaulted, the reverse flow began. A net of about $50 billion currently moves in this "wrong" direction, much of it from the very countries least able to pay. Each year Latin America alone exports more than $400 billion of its capital—more than the region spends on education.[3] "Under such conditions," asks Alvaro Umaña Quesada, a former Natural Resources Minister of Costa Rica, "how can we expect to have development of any sort?"

Some of the debt is owed to banks, some to nations, some to multilateral agencies. Fifty percent of it is considered beyond the capacity of the borrowers to repay. Lenders, particularly the commercial banks that had bestowed the petrodollars so freely, realize they might never

---

3. Figure cited at the colloquium by Alvaro Umaña Quesada.

recover their loans. A lively global market has sprung up, in fact, in which deeply discounted loans (down to as little as ten cents per dollar of face value) are swapped for cash. In recent years the U.S. government has encouraged commercial banks to allow debtor countries, often working through nongovernmental organizations, to repurchase their debt at these discounted secondary-market rates. Debt-for-equity arrangements in which banks have converted debt into ownership of local enterprises in debtor nations have also become more commonplace.

Since the advent of the Reagan Administration's Baker Plan, which emphasized additional lending to developing countries to enable them to "grow out of debt," various mechanisms offering direct relief have also come into being. Under the Brady Plan in the United States, successor to the Baker Plan, some country-to-country loans have in recent years been forgiven. Several other nations have also given limited relief from bilateral debt. Canada has converted some loans to outright grants, and France has canceled some debts incurred by very poor African nations that in all likelihood could not repay them anyway. Although World Bank debts must be paid off if recipient countries wish to receive further loans, the Bank is the principal force in negotiating the structural adjustment programs that are designed to enable debtor nations to avoid defaults by means of export-led growth.

While any form of debt relief gives developing countries elbow room to address environmental problems if they wish to, in most instances they have no obligation to do so. Sometimes, in fact, an acceleration of environmental degradation has occurred in rural areas where the emphasis that adjustment assistance places on exports often translates very directly into larger harvests of trees from already depleting forests, more intensive cultivation in marginal areas, or speedier extraction of unrenewable minerals and oil. The need to export increases pressures on developing countries to farm lands that should be left untouched to protect watersheds or prevent erosion, and to use environmentally unsound agricultural chemicals that have negative effects ashore as well as on important marine environments in the coastal zone.

Cuts in government spending—another structural adjustment staple—inhibit the capabilities of environmental management agencies.

Without the staff to monitor and enforce them, environmental laws and regulations mean little. For want of funds, many national parks meant to protect biodiversity lack proper management. While Brazil's Collor government has shifted away from some policies that contribute directly to Amazonian devastation, José Lutzenberger, the nation's outspoken, cabinet-level Environment Secretary, must struggle forward on a ludicrously inadequate budget for reasons having much to do with debt burden. For want of personnel, most of the country's national parks are unmanaged and riddled with gold miners, slash-and-burn squatters, and others doing grave environmental damage even in areas that on paper enjoy special protection.

Nigeria provides a textbook example of how structural adjustment can lead to environmental instability. There, when oil revenues collapsed in 1986, a sharp currency devaluation provided strong incentives for agricultural exports and, according to the World Bank, had the positive effect of reversing "the strong urban bias that had developed during the oil boom."[4] But thanks to what the Bank termed the revitalization of the tree-crop sector, Nigeria's annual deforestation rate also became the world's second highest, far surpassing sustainable limits and heralding no more than vestigial forest cover by the year 2000. By the late 1980s, when Nigeria had become a net *importer* of timber products, the nation was ironically also making plans to prepare a Tropical Forestry Action Plan (TFAP) as part of a worldwide program to make tropical forestry sustainable.

In other countries, the pressure to export brings dire consequences even more swiftly. Thus, partly as a result of being compelled to shift from wheat to cotton for the export market, Sudan currently faces a severe grain shortage and a national food crisis. Difficulties often result from lack of preparedness. In sub-Saharan Africa, reports the World Bank, dependence on the export of primary products will be prolonged not only to meet adjustment assistance targets but also because weak infrastructures and lack of management capabilities inhibit the countries' ability to develop alternative export programs.[5]

4. The World Bank, *Sub-Saharan Africa: From Crisis to Sustainable Growth* (Washington, D.C., 1989), p. 48.
5. *World Development Report 1990*, p. 12.

As we have seen, within both the International Monetary Fund and the World Bank there is growing awareness that environmental effects must be considered when designing and implementing macroeconomic programs. But although new guidelines have been adopted for lending under adjustment agreements, they have been only partially incorporated into the actual lending process, and the consequences have not been carefully examined. As one environmental official at the Bank noted, "Although we want to look into it, we haven't had time."

While developing countries express little fondness for environmental conditionalities, direct linkages increase the likelihood that debt-reduction programs would pack an environmental punch. The pioneer idea of this sort is what is called the debt-for-nature swap, proposed in a 1984 *New York Times* Op-Ed article by the energetic biologist Thomas Lovejoy, who then worked at the World Wildlife Fund. In such a swap, one or more international conservation agencies raise funds to purchase a portion of a country's commercial debt at a discount or persuade the bank holding the debt to donate some of it; the debt is then forgiven in exchange for a commitment from the debtor government to use local currency or bonds to achieve local conservation objectives. In 1987, Conservation International, a private organization, completed the first such swap with Bolivia. By January 1991, conservation agencies had paid $16,654,765 to purchase debt with a face value of $97,726,106. While these sums do not seem impressive relative to the massive total Third World debt, the more than $60 million in local conservation bonds that the swaps generated is a substantial figure in the low-budget world of environmental protection.

Debt-for-nature swaps are beneficial to Third World countries in many ways. Lower indebtedness means higher creditworthiness. The swaps also liberate money that would have gone to debt servicing, a shift that can be significant even if the sums involved are minimal. Jocelyn Rafidinarivo, Counselor for Financial and Public Affairs of Madagascar, which entered into an agreement with Conservation International in August 1990 to swap both bank and trade debt, commented in a *New York Times* article that although the amount to be swapped was a small part of the country's total debt, "the money saved will help farmers develop new techniques to grow their produce." In Costa Rica, says Alvaro Umaña Quesada, $40 million in swaps have attracted additional resources from donor nations, added weight to environmental goals in national planning, and encouraged long-term stability since only the interest on the long-term bonds is spent. In one deal, an investment of $5 million bought $33 million in debt. At its end of the swap, Costa Rica launched a program in which up to $10 million in credit would be extended to small farmers investing in commercial reforestation projects; returns from the eventual sale of these tree crops, it is hoped, will pay for the loans. "The program creates a *culture* of planting," says Umaña. "Once the farmers learn how much it costs for these things to grow, they're less likely to deforest."

Yet even in Costa Rica, the world's most enthusiastic debt-for-nature advocate, the swaps represent only a small fraction of the overall debt-reduction program, from $4 billion to $3 billion in face value, which consists almost entirely of direct government repurchases. Elsewhere, obstacles stand in the way of the widespread use of the swaps. The Third World countries fear the inflationary effect of printing large amounts of money to redeem debt in local currency. They also regret the loss of sovereignty when outside agencies gain control of their land in the course of some of the transactions. Says Umaña: "The swaps were portrayed as a way for the conservation groups or foundations buying out land in the developing countries to set it aside for conservation. That brought into the matter the whole idea of sovereignty, and it aroused a lot of negative feelings. That's why it did not spread very fast."

This sort of reservation can be overcome by issuing bonds instead of currency swaps (as in the 1987 swap between Ecuador and the World Wildlife Fund) and maintaining government or local NGO control of nature reserves. Limits on the size of the swaps would also help. Recently the U.S. Treasury made it more attractive for banks to donate portions of their Third World debt to environmental agencies by ruling that they may deduct the full face value rather than the deeply discounted market value of the amount donated. This should accelerate action at the commercial end of the debt-for-nature market. Still, those seeking to link the environment to major increments of debt relief will want to develop different mechanisms involving public as well as private-sector debt.

Several such ventures have been undertaken. The United States' Enterprise for the Americas Initiative, undertaken in 1990, allows for some official U.S. debt to be forgiven or "restructured" in return for environmental commitments from debtor Western Hemisphere nations. Though only a small portion of Latin America's approximately $12 billion in debt to the United States government was negotiable under the initial legislation, which limited the field to some concessional loans under the PL480 food-assistance program, the Bush Administration anticipates wider applicability. Eventually, it is hoped, loans through USAID, the Export-Import Bank of the United States, and the Commodity Credit Corporation will all qualify if debtor countries abide by stringent Enterprise for the Americas conditionalities. Among multilateral lenders, the Inter-American Development Bank has begun to make loans for purchases of commercial debt provided that the local funds generated are allocated to environmental purposes. A $150 million reforestation program in Mexico City is one of the initial results of this new effort.

The World Bank, which has a policy against renegotiating its loans, is considering a scheme whereby debtor countries would use Bank resources to buy commercial debt that is not their own, then once again allocate local funds to environmentally sound development projects. Joan Martin-Brown of UNEP suggests that all nations pledge to relieve developing countries of up to half their debt in return for their commitment to establish biosphere reserves and conduct village-level programs of sustainable development; competent observers would monitor to assure compliance, and increments of relief would be withheld in the event of defaults. Multilateral aid donors are considering an expansion of the World Bank–directed Global Environment Facility into a larger Environmental Fund to finance linked efforts that relieve debt and support environmental quality.

Since any form of debt relief gives developing countries a better opportunity to address environmental problems, schemes that include no specific conditionalities may also prove to be helpful. One such is the suggestion that the World Bank and the International Monetary Fund act as "bankruptcy judges," passing binding rulings on the maximum percentage of its total debt that a particular country would be required to service before special assistance would be extended. Gareth Porter, of the Environmental and Energy Study Institute in Washington, suggests creating "a new institution aimed at debt reduction, called an 'international debt facility,' that would assess how much debt repayment each debtor country can realistically pay without adversely affecting its chances for economic development," and, according to Porter's plan, concerned NGOs would then pressure banks to reduce debt to that level.

Trade, investment, debt—it is hard to overestimate the complexity of what is involved in breaking down the rigidities of the current global biases and constructing new arrangements between North and South that would encourage more attention to the environment in poor countries. Large-scale creative thinking, of the sort that produced the Marshall Plan, the Bretton Woods agreement, and the new institutions that served the world so well in the years following World War II, seems now in very short supply. The next and final chapter examines our readiness to pick up the gauntlet.

꙰

CHAPTER II

The View
from the Kitchen

It is on fateful January 16, 1991, that I begin to write these lines. In our living room, ironically, an amaryllis that my wife has been nurturing for more than a month is finally about to spring into bloom as war unfolds in the Persian Gulf. I thought last night of a time years ago when a distinguished professor in Tokyo was asked what role he felt Japan should play in international affairs. "Absolutely none," he replied. Then I thought of Richard Darman, director of the U.S. Office of Management and Budget, who in 1990 told a Harvard audience that "Americans did not fight and win the wars of the twentieth century to make the world safe for green vegetables." In any determined effort to exchange obsessive militarism for a new environmental order, I reasoned, Tokyo will need to attach principles to its interests and step into the world with improved sensitivity. Washington will need to become more reflective, more innovative. All the nations of the North, particularly those occupying the bubble of Western Europe, will need greater resolve to shape not just pampered districts but a more equitable planet. The quiet wisdom of an Adlai Stevenson, the inspiring voice of a Barbara Ward, are greatly in demand, for our most powerful leaders must appreciate the values that come to the fore when we con-

Norway's Prime Minister Gro Harlem Brundtland,
pioneer promoter of sustainable development

sider international affairs from the standpoint of biology rather than machismo or image or short-term politics.

If the end of the Cold War represents anything more positive than the beginning of a new one, and if, as is often forecast, a new concern for North-South equity will preoccupy us as the long-running confrontation between East and West once did, then stabilizing the global environment is a powerfully attractive organizing principle. The groundwork for this is well laid—not only through the convergence of environmental and development concerns that this book has traced but also as a result of several quite dramatic recent events. The world's resolve to end all CFC usage demonstrates that people with radically different views about a shared environmental problem, working in good faith, can find common cause. Since 1987, the world has also been considering the challenge of *Our Common Future,* the much-discussed Brundtland report. It posited a broad reordering of the world's economic systems and relationships for the sake of environmental equilibrium and intergenerational equity, and it emphasized the rural tropics. Preliminary discussions about implementing the Brundtland agenda point toward the United Nations' pivotal "Earth Summit." Sustainability lies at the very heart of the agenda for this meeting, and for many ensuing rounds of discussion and negotiation.

Environmental experts and lay leaders have for years been sketching the outlines of the ecological "global bargain" between developed and developing nations that could emerge from UNCED's comprehensive Agenda 21 (which will provide a framework for future action) and subsequent negotiations. For their part, developing countries would pledge to address the population question with new determination and sharply curtail deforestation and other environmentally destructive practices. Fundamental change, not only political and economic but cultural as well, would be required of them. Sharing power with the grass roots will never come easily to many of its rulers, but it is necessary if ecological needs are to be efficiently met. Nationalists will need to balance their distrust of foreigners with appreciation for their enthusiasm, skills, and technologies. And in the South as well as in the North, new standards of morality will have to enter the public domain.

The South not only will need to stop doing things that have negative consequences but also (with Northern help) will have to start doing things in new ways. Technology is critical. "What is required is not simply more of the same," writes Robert W. Fri, president of Resources for the Future, a research institution in Washington,

> but new technologies that produce more food and fiber without the environmental consequences of the current ones. . . . Energy analysts argue that we can meet future energy needs and solve the pollution problems that energy creates, but not with yesterday's technology. We need not cut old-growth and tropical forests to have adequate timber supplies, but it will take an approach different from today's. The world's water resources are ample to sustain a much larger population, though not if we manage these resources as we do now.[1]

Planners, presidents, and citizens will need to accept the compromises between economic and environmental objectives that will sometimes

1. Robert W. Fri, "Sustainable Development: Principles into Practice," published in his organization's newsletter, *Resources*, No. 102 (Winter 1991).

be required even in a distinctly greener world. As environmental a government as Brazil is ever likely to get will still probably decide in favor of damming the Xingu River in the Amazon, a painful move whose cost-effectiveness is also evident, over the protests of local indigenous people. But application of the principles of resource accounting, in which today's "externalities" will at last be counted as part of economic costs, will sharply tilt the scales toward environmental benefits. Environmentally negative trade-offs will consequently become far more difficult to justify. Yesterday's conflicting objectives will, if these changes come to pass, become tomorrow's synergies.

In return for a broad commitment from the South, Northern nations would reduce atmospheric pollution so that overall greenhouse stability can be achieved even as developing countries increase their emissions enough to accelerate their growth rates. Despite coal-reliant China and India, burning tropical forests, and methane-producing rice paddies and cows, industrial nations continue to emit the preponderance of greenhouse gases.[2] Even countries such as the Netherlands, which has already demonstrated firm resolve, would need to make the further painful improvements in energy efficiency that will be expected of them. The United States, with 5 percent of the world's population and 30 percent of its annual consumption of fossil fuels, and a pollution champion in many other respects, would have to express far greater resolve to conserve energy than that drafted into the insipid energy program announced by the Bush Administration early in 1991. "The best contribution that the United States could make," says William Nitze, "would be to embark on a domestic program of sustainable development." Controls on greenhouse gas emissions, a matter already under intense international scrutiny, would represent only part of the

2. According to authors Mark C. Trexler, Irving M. Mintzer, and William R. Moomaw: "Industrialized countries are likely to be responsible for over 90 percent of the global warming to which we became committed through 1986." The authors also warn, however, that the proportion of emissions from developing countries threatens to "grow dramatically" unless those countries adopt preventive energy strategies. These findings were reported in a paper entitled "Global Warming: An Assessment of Its Scientific Basis, Its Likely Impacts, and Potential Response Strategies," presented at the U.S. Environmental Protection Agency's Workshop on the Economics of Sustainable Development, January 23–26, 1990.

Northern commitment. Greater equity would also result from new forms of Northern assistance to alleviate Southern distress on the debt, trade, and investment issues. New institutions, or a broad revamping of existing ones, would be required to grapple with these daunting tasks.

It is not easy to calculate the cost of achieving a global restructuring of this magnitude, but some analyses find it manageable. As of 1990, the world was still spending about $1 trillion a year—almost as much as the developing world's entire debt—on armaments. For only 15 percent of that, or $150 billion a year during the latter 1990s, according to the Worldwatch Institute, the world could take the steps "required to achieve sustainable development between 1990 and 2000," in such fields as preventing soil erosion, reforestation, increasing energy efficiency, and addressing the population question.[3]

Even if the costs greatly exceed these estimates, a large portion of them could still be defrayed through simply passing them on—as usual—to consumers. Much of the total public investment required could also come, not from newly minted coin, but through reprogramming of what is already in the budget or forecast. Bold decisions such as that taken early in 1991 by U.S. Defense Secretary Dick Cheney to cancel the $57 billion A-12 attack aircraft, after only $1.2 billion had been spent, would carry the world far toward the goal. Though the Gulf War prolonged indefinitely the time when deep cuts in tactical weapons such as the Patriot missile will be politically negotiable in the United States, countless billions could be free for other purposes if the principal nuclear powers were to consummate the dramatic reductions in strategic arms that are currently proposed.

Ideas abound about how the United States, rather than dismantle military and intelligence capabilities, could convert them to other purposes: recycled barracks to house the homeless, the mentally ill, or convicts; army supercomputers to help analyze climate change; mothballed Sturgeon-class nuclear submarines to study the mysteries of the deep ocean; former spy planes to probe the ozone layer. Career personnel could be retrained to carry out alternative tasks. Already, the American corporations that have relied heavily on arms sales are

3. According to data presented in its publication *State of the World 1988*.

scratching hard to find new tasks for their engineers and technocrats. Business generally is far readier to pitch in. Refocusing these capabilities on the growing environmental market would help make the earth cleaner, maintain United States leadership in environmental technology, and keep exports growing.

There are, moreover, many basic political reasons for the North to want to pay an affordable price for global sustainability. Environmentally as well as economically, the relationship between Northern security and a healthy South draws ever closer. With natural resources looming as the probable *casus belli* of many regional conflicts in the future, and with nuclear proliferation making inexorable progress from land to land, local environmental wars could pose grave threats to all people. Use of the environment itself as a tool of war, an old practice that Saddam Hussein escalated from the battlefield to the ecosystem level by setting fire to Kuwait's oil wells and pumping vast quantities of oil into the Persian Gulf, will remain an ever more lethal threat. The South, with its fast-growing population, holds great potential as a market for Northern exports—if it can afford to pay for the goods it will want to buy. Ecological distress would, on the other hand, increase the flow of environmental refugees from Asia, Africa, and many parts of the Western Hemisphere into nations of the developed world that find it difficult to provide adequate services for their existing populations.

For all the appeal of these sorts of arguments, their chances of prevailing seem limited. Beyond the more specific constraints on Northern action already covered in previous chapters, even the extent of our widely heralded general commitment to pursuing the new environmental agenda remains questionable. The ease with which U.S. voters turned their backs on the spring 1990 Earth Day and voted down environmental proposals in the November 1990 balloting is but one indication of where the goal of sustainability really stood, when push came to shove, even before the Gulf War. "The electorate is becoming too sophisticated for the gibberish of the 'greens,' " said Donald Feldstein of Teaneck, New Jersey, in a letter to *The New York Times Magazine.* In the war's aftermath, environmental priorities in the United States will surely suffer further attrition in proportion to the prolongation of the traditional values of the military-industrial complex. Already, the protection offered wetlands under the Clean Water Act has come under heavy attack.

Leaving aside the effects of the war, leaving aside such gestures as the Enterprise for the Americas Initiative, official encouragement for debt-for-nature swaps, and the accentuation of environmental values among the aid donors, the underlying basis of U.S. foreign economic policy in the 1990s has precious little to do with the needs of the poor in developing countries, let alone the health of their environments. "Competitiveness" is the broad term that dominates the economic "vision" at the White House, which is weary of not having a "level playing field" for global commerce. Even within the skimpy development assistance portion of the foreign aid budget, as we have heard from close observers such as Joseph Wheeler and Robert Blake, export considerations loom far larger than sustainability (ideally, of course, these vastly different goals should be housed in separate agencies). In 1991, reports circulated that the Export-Import Bank of the United States, an agency that could serve economic development interests of Third World nations as well as those of the United States, would revert to its Vietnam War–era practice of financing arms sales. Foreign aid can gain the new support it needs in the United States only if both the rationale and the administrative bureaucracy get long-needed overhauls. Internationally, fast-expanding green movements everywhere have not yet deeply affected the behavior of national development assistance agencies, let alone the economists and engineers of the World Bank. For all the brave global talk, the inordinate amount of time that UNEP's leaders need to spend each year trying to raise the agency's paltry annual budget (less than $36 million in 1991) underscores the shallowness of the world's environmental pocket.

Even if the North and particularly the United States were willing to embark on an enthusiastic global environmental dialogue, sharply differing perceptions about what comes first would have to be overcome. Edward Seaga, former Prime Minister of Jamaica, who while in office symbolized economic orthodoxy and submitted his struggling country to adjustment assistance without a human face, put it well in his January 7, 1991, address at the Council on Foreign Relations colloquium in New York. "The drumbeats of the North," he warned, "do not automatically translate into rhythms in the South, even where there is conviction and willingness and the means are provided." His conclusion reflected the sentiments of this book:

> Too much of the programming and formulation of policies to deal with complex global issues tends to reflect macro views without sufficiently considering the microcosm of society, the household, and its perceptions of the problems and solutions as seen through the demands of the kitchen economy. Any Third World agenda on environmental issues will place shelter, fuel, water, and energy at the top of the list. Likewise, deforestation in the mindset of environmentalists everywhere is a major issue contributing as it does to the feared greenhouse effect of atmospheric warming; depletion of water resources and the massive loss of topsoil through soil erosion.
>
> The industrial world, accomplished as it is in putting men on the moon, orbiting the earth, telecommunicating from one end of the world to the other, building tunnels under the sea, harnessing nuclear power, biogenetically creating new life forms and creating computers with awesome capacity, cannot be held to be seriously concerned about the environment if in this advanced technological age it still cannot light a poor man's home atop a distant hill or allow him to cook his meals without denuding his own landscape.

Beyond priorities and money lie fundamental questions about how people approach life. In negotiating the global bargain, impatient Northerners may find it hard to adjust their thinking to sharply contrasting ideas about space, time, and distance that still prevail in the villages of the Third World. For all the blinding speed of modern communications, the gap in perceptions about values and cadences remains wide. Even today there is much to be learned from the old story about the USAID official who once tried to instruct a northeast Brazilian fisherman about the virtues of investing in a larger vessel and fancier equipment. "Your business will grow and prosper," says the USAID man. "Why would I want my business to grow and prosper?" asks the fisherman. "You will be able to afford more and more," answers the USAID missionary. "Someday you may even have a house on the beach." Says the fisherman: "I already have a house on the beach."

During the 1970s, the world debated the so-called New International Economic Order (NIEO), which, with little reference to environmental issues, would have involved major financial transfers from North to South to bring about greater global harmony. But the North proved unwilling to loosen its purse strings, the talks failed, and the developing world was condemned to the stagnation of the 1980s. Now again, as Mahbub ul-Haq and other leaders of the South make amply clear, the developing world expects a payoff in return for environmental pledges. But even with more at stake, the North seems little readier than it was two decades ago to pump large amounts of unrestricted cash into Southern coffers.

The situation is cause for grave apprehensions about how the broad global bargain will fare at UNCED and beyond. But despite it all, I still fervently believe that we must somehow agree at least on this basic piece of it: taking to heart the lessons from the villages of the rural tropics, emphasizing grass-roots, bottom-up styles of rural development, and providing the forms of support from the North that will often be needed for their success. Out in the Third World's countryside, local shifts in emphasis, of the sort advocated by such wise citizens as Dalmiro Cortez and Jorge Orejuela and Yves Renard, Ackim Mwenya and Surapon Duangkhae, would be sought. On existing farmlands, Northern expertise would help increase the efficiency of crop production and reduce to a minimum the environmental damage caused by intensive agriculture. Local food security would rank as a higher priority than agricultural exports. The arrival of new technologies, and unprecedented educational opportunities, would assist villagers in making the transition from despair to stability, gaining distance from the hopelessness of the poverty trap. The world would cooperate in tearing down the Berlin Walls that still separate the planet's usually urban rich from the Third World's ignored and stifled rural poor.

I do not propose a neo-arcadian scenario, for this is out of the question. "Before they came from outside to get our timber we had no poor people," says Margaret M. Taylor, ambassador of Papua New Guinea to Washington. Then she saw the shift as more and more newcomers arrived. Few frontiers or enclaves remain. Money has become a requisite among the crafty indigenous people of Panama's tiny San Blas Islands, who still value the self-sufficiency of their fishing and farming traditions even as they sell *molas* (brightly colored, hand-embroidered textiles) to cruise-ship passengers. If Africa and many parts of Asia remain heavily rural, rapid urbanization is a universal phenomenon. Dangerous Nairobi, a placid town of fifty thousand only two decades ago, now has a seven-figure population. Demand for the consumer paraphernalia of modern society will only increase.

A new deal between the rich of the North and the poor of the rural South must take into account such powerful trends. But even factoring them in, I believe that much could be accomplished without the mighty new burst of economic activity that Jim MacNeill and others prescribe. Achieving a decent level of subsistence for the world's absolutely poor rural people, by means of activities that do not cause further environmental damage and that may require moderate but not explosive or destabilizing economic growth, would in itself be a dramatic and not inordinately expensive victory.

Should the changes I propose come to pass, human nature being what it is, people will no doubt invent new things to fear and new ways to inflict harm on one another. But we would all have gained in many ways—from lower prices for farm goods and from eased tensions and healthier economies in developing countries. Some of the gravest dangers for human welfare that we currently foresee would be eliminated or diminished. The outlook for the planet's nonhuman biota would be improved. The resulting world would be cleaner, fairer, more efficient. We would be more likely to have a future to worry about.

Acknowledgments

William K. Reilly, administrator of the U.S. Environmental Protection Agency, launched this project. In 1988, while serving as president of the World Wildlife Fund and the Conservation Foundation, he, along with R. Michael Wright, now senior fellow, invited me to undertake the extensive travel that led to the reports on which Chapters 5, 6, and 7 of this book are based—and, though not directly, to the ideas and judgments that lie at its heart.

My initial thanks must therefore go to them. Of the many other colleagues then in place at WWF and CF who gave important assistance in producing the field reports and developing the book, I must particularly mention Bob McCoy, director of publications, a sensitive "handler" and valued friend. Others there who merit special thanks are librarians Barbara Rodes and Carla Langeveld; computer experts Tim Sivia and Kathy Dale; and these people from many branches of the organization: Katrina Brandon, Bruce Bunting, Bob Buschbacher, Connie Fraser, Curt Freese, Kathryn Fuller, Nancy Hammond and her capable assistants, Sally Karwowski, Fannie Mae Keller, Jeff Leonard, Paige MacDonald, Doris McClanahan, Emilie Mead, Gus Medina, Tracey Messer, Carlos Saavedra, Natalie Waugh, and Diane Wood. At the World Wide Fund for Nature in Gland, Switzerland, my thanks go to Charles De Haes, director-general, and to MaryRose Rudaz for her kind assistance in arranging appointments there and elsewhere in Europe.

Although the World Wildlife Fund commissioned this project, it could not have been completed without the assistance of many others located elsewhere. Any such list must begin with the Council on Foreign Relations in New York City, which awarded me its Whitney H. Shepardson fellowship for 1990–91. Peter Tarnoff, the Council's president, Nicholas X. Rizopoulos, director of studies, and a fine disciplinarian, and Kenneth Keller, senior fellow for science and technology, all tried hard and faithfully to help me focus my scattered thoughts. Although I, of course, am solely responsible for what appears on these pages, their efforts are greatly appreciated. Many others of the Council's staff in New York and in Washington, where I did much of the work, assisted in many ways. Principal among them are Alton Frye, Judith Gustafson, Linda Harsh, John Millington, Carol Rath, and John Temple Swing. Through the Council I was able to take advantage of the facilities of the Carnegie Endowment for International Peace, and I extend warm thanks to its librarian, Jennifer Little, and her colleagues.

Others who merit signal recognition are: Martha H. Coolidge; Hope Patterson; Susan Fletcher of the Congressional Research Service of the Library of Congress; Peter Thacher of the World Resources Institute; Ernst Lutz of the World Bank; Lillian Calo of Democracy Travel; and Flo and Leslie Stone.

For financial support I owe the deepest gratitude to the Marpat Foundation of Washington, D.C., and particularly to Mrs. Jefferson Patterson, Marpat director, and Mrs. Joan F. Koven, secretary and treasurer, for their generosity in enabling me to carve out the time I needed to complete this work. Funding for the colloquium that was critical to the book's final chapters came from the John D. and Catherine T. MacArthur Foundation, Citicorp, and the World Resources Institute. Within these organizations, I extend thanks to these individuals: Daniel Martin and Marta Iturrieta at the MacArthur Foundation; John Reed, Paul Ostergard, and William Kaplowitz at Citicorp; and James Gustave Speth and Walter Arensberg at WRI.

Special appreciation must go to Eve Hamilton, my unflagging research assistant; to my patient and always responsive agent, Tom Wallace; and to Elisabeth Sifton at Alfred A. Knopf, a talented editor who absorbs vast amounts of information and somehow manages never to forget *any* of it. Finally, and most of all, I thank the scores of people who led me through the fields, forests, and byways of the Third World and taught me much about life.

Notes

꙰

My reading for this book spanned a curious range, from the Book of Genesis to Edward Abbey's *Desert Solitaire*. Presenting a conventional bibliography would, therefore, serve little purpose. In this section I attempt instead to summarize the sources for my information. For technical data I relied heavily on the publications of the United Nations Development Program, the World Bank, and the World Resources Institute, as well as on individuals whose works and identities are noted in the text. As noted both in Chapter 10 and in the pertinent section of these Notes, much of the data and reasoning contained in that chapter came as a result of the Colloquium on Global Economics and Sustainable Rural Development that I was able to organize under the joint sponsorship of the Council on Foreign Relations and the World Resources Institute. I myself compiled most of the field information included in Chapters 5–7 and in briefer passages in other chapters during the course of many research trips to distant places. Some were undertaken many years ago: I first visited Amazonia in 1965. Most, however, took place during a period of very intensive travel and study in late 1988 and early 1989 that was sponsored by the World Wildlife Fund. Its program staff and the project files at its headquarters in Washington, D.C., also yielded much useful material. What follows is a chapter-by-chapter breakdown of my principal sources.

CHAPTER I

Specifics are based on reports and proposals in World Wildlife Fund project files and my own field observations. Sources of more general information are listed below.

CHAPTER 2

In his *Economic Development: The History of an Idea* (Chicago: University of Chicago Press, 1987), the economist H. W. Arndt well summarizes his field. David Morawetz adds detail about the post–World War II era in his *Twenty-five Years of Economic Development, 1950 to 1975* (Washington, D.C.: The World Bank, 1977). A long series of occasional papers issued by the Overseas Development Council, a private organization in Washington, D.C., was very helpful as well.

Development efforts were barely under way when scientists gathered at UNESCO's International Technical Conference in Lake Success, New York, in 1949. This meeting's proceedings gave fair warning of the threats to the environment that development would pose. Two decades later the Conservation Foundation brought together an eminent group at Airlie House, Virginia, to review similar themes. The resulting publication, entitled *The Careless Technology: Ecology and International Development* (Washington, D.C.: The Conservation Foundation, 1969), contains views and passages that ring true to this day.

The notes for Chapter 8 supply more about publications having to do with bottom-up, grass-roots-based modes of development. A pioneer among these is *They Know How: An Experiment in Development Assistance,* a slim but influential volume issued in 1977 by the sprightly Inter-American Foundation, a public agency based in Rosslyn, Virginia.

CHAPTER 3

Donald Worster's *Nature's Economy: A History of Ecological Ideas* (San Francisco: Sierra Club Books, 1977) is essential reading. The works of the historian Roderick Nash, particularly his classic *Wilderness and the American Mind* (New Haven: Yale University Press, 1973), are also of fundamental importance. This chapter owes much to an index summarizing the life and work of the dauntless American conservation leader Harold J. Coolidge, Jr. Robert Boardman's *International Organization and the Conservation of Nature* (Bloomington: Indiana University Press, 1982) and Lynton K. Caldwell's *International Environmental Policy: Emergence and Dimensions* (Durham, N.C.: Duke University Press, 1984) review the evolution of an institutional framework in the field.

The relationship between environment and development was deeply explored at the warm-up meeting for the 1972 Stockholm Conference on the Human Environment. The "prep" session was held in Founex, Switzerland, June 4–12, 1971. Its results were published by the United Nations Conference on the Human Environment in a book entitled *Development and Environment* (Mouton, Paris, and The Hague, 1972). The following year the classic *Ecological Principles for Economic Development* (London: John Wiley & Sons) made its appearance. Its co-editors are the ecologist Raymond F. Dasmann, John P. Milton, and Peter H. Freeman.

CHAPTER 4

While working on my previous *Dreams of Amazonia* (New York: Elisabeth Sifton Books/Viking, 1985), I encountered an already long bookshelf of writings on environment and development in that region. Of these I recommend: the pioneering *Amazon Jungle: Green Hell to Red Desert?* by Robert J. A. Goodland and Howard S. Irwin (New York: Elsevier Scientific Publishing Company, 1975); numerous articles on land use by Susanna Hecht of the Department of Architecture and Urban Studies, University of California at Los Angeles; and several works by the sociologist Stephen G. Bunker, who has undertaken deep studies in the Marabá region. The summary monograph entitled "Government Policies and Deforestation in Brazil's Amazon Region," written by Dennis J. Mahar (Washington, D.C.: The World Bank, the World Wildlife Fund, and the Conservation Foundation, 1989), offers a succinct overview.

The latter part of the chapter is based on many interviews, as well as on reports and other publications that aid agencies, environmental organizations, and other sources kindly made available. My personal experience at the World Wildlife Fund, which began with my election to its board of directors in 1976, encompasses the period under discussion.

CHAPTERS 5–7

Abbreviated reports of the six essential field visits included in these three chapters were first published, in 1988 and 1989, as a series of eight-page WWF Letters, and in 1991 in a WWF paperback entitled *Wildlands and Human Needs*. The information in them was gathered on-site, from WWF program staff members at the organization's Washington headquarters, and from project files. Books supplementing my deficient prior knowledge of Africa include *How Can Africa Survive?* by Jennifer Seymour Whitaker (New York: Harper & Row, 1988), *Squandering Eden* by Mort Rosenblum and Doug Williamson (New York: Harcourt Brace Jovanovich, 1987), and *The Greening of Africa* by the British journalist Paul Harrison (London: Earthscan/Penguin, 1987). The World Bank's *Sub-Saharan Africa: From Crisis to Sustainable Growth* (Washington, D.C., 1989) and its overall assessment entitled "Rural Development—World Bank Experience, 1965–86," published in 1988, were key references. So was the U.S. Congress's Office of Technology Assessment's 1988 analysis of the relationship between African agriculture and U.S. development assistance.

CHAPTER 8

Any listing of important literature about grass-roots development must include the trenchant observations of the economist Albert O. Hirschman of Princeton University. Among many, the book he prepared under the auspices of the Inter-American Foundation, entitled *Getting Ahead Collectively: Grassroots Experiences in Latin America* (New York: Pergamon Press, 1984), was especially pertinent. Other authors whose field observations gave valuable guidance include Roland Bunch of the World Neighbors organization *(Two Ears of Corn: A Guide to People-Centered Agricultural Improvement,* Oklahoma City, 1982) and Robert Chambers of the University of Sussex *(Rural Development: Putting the Last First,* Harlow, Eng.: Longman Scientific and Technical, 1983).

Race to Save the Tropics (Washington, D.C., and Covelo, Calif.: Island Press, 1990), a volume of essays edited by the ecologist Robert J. A. Goodland of the World Bank, offers pioneer information about the workings of applied ecology. The same is true of Jeffrey A. McNeely's *Economics and Biological Diversity: Developing and Using Economic Incentives to Conserve Biological Resources* (Gland, Switz.: International Union for the Conservation of Nature and Natural Resources, 1988). Another valuable Overseas Development Council publication is *Environment and the Poor: Development Strategies for a Common Agenda,* edited by H. Jeffrey Leonard, then of World Wildlife Fund and the Conservation Foundation, and published in 1989.

CHAPTER 9

Two benchmark works are *Our Own Agenda,* the report of the Latin American and Caribbean Commission on Development and Environment (Washington, D.C.: Inter-American Development Bank, 1990), and *The Challenge of the South,* the report of the South Commission (New York: Oxford University Press, 1990). The United Nations Development Program's *Human Development Report 1990* (Oxford and New York: Oxford University Press, 1990) contains important data and insights.

Eve Hamilton, who acted with distinction as my research assistant during most of the time that this book was taking shape, canvassed many sources to assemble the information about the effects of developing countries' export programs that appears in the latter part of the chapter, in her own words from place to place. The section of the chapter that discusses the development of St. Lucia's Pitons region stems from several visits I have made to the island in recent years.

CHAPTER 10

Once again, this chapter is greatly indebted to Ms. Hamilton's research. In part it is also the result of the colloquium mentioned in the text. What the participants said at the meeting greatly influenced my thinking about the matters under discussion. I alone am responsible for the chapter's content. In addition to Ms. Hamilton and myself, those who attended were:

Walter Arensberg, World Resources Institute; Robert O. Blake, Committee on Agricultural Sustainability for Developing Countries; Sharon L. Camp, Population Crisis Committee; Nomsa Daniels, Council on Foreign Relations; Arba Diallo, United Nations Conference on Environment and Development; Marc Dourojeanni, Inter-American Development Bank; Maria de Lourdes Davies de Freitas, Instituto Brasiliero do Meio-Ambiente e Recursos Naturais Renováveis; Michael Gucovsky, United Nations Development Program; Peter Hakim, Inter-American Dialogue; John Maxwell Hamilton, World Bank; William A. Hewitt, former chairman, Deere & Co.; Shafiqul Islam, Council on Foreign Relations; Stephen Kass, Berle, Kass & Case; Kenneth H. Keller, Council on Foreign Relations; John D. Macomber, Export-Import Bank of the United States; Joan Martin-Brown, United Nations Environment Program; Audrey McInerney, Council on Foreign Relations; Hassan Ali Mehran,

Economic Adviser to the Government of Aruba; William A. Nitze, Alliance to Save Energy; John R. Petty, Petty-FBW Associates; Gareth Porter, Environmental and Energy Study Institute; Jack Raymond, JR Consulting Services, Inc.; Robert Repetto, World Resources Institute; G. Edward Schuh, Hubert H. Humphrey Institute of Public Affairs, University of Minnesota; The Rt. Hon. Edward Seaga, PC, MP, former prime minister, Jamaica; S. Bruce Smart, World Resources Institute; Mark J. Smith, Council on Foreign Relations; James Gustave Speth, president, World Resources Institute; John Temple Swing, Council on Foreign Relations; Peter Tarnoff, president, Council on Foreign Relations; Margaret M. Taylor, ambassador of Papua New Guinea to the United States; Eleanor Tejirian, the American Assembly; Sarah Timpson, United Nations Development Program; Alvaro Umaña Quesada, Instituto Centroamericano de Administración y Empresas, Costa Rica; Joseph C. Wheeler, Organization for Economic Cooperation and Development.

CHAPTER 11

What influenced me here encompasses the thought of many people and institutions. Reinforcement for the points made in this summary comes from conversations with Thomas Lovejoy, George M. Woodwell, and Edward O. Wilson; from the Worldwatch Institute's absorbing series of *State of the World* reports; and from the comprehensive *World Resources* report issued annually by the World Resources Institute. For many years the London-based International Institute for Environment and Development, now functioning under the auspices of the World Resources Institute, published important material under the imprint of Earthscan Publications, Ltd. *Signs of Hope* by Linda Starke (Oxford: Oxford University Press, 1990) traces the institutional path from the Brundtland report to the United Nations' 1992 Conference on Environment and Development. The work was commissioned by the Centre for Our Common Future, an organization founded to carry forward the Brundtland agenda. Other essential literature includes works by Gilbert White, Aldo Leopold, Fairfield Osborn, William Vogt, Denis Goulet, and Edward O. Wilson. No book of this sort could have been put together without repeated reference to *Our Common Future* (New York: Oxford University Press, 1987).

Many wise people kindly discussed with me their views about the broadest issues. There is no such moment that I treasure more than the hour I spent in Coconut Grove, Florida, at the home of Marjory Stoneman Douglas, indefatigable protector of the Everglades. "I can't hear anymore, and I can't see," she said on the eve of her one hundredth birthday. "But I can still talk." As long as she lived, she promised me, she would keep up her fight to save the Glades from unwise development. I can only hope to live so long or work so hard for the values we share.

Index

PHOTOGRAPHIC CREDITS

Grateful acknowledgment is made to the following for
permission to reprint photographs on the pages indicated:
Department of Library Services, American Museum of
    Natural History/D. Finnin: 53 (right)
The Bettmann Archive: 52, 53 (left), 55
Inter-American Foundation/Mitchell Denburg: 32
Stephen Nash: 123
Andrew Posner: 75, 77
Reuters/Bettmann Newsphotos: 217
Roger Stone: 8, 9, 11, 12, 16, 18, 19, 74, 100, 101, 104,
    121, 135, 137, 147, 149, 151, 153, 159, 166, 167, 169, 170,
    180, 182, 185, 219
United Press International: 260
World Bank Photo Collection: 234, 240
Wide World Photo: 215, 216

A NOTE ABOUT THE AUTHOR

A frequent writer and commentator on the global environment, Roger D. Stone is Consultant on Environmental Issues at the Council on Foreign Relations and a Senior Fellow at the World Wildlife Fund. He has been Whitney H. Shepardson Fellow at the Council on Foreign Relations, a vice president of the World Wildlife Fund, president of the Center for Inter-American Relations, a vice president of Chase Manhattan Bank, and a foreign correspondent and news bureau chief for *Time* magazine. The author of two previous books, Mr. Stone lives in Washington, D.C.

A NOTE ON THE TYPE

The text of this book was set in Sabon, a type face designed by Jan Tschichold (1902–1974), the well-known German typographer. Based loosely on the original designs of Claude Garamond (c. 1480–1561), Sabon is unique in that it was explicitly designed for hot-metal composition on both the Monotype and Linotype machines as well as for film setting. Designed in Frankfurt, Sabon was named for the famous Lyon punchcutter Jacques Sabon, who is thought to have brought some of Garamond's matrices to Frankfurt.

Composed by Creative Graphics, Inc., Allentown, Pennsylvania. Printed and bound by The Courier Book Companies, Westford, Massachusetts.

Designed by Peter A. Andersen